Ainmeil thar Cheudan

Presentations to the 2011 Sorley MacLean Conference

21 Feb.
Moscow '84

Ainmeil thar Cheudan

Presentations to the 2011
Sorley MacLean Conference

Edited by
Ronald W. Renton
and Ian MacDonald

Clò Ostaig

2016

Ainmeil thar Cheudan: Presentations to the 2011 Sorley MacLean Conference
air a dheasachadh le/edited by Ronald W. Renton agus/and Ian MacDonald

Air a fhoillseachadh le/Published by Clò Ostaig
Sabhal Mòr Ostaig, Slèite/Sleat
An t-Eilean Sgitheanach/Isle of Skye IV44 8RQ

www.smo.uhi.ac.uk/gd/rannsachadh/clo-ostaig/

Air a chlò-chumadh le/Typeset by Duncan Jones
Air a chlò-bhualadh le/Printed by Bell and Bain Ltd, Glasgow

A' chiad fhoillseachadh an 2016/First published in 2016

Bu mhiann leis an fhoillsichear taic fhialaidh Urras an Eilein
mu choinneimh cosgaisean an leabhair seo aithneachadh/
The publisher would like to acknowledge the generous support of
Urras an Eilein (the Isle of Skye Gaelic charity) towards the costs of this book.

Chuidich Comhairle nan Leabhraichean am foillsichear le cosgaisean an leabhair/
The Gaelic Books Council assisted the publisher with the costs of the book.

Gheibhear catalog CIP airson an tiotail seo bho Leabharlann Bhreatainn/
A CIP catalogue for this title is available from the British Library.

ISBN 978-0-9562615-4-0

An dealbh-toisich: Somhairle MacGill-Eain le Alberto Morrocco, air
ath-riochdachadh le cead còir teaghlach Shomhairle MhicGill-Eain

Frontispiece: Sorley MacLean by Alberto Morrocco, reproduced by
kind permission of the family of Sorley MacLean

Dealbh a' chòmhdaich: dealbh-toisich William Crosbie dhan leabhar
Dàin do Eimhir agus Dàin Eile (1943), air ath-riochdachadh
le cead còir oighreachd an fhir-ealain

Cover image: William Crosbie's frontispiece to the book *Dàin do Eimhir
agus Dàin Eile* (1943), reproduced by kind permission of the artist's estate

Clàr-Innse / Contents

DVD PRESENTATIONS

Facal-toisich

Bha dlùth-cheangal aig an t-sàr bhàrd Albannach, Somhairle MacGill-Eain, ri Sabhal Mòr Ostaig. Bha e mar aon dhen chòignear a bha nan urrasairean air a' Cholaiste aig an fhìor thoiseach, b' e a' chiad neach a bha na Sgrìobhadair air Mhuinntireas aig an t-Sabhal agus bhiodh e tric is minig a' frithealadh thachartasan aig a' Cholaiste. Bha e iomchaidh mar sin gun deach cruinn-eachadh sònraichte a chumail aig an t-Sabhal airson ceud bliadhna bho àm a bhreith a chomharrachadh san Ògmhios 2011. Chaidh an cruinneachadh a chur air dòigh le sgioba bho Oilthigh Taobh Siar na h-Alba agus bho Shabhal Mòr Ostaig.

Bha e nar rùn gum biodh an tachartas na mheadhan air beatha, obair agus dìleab Shomhairle a chomharrachadh le spiorad subhachais agus gum biodh gach taobh dhen duine air fhoillseachadh. Gus sin a thoirt gu buil, chaidh diofar eileamaid fhilleadh dhan phrògram. Thòisich an cruinn-eachadh le cuirm chiùil is bàrdachd is chrìochnaich e le turas gu Ratharsair, eilean àraich a' bhàird. Eadar iad sin bha co-labhairt le pàipearan acadaim-igeach air caochladh chuspair mu na sgrìobh is na rinn Somhairle, mar a tha air aithris san Ro-ràdh aig an luchd-deasachaidh. Mar phàirt dhen cho-chruinneachadh chaidh am film mu Shomhairle a rinn Tim Neat dhan BhBC ann an 1986 a shealltainn agus chaidh dà sheisean a chumail anns an robh panailean de thriùir a' dèanamh luaidh air mar fhoghlamaiche agus mar fhilidh. Fhuaireas tro gach snàithlean eadar-dhealaichte a bha sin dealbh anabarrach farsainn is domhainn air Somhairle am bàrd, an sgoilear, an duine, am maighstir-sgoile agus an Gàidheal.

Bha sinn a' meas gur e call a bhiodh ann mura biodh cothrom aig daoine nach robh an làthair aig an tachartas ainmeil seo blasad fhaighinn dhe na h-òraidean is na taisbeanaidhean a thugadh seachad aig a' cho-labhairt, agus tha sinn taingeil gu bheil an leabhar seo agus an DVD a tha na chois a' dèanamh sin comasach. Tha sinn fada an comain an luchd-deasachaidh, Ronnie Renton agus Iain MacDhòmhnaill, airson am mòr-shaothrach, an ealantais agus am foighidinn ann a bhith a' trusadh agus a' cur ri chèile nan diofar phàipearan agus stuthan faicsinneach a tha sa phasgan inntinneach is luachmhor seo. Cha phàigh taing iad.

Bu mhath leinn cuideachd ar buidheachas a chur an cèill do theaghlach Shomhairle, do gach neach a ghabh pàirt san tachartas agus do ar co-obraichean a rinn uimhir airson tachartas cho soirbheachail a chur ri chèile.

Anne Gifford, An t-Iar-Dheadhan, Oilthigh Taobh Siar na h-Alba
Boyd Robasdan, Am Prionnsapal, Sabhal Mòr Ostaig

Foreword

The distinguished Scottish poet, Sorley MacLean, was closely associated with Sabhal Mòr Ostaig. He was one of the five original trustees of the College, the first Writer in Residence at Sabhal Mòr and a frequent visitor and contributor to various events at the College down through the years. It was, therefore, fitting that a special event was held at Sabhal Mòr Ostaig in June 2011 to commemorate the centenary of his birth. The gathering was organised jointly by a team from the University of the West of Scotland and from Sabhal Mòr Ostaig.

Our aim was to stage an event that would both mark and celebrate Sorley's life, work and legacy and shed light on all facets of the man. In order so to do, a variety of elements were built into the programme. The gathering began with an evening of music, song and poetry and ended with a trip to Raasay, the bard's native isle. Between these bookends there was a conference with a range of academic papers on topics related to Sorley's literary and other activities, as outlined in the Introduction by the editors. A screening of Tim Neat's film about Sorley, originally broadcast by the BBC in 1986, and two panel sessions in which three individuals who knew him well discussed and explored his role as an educationalist and as a bard, formed other significant strands of the event. Each of these differing inputs augmented and enhanced our understanding and appreciation of Sorley the man, the poet, the scholar, the schoolmaster and the Gael.

We felt that it would be a shame if people who were unable to attend so rare an occasion could not sample some of the lectures and presentations given at the conference and we are glad that this book and the accompanying DVD makes that possible. We are deeply indebted to the editors, Ronnie Renton and Ian MacDonald, for their industry and tenacity in gathering papers and visual materials from contributors and their skill in preparing them for publication in this fascinating and valuable production.

We would also wish to express our gratitude to Sorley's family, to all who contributed to proceedings and to our colleagues who did so much to plan and deliver such a successful event.

Anne Gifford, Asssociate Dean, University of the West of Scotland
Boyd Robertson, Principal, Sabhal Mòr Ostaig

Introduction

The *Ainmeil thar Cheudan* conference to mark the centenary of the birth of Sorley MacLean was held at Sabhal Mòr Ostaig between 15 and 18 June 2011, and what follows is some of the material presented there. As often happens after conferences, in the end not all the papers given reached us, but we have published all those that were made available. They are printed in the order in which they were delivered at the conference, and we are grateful to contributors to the book for their patience and co-operation. We also thank those who allowed us to include their presentations on the accompanying DVD. We thought it appropriate to present them in this format because they contain images and voices not readily available otherwise.

The magisterial opening essay by Douglas Gifford reflects on the fact that the Scottish Renaissance movement is paradoxically full of decline and loss. And at one point MacLean himself, when speaking of the state of Gaelic, endorses this. Gifford then goes on to locate MacLean as a great war poet in the context of his contemporaries Hamish Henderson and George Campbell Hay.

Alan Titley's chapter describes the thrill, the excitement – the 'buzz' – of poetry, and exemplifies this with quotation from the eighteenth century Scots Alasdair Mac Mhaighstir Alasdair and Donnchadh Bàn and from Irish poets such as Eoghan Rua Ó Súilleabháin. He claims that MacLean is the heir of their tradition and that he experiences the same 'buzz' when reading MacLean's 'Coilltean Ratharsair' ('The Woods of Raasay'). That same poem is the subject of Peter Mackay's insightful contribution, during which he conducts a fascinating examination of MacLean's use of the classical myths of Actaeon and Artemis and analyses the structure of the poem in terms of paradise, fall and realisation of the fall; and also, at another level, as the cycle of growth and decay.

Emma Dymock then discusses the correspondence between MacLean and his friend and great encourager, the nationalist poet Douglas Young. These letters give the men's historical perspective on the times they lived in, their opinion on the state of Gaelic, the suitability of the Scots language as a medium for poetry and their views on the intellectual climate of the

1930s and 40s. The correspondence sheds great light on the relationship that existed between these two men and on the literary affairs of the Scotland of their time.

In 'Sorley MacLean and the Modern Panegyric' Timothy Neat quotes in full the eulogy MacLean gave at the unveiling of the Hugh MacDiarmid Memorial at Langholm on 11 August 1985 and describes the manner of its delivery, while John Purser, in 'Guth Shomhairle' ('Sorley's Voice') describes the mesmeric features of MacLean's performance of his own poetry and demonstrates the relationship between his oral delivery and the musical tradition of the *pìobaireachd* of his own country.

In Timothy Neat's second piece he discusses the making of the film *Hallaig: the Poetry and Landscape of Sorley MacLean* and its two versions. He also includes correspondence with Nessa Doran, the Irish Eimhir, and Seamus Heaney, and suggests connections between MacLean's poetry and that of Samuel Taylor Coleridge. In his lecture Murdo Macdonald praises William Crosbie's modernist interpretation of MacLean's poetry in his frontispiece painting in *Dàin do Eimhir agus Dàin Eile* (1943) and goes on to show the connection between Celtic art and literature from the Book of Kells until the present day. He has special praise in this regard for the vision and enthusiasm of Walter Blaikie, director of the Edinburgh printers T & A Constable, and of William MacLellan, the publisher of the 1943 collection.

The first of the Gaelic essays here is by Maoilios Caimbeul, and its title might be translated as 'Sensibility in the Poetry of Sorley MacLean'. Having established the factors which have conditioned MacLean's philosophy of life, Caimbeul compares MacLean's view of the world with that of some traditional Gaelic poets and seeks to identify where he is radically different from them. His is a powerful new humanist voice in Gaelic poetry that rejects traditional Christian beliefs. In a comparison with the Christian philosophy of the scholar Derek Prince, Caimbeul considers that a strand is missing from MacLean's world view: the strand which integrates *rudan ana-ghnàthaichte* – in this case, the spiritual experience of human beings – with the naturalistic. The second Gaelic essay is by Màiri Sìne Chaimbeul, and in 'Songs of Lochalsh and Kintail' she describes the singers and songs of the area at the time when MacLean was headmaster of Plockton High School. MacLean's own teaching made the songs and poems come alive for his pupils and enhanced the status of Gaelic.

Hugh Cheape's minutely researched paper turns to another side of MacLean's work and focusses on MacLean as historian, tradition-bearer and literary critic. He points out how MacLean interprets the past through its poetry. MacLean's essay on 'The Poetry of the Clearances' is many years ahead of its time, whilst his perceptive analysis of seventeenth-century Gaelic poetry demonstrates the richness of the culture of that era.

Norman Bissell may not have Gaelic, but in 'Nature, Socialist Politics and Love in the Poetry of Sorley MacLean' he shows real insight into the poet's work. He explores succinctly the major issues which deeply affected MacLean, and to someone coming to MacLean for the first time, with or without Gaelic, this short essay would be an excellent introduction. By contrast, Máire Ní Annracháin's is a highly sophisticated and deep analysis of five major poems ('Coilltean Ratharsair', 'Hallaig', 'Uamha 'n Òir', 'Coin is Madaidhean-allaidh' and 'Fuaran') that demonstrates that they adhere in very different ways to a vision and quest structure and argues that this may be found in many other MacLean poems.

In the last item in the book Ian MacDonald conducts a relaxed but extensive interview with Christopher Whyte, editor of the 2002 *Dàin do Eimhir* and of *An Cuilithionn 1939 and Unpublished Poems* (2011). Here Whyte tells us of his first encounter with MacLean and discusses the huge importance of the first version of 'An Cuilithionn', stressing that the 1989 work is an abridgement of the earlier poem. He emphasises the urgent need for an open biography of MacLean, asserts that it was right to restore the *Dàin do Eimhir* sequence and feels that a concordance of the poet's work would be of immense help in MacLean studies. He discusses important issues connected with the translation of MacLean's poetry and concludes by pointing out the advantages of *Caoir Gheal Leumraich / White Leaping Flame*, the new collected edition edited by himself and Emma Dymock and published in November 2011, some months after the conference.

Most references to the poetry in this book are, in fact, to *Caoir Gheal Leumraich*, but with some papers it was more practicable to refer to an earlier edition, *O Choille gu Bearradh / From Wood to Ridge*, first published in 1989.

Our thanks go to Mrs Anne Crosbie for permission to use the illustration from the cover of the 1943 collection *Dàin do Eimhir agus Dàin Eile* by her husband, the late William Crosbie, on the cover of this book and on that of the DVD; to Mr Gordon Wright for the photograph of Sorley MacLean before track 4 of the DVD; to Ms Jessie Ann Matthew for the photograph after track 5; and to the MacLean family for the other photographs used on the DVD and for the portrait drawing by Alberto Morrocco which forms the frontispiece to this book.

We are grateful to Ms Sandra Byrne at Sabhal Mòr Ostaig for gathering useful preliminary information for us; to Mr Duncan Jones of the Association for Scottish Literary Studies for typesetting the book and for his sound practical advice; and to Mr Tony Grace of the University of the West of Scotland for making the DVD and to Mr Greg Friel of Frielance for final editing work on it. In conclusion, we would like to thank Professor Boyd Robertson of Sabhal Mòr Ostaig and Mrs Anne Gifford of the University of the West of Scotland for inviting us to prepare this celebration of the life and work of Sorley MacLean. It has been an honour and a privilege.

Tha sinn an dòchas gun leudaich an leabhar seo tuigse is meas air saothair Shomhairle MhicGill-Eain.

RWR and IMD

1. The Paradox of Renaissance and The Pity of War

DOUGLAS GIFFORD

My extended title is 'The Paradox of Renaissance and The Pity of War', for reasons I'll try to explain. Is it not striking, however, that the three finest Scottish poets of the Second World War, Sorley MacLean, George Campbell Hay and Hamish Henderson, born in 1911, 1915 and 1919 respectively, should have found their way separately to the same theatre of war in North Africa, albeit that Hay was in Algiers, almost a thousand miles from Henderson in Cairo and MacLean in the desert (and the actual fighting) around El Alamein, arguably the site of the most significant battle of the Second World War?

I found myself widening the terms of 'war', realising that its violence and psychological impact began long before the invasion of Belgium, and raised profound issues for our three poets long after. And the effects of war in its most far-reaching sense affected the course of literary Renaissance and social revival in Scotland, arguably withering and bringing to an end around 1950 the life of what had been seen as a coherent cultural movement. When we add to this that the bulk of Renaissance writers had gathered around supporting varieties of 'national socialism', which after the Third Reich would become an untenable concept, post-war ideological debilitation can be understood.

I have to admit to some hesitancy in addressing you, since I have no Gaelic and I'm sure most folk here are far more knowledgeable regarding Sorley MacLean and Gaelic poetry. But I'd argue that, if I find greatness in translation, how much more must lie in the originals with their effects of rhythm and subtleties of nuance! And since we are celebrating Sorley MacLean's life and achievement, please take my discussion of the English translations, made by the poets themselves, in the spirit of respect and admiration intended.

*

The 'Scottish Renaissance' is generally accepted to run from the 1920s and MacDiarmid's early Scots poetry from *Sangschaw* and *A Drunk Man* down to around 1950.[1] This is the age of MacDiarmid, Muir, Soutar, Lindsay, Bruce,

Scott and so many others in poetry, and Gibbon, Gunn, Linklater, Mitchison, MacColla and a host of others in fiction, Bridie and McLellan in drama. While many writers like Scott, Lindsay and Bruce continued, in poetry rather than fiction or drama, I think it's fair to say that Scottish literature surged up to an impressive height in the Twenties and Thirties – until war once again thrust its obsessive claims upon so many. Arguably, war itself and the harsh realities of its impoverished British aftermath, together with the new fears of war with the USSR and the divisions in interpretations of socialism, brought an end to the predominantly rural and essentialist mythologies of Gunn, Gibbon, Linklater and so many of the poets from early MacDiarmid, Muir and Soutar to Henderson and Campbell Hay. This is one aspect of what I've termed 'the pity of war'; there is of course the corollary of the personal damage it inflicted – outstandingly on George Campbell Hay, but unquantifiably on so many others.

What were Renaissance values and aims? The revival based itself around four or five outstanding concepts: the shared need to rediscover indigenous roots and traditions; the need for re-assertion of the two older languages of Scotland; and to aid this (going beyond the older Irish and Celtic revivals, given the later work and Freud and Jung), a recognition of racial memory as suggested by Jung in his idea of 'the collective unconscious', and so vividly present in, for example, the profound moments of spiritual timelessness in Gunn and Gibbon – to the extent that what we can loosely term 'supernatural' epiphany is often a point of realisation of aims in writers like Gunn, Gibbon and Mitchison – though arguably much more restrained in Gaelic poetry.

These ideas of quest for self-discovery in terms of tradition and place and past put recurrent and emphatic emphasis on home, and its local landscape and topography, and its traditional sense of community and its self-renewal (or not!) through cultural traditions and its economic bases in farming and fishing. My fifth tenet is harder to specify – but broadly, virtually all major writers of 'Renaissance' were in opposition to the Establishment status quo, questioning Imperial British – and specifically English – values to greater or lesser degrees, and – to greater or lesser degrees – seeing communism and the Red Army, or national socialism, as having the potential to bring about their longed-for changes.

Nor was this changing to be purely MacDiarmid- and Lowland-based; there were three or four territories of Renaissance: Lowland, Highland,

North-East and Orkney. We should be wary of compartmentalising Highland and Lowland revivals, since border lines are constantly permeable. Hay's father's great novel of 1914, *Gillespie*, belongs as much with the Lowland tradition of *Weir of Hermiston*, *The House with the Green Shutters* or *Hatter's Castle*; Mitchison lived and worked at length in Kintyre; Gunn created his greatest work interpreting Highland *and* Lowland culture; and Gibbon and his heirs like Jessie Kesson can hardly be called Highland or Lowland. Henderson was born and lived for ten years on a Highland–Lowland borderland, at Spittal of Glenshee and Blairgowrie, with Gaelic and travellers' borderland links of language and culture, and used this home-country (after an English public school education, Cambridge and war experience) to form a Graeco-Gaelic and even druidic ideal of life broadly based on a Highland cultural identity. Campbell Hay constantly cited the fishing village of Ayrshire, Dunure, the Lowland fishing port mirror of Carradale in Kintyre, as his family's starting-point, along with his beloved Tarbert, again on something of a territorial borderline, as a personal taproot – but, like Henderson, moved, in his case in his teens to the Edinburgh public school Fettes ('England in Scotland', where he and friends were 'whipped like dogs'), and thence, like Henderson, to Cambridge and, through scholarship, to Oxford.[2] And Highland–Lowland borders were constantly breached for MacLean and Hay in their deeply productive friendships, not just with MacDiarmid but with a huge range of Lowland writers, pre-eminent being Douglas Young, Sydney Goodsir Smith, Robert Garioch, Tom Scott and so many others. MacDiarmid, however, broods over all.

MacLean was born in 1911, Hay in 1915, and Henderson in 1919 – and so there are time-lags between their various experiences of MacDiarmid and Renaissance, though it is clear that at different stages MacDiarmid 'adopted' all of them as allies or potential heirs to the bearing of his Renaissance standard. Yet the relationship was two-way: MacDiarmid's re-creation of himself as an overarching Scot-Gaelic bard was based on MacLean's inspiration, with MacLean providing the translations of MacDonald's 'The Birlinn of Clanranald' and MacIntyre's 'In Praise of Ben Dorain' for MacDiarmid's Scots versions, of which MacLean thought very highly. (It is clear that at this stage MacDiarmid thought of MacLean as his Gaelic counterpart in Scottish Renaissance – and we should remember that MacLean was studying at Edinburgh University from 1929 to 1933 and, after an unhappy year in Mull in 1938, living and teaching in Edinburgh in 1939, while beginning the great long poem 'An Cuilithionn', its form inspired by MacDiarmid's *Drunk Man*.) For MacLean, strong and influential friendships included those with Mitchison, Goodsir Smith, Garioch – and, given MacLean's self-criticism and its inhibiting effect on publication, it was to be these Lowland friendships which belatedly brought him into proper recognition. It was with fellow-poet and friend Robert Garioch that MacLean's early poetry appeared in *17 Poems for 6d* in 1940; poet Douglas Young was crucial in encouragement and in bringing about publication of the first edition of *Dàin do Eimhir agus Dàin Eile* in 1943, while also translating him into Scots in his *Auntran Blads* in the same year – dedicating the volume to MacLean and Hay. In 1970 poet Tom Scott pushed MacLean into much greater prominence with his *Four Points of a Saltire*, which deplored MacLean's lack of recognition. 'How many people,' wrote Scott, 'know that the best living Scottish poet, by a whole head and shoulders, after the two major figures in this century, Edwin Muir and Hugh MacDiarmid, is not any of the English writing poets, but Sorley MacLean?'[3] A year later came Iain Crichton Smith's translations of *Dàin do Eimhir*, the poem sequence which Smith described as 'miraculous'.[4]

Something of the same importance of Lowland friendship is the case with Hay, who encouraged Young to learn Gaelic, and who shared the same friends as MacLean. MacLean was his friend – although intriguingly MacLean saw himself as *personally* closer to Muir and MacDiarmid than to Young (the most aristocratic man he'd encountered) and Hay and philosopher George Davie.[5] Significant, this: arguably, despite recognising the worth of all, MacLean drew a line of class and heritage which put the first two as belonging to a different tradition of upbringing and identity compared to the public school and Oxbridge background of the others. That said, as early as 1943 Hay was a dedicatee of Young's *Auntran Blads*, and in 1970 was with MacLean in Tom Scott's *Four Points of a Saltire*. MacDiarmid rated his work almost as highly as MacLean's (as did Young and MacLean himself), and MacDiarmid published Hay's poetic manifesto in his quarterly *The Voice of Scotland* in 1939.[6]

But it's with Henderson, the youngest of the three, that we see the cracks which split the later Renaissance after 1945. We remember that Henderson was just over twenty as war began, and he is without doubt the most romantic of the three, clearly entering into war and new experience with enormous gusto. This is not in the least to say that he did not mean what he wrote regarding the waste of war and the need for a post-war revolution; but it is a young poet of enormous energy, charisma and talent, with languages and people, who will enter Sicily in triumph (using jeeps and horses to add dramatic enthusiasm for undoubted achievement), accepting personally the Italian Marshal Graziani's surrender. The question arises: how does such a young man move on after such heroic involvement and such an extended high pitch of experience?

Timothy Neat's two-volume biography, *Hamish Henderson* (2007–2009), hugely sympathetic to Henderson, reveals the frustrations Henderson was to encounter as his war experience counted for less and less in post-war Scotland.[7] Particularly galling was to be his exclusion from the BBC, probably due to increasing doubts in the Establishment about his political involvement in dubious activities, such as the Scottish Republican Army. Unlike Hay, Henderson perhaps was involved with too many people and a superfluity of social and political causes and commitments. And the hostilities between his Folk Renaissance and that of the revival of modern Scottish literature were deep. There was the flyting relationship with MacDiarmid and MacCaig, and, for Henderson, the more serious battles, concerning what he saw as the complete disregard of traditional music, with the BBC and George Bruce and Maurice Lindsay. And while Edinburgh University's new School of Scottish Studies rescued Henderson from his years of unemployment after the war, there were also serious differences with many of the School's early policy-makers. Neat suggests that perhaps Henderson was seen as politically and socially safer inside the Establishment. Despite all this, somehow, Henderson, despite his many flytings, maintained a huge number of enthusiastic friendships, very much including MacLean and Hay, and endlessly promoting their work at home and abroad.

This is the national context; but the international context must be remembered also. Scottish poets of the Renaissance years were acutely aware of and influenced by political and cultural developments in Ireland, as well as the revolutions in English poetry being brought about by Eliot and Pound in particular (with most Scottish poets contemptuous of the dominant English poetry of 'MacSpaunday': MacNeice, Spender, Auden). This contempt – especially in the case of our three poets – was hardly parochial, since wider European and world poetry attracted them to translation of poets like Blok, Fuernberg, Govoni, Angiolieri. All three poets were brilliant linguists. In addition to the Gaelic, English or Scots of their main poetic tongue, MacLean knew Latin and French, while Henderson had Gaelic, French, German and Italian, as did Campbell Hay – who also wrote original poetry in French, Italian and Norwegian. All three deeply respected, helped and promoted each other.

In summary: all three acknowledged the claims of the broad Renaissance movement: roots, language and race memory of community tradition. Their poetry is intensely bound to a creatively obsessive quest for validity and meaning and their own place in all of these. But there is more: all three have a profound sense of the threat of the possibility in a post-war world of the tragic extinction of traditional ways of life, together with their communities' poetry, song and culture. And this is the basis of my title's 'The Paradox of Renaissance'.

So what *of* the *paradox* of Renaissance? This seems to me to lie in the recurrent subject-matter of so many of the major writers. Consider Gibbon's title, *Sunset Song*. Doesn't it seem strange that our most well-known and popular native novel is hardly about rebirth, but – and in its sequels even more so – about loss of tradition, song, community? Gunn likewise, although his great trilogy concludes with a very temporary rebirth in *The Silver Darlings*: most of his Twenties and Thirties work, like *The Lost Glen*, *The Grey Coast* and *Butcher's Broom*, is about such loss, as is MacColla's *And the Cock Crew*, just as so much of the poetry of Hay and MacLean laments Clearance and decline of tradition. By the Thirties MacDiarmid himself had turned away from his early and wonderfully humane poetry of community and tradition in Scots to a bleak and distanced poetry of impersonality and fact in English.

After the war, Renaissance aims and values were rapidly dispersed with post-war scepticism, and a mood of ideological negativism and disillusion set in which was to persist till the mid-Sixties and the new work of writers like Crichton Smith, MacCaig, Mackay Brown and Morgan. The immediate post-war disenchantment is most vividly seen in the novel and the Fifties and Sixties work of Robin Jenkins, Dorothy Haynes, James Kennaway and Gordon Williams. Their themes are predominantly tragic, set in Scottish urban, rather than rural, decay, with rural tradition often mocked for its irrelevance to present stagnation, just as so often in drama, with the plays of

Ena Lamont Stewart, Robert McLellan and Joe Corrie, and outstandingly in James Bridie's most serious play of post-war urban despair, *Mr Gillie* (1950).

With all this in mind, can we deny that the term 'Renaissance' is something of a paradox? And wherein lie the reasons underlying the paradox and oxymoron of a literary revival which is preoccupied with elegy? Surely we must look to the earlier effects of the Great War, the decimation of the big men of communities, the impact of Depression, the decline of Gaelic and Scots? Nowhere does the sense of loss express itself more trenchantly than in MacLean's fiercely realistic assessment of the contemporary position of Gaelic to Douglas Young in 1943 (there's no doubting his sincerity, even if, thankfully, he was to be proved wrong):

> The whole prospect of Gaelic appals me, the more I think of the difficulties and the likelihood of its extinction in a generation or two. A highly inflected language with a ridiculous (because etymological) spelling, no modern prose of any account, no philosophical or technical vocabulary to speak of, no correct usage except among old people and a few university students ... full of gross English idiom lately taken over, exact shades of meanings ... not to be found in ... its dictionaries ... Above all, all economic, social and political factors working against it ... the notorious moral cowardice of the Highlanders themselves.[8]

And yet, holding this view, MacLean simultaneously writes the poetry which, like MacDiarmid's Scots lyrics, so impressively breaks the bonds of nostalgic simplification and custom, so that their work in Gaelic and Scots respectively become the mediums of a magnificently international poetry! But what of the other half of my title, 'The Pity of War'?

I begin with Henderson, the youngest of my three poets. Hamish Henderson's *Elegies for the Dead in Cyrenaica* appeared in 1948, and gained the Somerset Maugham award in 1949.[9] The ten elegies, followed by 'Song for the Heroic Runners', are, however, only a fraction of Henderson's war poetry, which is the most extensive poetry of the Second World War of any Scottish poet. '11 September 1941' (National Library of Scotland) follows young Henderson from the death of his mother to school in Dulwich and, in '4 September 1939', the loss of innocence – 'an incendiary dawn is prelude to this soft morning / First morning of the new war'. Shortly after, just turned 21, he was in uniform in Lancashire; a year later, a new Second Lieutenant, he was at sea in convoy to Freetown; thence by air to Cairo.

The early poetry feels its way into new worlds – in 'En Marche', Henderson is 'unsiccar o the foe I seek'. But soon he is lampooning fellow soldiers, with affection and respect, but is trenchant towards backsliders, as in many rollicking send-ups like 'Pioneer Ballad of Section Three' or 'Ballad of the Creeping Jesus' (which reveal Henderson's instinctive love of and facility with the irreverent and satiric traditional ballad form which was to be the hallmark of his post-war poetry). Here, in deceptively jovial ballad doggerel, is Rommel and his 'stubby guns on bulgy tanks', with the 'Fall of Tobruk' facing Allied disaster unflinchingly:

> Tommy thinks he holds Tobruk,
> along the road comes Rommel.
> Inside two shakes Tobruk is took
> and Tommy's on the bummel.

And the second verse clearly aligns Henderson and his communist sympathies with MacLean's early hope and belief in a Russian Red rising:

> I think old Timoshenko's fine.
> Thank God for the Red Army.

But with 'Lines to a Fool' the poetic mood darkens. In 'Ballad of Snow-White Sandstroke' the realities of dust and prickly heat take their toll, and Henderson finds 'A curse of sandy hell's on me', while 'We Show You that Death as a Dancer' sardonically describes how Death revels in his wartime 'dance into his promised land' – 'When we lie stickit in the sand'.

The early ballad doggerel was followed by poetry of a very different order, in the far more ambitious, profound and unified grouping of the ten great elegies, arguably the finest extended poetry to come out of the war (given that Campbell Hay's magnificent 'Mochtàr is Dùghall' remained unfinished). It was Sorley MacLean, when introducing the revised 1977 edition, who recognised, with his own desert experience, how Henderson's poems were centred on the weird doppelganger effect of desert war, in which the enemies seemed to mirror each other, and where mind gave way to mirage.

Their poetic Prologue sets out Henderson's aim: to hold on to 'my human barrier', and 'Maintain my fragile irony', to create 'A true and valued testament' for the dead. Paradoxically, the First Elegy, 'End of a Campaign', begins at the end with the 'many dead in the brutish desert'. Taking a position close to that of MacLean, Henderson, seeing that 'There were no gods and precious few heroes', adds that the dead 'saw through that guff before the axe fell'. And, like MacLean, Henderson constantly moves his mind from desert to Scotland and its little wars – warning us that we should be ever 'minding the great word of Glencoe's / son, that we should not disfigure ourselves with villainy of hatred'. Amidst the shifting sands and moralities Henderson clings to his humanity, as the Second Elegy, moving back into earlier war, develops the motif of nightmare displacement, as the nostalgic dreams of family and home give way to the reality of nightmare landscapes of the 'shabby lion-pelt of the desert'. Now Henderson presents his mirror/mirage world, where, across the desert laager, in sleep both sides are one, 'Friends and enemies, haters and lovers / both sleep and dream'.

The Third Elegy, 'Leaving the City' [Alexandria], sees distinctions of rank disappear under pressure of action, just as 'We send ... our greetings' to the advancing enemy – 'out of the mirror'. The elegy's invocation to courage, almost naively exulting in action at last, is then undercut by the Fourth's picture of renewed and bitterly cold inaction and endurance as the dead are buried, a desert wind again intermingling friend and foe in bleak endurance. The Fifth, 'Highland Jebel', again links Scotland in memory with the desert's moronic monotony, emphasising these links by describing Scottish dead in skirmish as 'Another falls for Hector' (the war-cry of the MacLeans to save their chief at the battle with Cromwell at Inverkeithing). And again, a link with MacLean: Henderson reveals his bitterness regarding 'the houses lying cold' back home through Clearance, but, like MacLean, setting national anger aside as secondary to the greater evil, so that the ideal of Highland heroic action will be sustained: 'we'll keep our assignation / with the Grecian Gael.'

The climax of the poem's action is of course the crucial battle of El Alamein. Paradoxical again, Henderson, rather than making this the climax of his poem, chooses to present the action under the holding title of 'Interlude: Opening of an Offensive', in three movements ('the waiting', 'the barrage', 'the Jocks'). But what an interlude! In the first movement, waiting for action, Henderson describes the last brew-up before battle, 'a silence not yet smashed by salvoes', as tanks in 'tourbillions of fine dust' move through 'the nervous fingers of the searchlights' (their crossing the signal for the next movement of the barrage). Here Henderson superbly captures the staccato violence and shattering rhythms of war, mingling sound and berserk subjective response:

> Let loose …
> the exultant bounding hell-harrowing of sound.
> Break the Batteries. Confound
> the damnable domination. Slake
> the crashing breakers-hurled rubble of the guns.
> Dithering darkness, we'll wake you! Hell's bells
> blind you. Be broken, bleed
> deathshead blackness!
>   The thongs of the livid
> firelights lick you
>   jagg'd splinters rend you
>   underground
> we'll bomb you, doom you, tomb you into grave's mound …

Then, in the second movement, the Jocks advance; and Henderson captures centuries of Scotland and war in what becomes almost a disjointed nightmare vision of the pent-up hatred of fascism and its doom, with the wild accompaniment of the Scottish pipes.

> They move forward into no man's land, a vibrant sounding
>   board.
>   As they advance
> the guns push further murderous music.
> Is this all they will hear, this raucous apocalypse? …
> No! For I can hear it! Or is it? … tell
> me that I can hear it! Now – listen!

> Yes, hill and sheiling
> sea-loch and island, hear it, the yell
> of your war-pipes, scaling sound's mountains
> guns thunder drowning in their soaring swell ...
> Now again! The shrill war-song: it flaunts
> aggression to the sullen desert. It mounts. Its scream
> tops the valkyrie, tops the colossal
> artillery ...

> We'll mak siccar!

Amidst this murderous music, war's hysteria has taken over, and now the enemy are clearly recognised as German fascists, 'doomed in their false dream', and Henderson now repeats the cry of 'We'll mak siccar!' against 'the tyrannous myth' of fascism.

Thus ends Part One; significantly, Henderson opens Part Two by quoting verses from MacLean's 'Death Valley', thus modulating battle hysteria to pity, in the manner of MacLean's sorrow for the dead German boy. And now, where Part One moves through mirage to wild battle, Part Two moves through its second set of five Elegies to a calmer, more humane, yet resolute conclusion. This second movement begins by accepting commitment; but now, in the Sixth Elegy, Henderson begins to wrestle with guilt and the meaning of such sacrifice, so that while accepting its necessity, he asks where healing and forgiveness may be found – and no immediate answer comes.

The Seventh and Ninth movingly present cameos of good – and dead – Germans, ironically reversing the cruel cliché to reveal humanity, in a compassionate recognition found also in MacLean's 'Death Valley'. The essential decency or honest delusion of the seven, from Lieutenant and Corporal to Volkdeutscher Pole and young swaddy, is revealed in their mundane notebooks, or simply imagined. 'The fifth a mechanic' wants only his girlfriend – and 'All the honour and glory, / the siege of Tobruk and the conquest of Cairo / meant as much to that Boche as the Synod of Whitby'.

The Ninth Elegy movingly combines Henderson's barrack-room style with genuine meditation on war, as he imagines the thoughts of a British soldier 'looking at the grave of a fallen enemy'. Henderson recreates his thoughts about the eighteen-year-old – the mirror effect again, as a common sardonic humanity is found:

> Cheerio, you poor bastard.
> Don't be late on parade when the Lord calls 'Close Order'.
> Keep waiting for the angels. Keep listening for Reveille.

But it is the Eighth and Tenth, intermingled, like war itself, with very different moods and situations, which, standing aside from the immediacy of war, move towards a more conciliatory humanity. The first, 'Karnak', ostensibly evokes a holiday of ancient time, the King paying homage to Osiris, with scenes of harvests, peasants and prisoners, of the King boating and Bedouins coming from the South. But other and ancient times begin to emerge, from 'the Horsemen of Amir' to Cavafy's 'barbarians', and statues to ancient gods, so that now Henderson suggests that all present wars have happened endlessly before, implying that Rommel and the Allies are merely the latest to disturb the desert. The Tenth Elegy fittingly completes the sequence. The Allies have finally won – and now, passengers in airliners will look down on 'the ennui / of limestone desert ... certain / they've seen it, they've seen all' but seeing nothing, not seeing the 'recces and sorties, / drumfire and sieges', the ambushes and supply lines forgotten. The elegies are seen now as a duty, Henderson seeing himself as 'Remembrancer', fighting on to build for the living, but also for the dead. Henderson concludes this greatest of war sequences with an invocation to 'build for the living / love, patience and power to absolve'.

As with Hay and MacLean, however, we should not miss the other, deeply political invocation to post-war revolt against Western capitalism and bourgeois repression:

> ... carry to the living
> blood, fire and red flambeaux of death's proletariat.
> Take iron in your arms! At last, spanning this history's
> apollyon chasm, proclaim them the reconciled.

Henderson continued to write powerful war poetry, such as 'Heroic Song for the Runners of Cyrene', almost a reprise to the Elegies in its timeless and Edwin Muir-like allegory picture of endless war in history, 'history the doppelgänger / running to meet them', and the desert's heat a 'trembling mirror', reflecting humanity's endless engagement with war and the Endless Other.

'So Long' is a fitting coda – like 'Heroic Song', not in itself a formal part of the ten elegies – to this extended mixture of brutality and meditation.

> To the war in Africa that's over – goodnight.
>
> To thousands of assorted vehicles, in every stage of
>   decomposition
>   littering the desert from here to Tunis – goodnight.
>
> To thousands of guns and armoured fighting vehicles
>   brewed up, blackened and charred
>   from Alamein to here, from here to Tunis – goodnight.
>
> To thousands of crosses of every shape and pattern
>   alone or in little huddles, under which the
>   unlucky bastards lie –
>   goodnight …
>
> To the sodding desert – you know what you
>   can do with yourself.
>
> To the African deadland – God help you –
>   and goodnight.

'So Long' is not just Henderson's laconic farewell to Africa. In another sense, together with some similarly laconic and elegiac poems of the same period, it is arguably a farewell to his best poetry. 'Song for An Irish Red Killed in Sicily', 'From the Serbian Spring 1941', 'Lament for The Son', in which Henderson imagines a father's grief, 'Requiem for the Men the Nazis Murdered', and the extended 'Dialogue of the Angel and the Dead Boy' show how deeply war experience had moved and changed Henderson, who never again attained the power and completeness of this early war poetry. Arguably, his famous 'The 51st Highland Division's Farewell to Sicily' (which gains so much of its elegiac power from its combination of words and pipe tune) marks a turning-point in Henderson's creativity. There are still stirring ballads for singing, written for fellow-soldiers, like his contemptuous response to Lady Astor's implied criticism of the Eighth Army, 'Ballad of the D-Day Dodgers', but the first group of poems have a metaphysical depth and a constant insistence on the crucial importance of civilised humanity, while the second are poems of camaraderie and encouragement.

That said, in his fascinating and mammoth biography – in itself a kind of guide to Scottish culture and politics in the post-war years – Timothy Neat argues on Henderson's behalf that the influence of the Italian communist philosopher Antonio Gramsci (whose *Letters from Prison* Henderson was to translate), together with his identification with the folk and culture of his Blairgowrie childhood, led him to see folksong and political song as just as necessary for the cultural and political reform of Scotland, and for international political awakening – and it cannot be denied that Henderson has written some of the world's greatest songs of this kind, such as 'The John MacLean March', 'The Flyting o' Life and Daith' and 'The Freedom Come-All-Ye'.[10]

*

George Campbell Hay had a very different view of war.[11] Sharing, with qualifications, Henderson and MacLean's loyalty to tradition, nationalism and a socialist-communist anger at the dead hand of Westminster, he had none of Henderson's energetic participation or MacLean's praise of enduring heroism, instead seeing war as the meaningless madness of dictators, almost a living force of Evil, blindly predestining its victims. Onlooker rather than participant in war, Hay originally intended to stay out of involvement of any kind, his cause being that of nationalist friends like Douglas Young, who saw their quarrel as being with England before Germany. After going 'under the cairn' – that is, hiding out rough in Argyll – he gave in to save his mother being harassed, and went with Ordnance to Tunisia, where his language skills brought him respect for and from the Arabs – 'Atman' expressing his preference for the humble Arab fellaheen victim rather than for his judge. The actual war poems are few – barely a dozen – yet 'Bisearta'/ 'Bizerta' has an astonishing intensity in its vision of violence and death ('and who tonight are beseeching / death to come quickly in all their tongues … who tonight is paying / the old accustomed tax of common blood?'). The last verse pans back from human suffering so that the fury of the blaze above the doomed city becomes animate Evil with a pulse and a heart.

> Uair dearg mar lod na h-àraich,
> uair bàn mar ghile thràighte an eagail èitigh,
> a' dìreadh 's uair a' teàrnadh,
> a' sìneadh le sitheadh àrd 's a' call a mheudachd,
> a' fannachadh car aitil
> 's ag at mar anail dhiabhail air dhèinead,
> an t-Olc 'na chridhe 's 'na chuisle,
> chì mi 'na bhuillean a' sìoladh 's a' leum e.
> Tha 'n dreòs 'na oillt air fàire,
> 'na fhàinne ròis is òir am bun nan speuran,
> a' breugnachadh 's ag àicheadh
> le 'shoillse sèimhe àrsaidh àrd nan reultan.

> *Now red like a battlefield puddle,*
> *now pale like the drained whiteness of foul fear,*
> *climbing and sinking,*
> *reaching and darting up and shrinking in size,*
> *growing faint for a moment*
> *and swelling like the breath of a devil in intensity,*
> *I see Evil as a pulse and a heart,*
> *declining and leaping in its throbs.*
> *The blaze, a horror on the skyline,*
> *a ring of rose and gold at the foot of the sky,*
> *belies and denies*
> *with its light the ancient high tranquillity of the stars.*

A young man speaks from the grave in 'An t-Òigear a' Bruidhinn on Ùir', wishing a great wind to blind the masters of war for the horrors they have brought about in Italy and Africa; and here Hay is close in ambition to Henderson. And if we wish to see war poetry at its highest, then Hay's magnificent 'Esta Selva Selvaggia'/'This Savage Wood' (the title, and the poem itself, draw on Dante's *Inferno*), developing themes introduced by 'Bizerta', shares with Henderson's 'Elegies' a common and international humanity. Its startling and savagely satirical juxtapositions of countries, languages and acts of atrocity show a modernist and internationally aware poet of the highest order. This is a nine-movement poem of Death, mingling the Clyde blitz with the crashed bomber who missed docks and destroyed a home; an Italian girl's posthumous and poisonous revenge on the soldiers who shot her; a French gendarme torturer; and other scenes of horror across the world, culminating ferociously in a nightmare confusion of ten world languages hate-filled, bitter and questioning. The horror reaches its climax in the fragmented cries of hateful self-justification of the seventh movement:

> *"Haus kaput – maison finie –*
> *kaput – capito? – familie.*
> *Alles ist kaput. Compris?"*

> *"Er hat uns belogen* – he told us lies."
> "Who wanted war? The poor man dies
> in war. He threw dust in our eyes."

> "Only the great make wars," they say,
> *"I pezzi grossi, gros bonnets,*
> *el-kebâr bass* make war to-day."

> *"Halûf! Βουλγαρικό σκυλί!*
> *Cretini 'e merda! Βρωμεροί!*
> *Τα Μακαρόνια! Sale Italie!"*

> *"N'âd dîn bâbak – salauds* – dogs!
> *Jene Scheisshernn!* Wops and Frogs,
> they're all the same, myte, like the Wogs."

Yet all of these international voices blame the Other, while the poet's conclusion sums up laconically and simply:

> "What crime was it we suffered for?"
> "They started it. We willed no war."
> *Listen to yourselves. Beware.*

War permanently scarred Hay; in an earlier poem, 'An Lagan'/'The Hollow', he had wondered if, on returning to his sacred places in Argyll, he would find his soul. Hay hardly ever referred to this turning-point, although Michel Byrne has speculated that it was perhaps the horrific experience in Greek Macedonia, where the bitter divisions of varieties of left and right wing allegiances meant that no-one trusted anyone else. As in Tunis, he favoured the ordinary people – which the right wing noticed, and which culminated in Hay barely escaping with his life; he tells of 'a terrific to-do' in a night of 'knives and carabines and all the rest – and that's the origin of my getting my pension'; and then the many years of mental illness which plagued him afterwards and led to hospitalisation in Carstairs and Lochgilphead and Morningside.[12] Did this prevent Hay from completing his most ambitious poem, 'Mochtàr is Dùghall'/'Mokhtâr and Dougall'?

The 'Prologue' begins with what could also have been the 'Epilogue'. The Arab in his homeland and the Scot who has come to the war in Africa are predestined to be killed by the same German sniper. The poem opens with a meditation on its conclusion:

> Mhochtàir is Dhùghaill, choinnich sibh
> an comann buan gun chòmhradh.
>
> B'iad fraighean an taigh chèilidh dhuibh
> an cactas ceusta, leònte.
>
> B'i 'n aoigheachd an dèidh furain dhuibh
> lan beòil den duslach ròsta.
>
> B'i fàilte an ùr-chomain sin
> guth obann, cruaidh a' mhòrtair ...
>
> A bheil fhios ciod e 'n dubh-chumhachd
> a chuir cruinn sibh air an sgòrr seo?
>
> A stiùir thar bheann 's thar chuan sibh,
> gur cruadhachadh le dòrainn?

Mokhtâr and Dougall, you have met
in an everlasting fellowship without conversation.

The walls of your gossiping house
were the tortured, wounded cactus.

The hospitality that followed welcome for you
was the fill of your mouth of hot dust.

The greeting of your new companionship
was the sudden, hard voice of the mortar ...

Who knows what black power
brought you together on this pinnacle,

Guided you over mountains and oceans,
hardening you with misery?

Hay has profound respect for the traditions and character of his Tunisian Arabs, and the poem, while tragic, is by implication a profound international celebration of difference and similarity between nations. This magnificent incomplete poetic account of the shared destiny of Arab Mokhtâr and Scottish Dùghall was to have been in two equally balanced parts, a thousand lines telling of Mokhtâr and his forefathers, their courage in defying oppressors and their search for spiritual truth, the first part balanced with a similar treatment of Dùghall and his Highland home and ancestry.

The first part is the measure of what we lost with incompletion. After a superbly ironic prologue, and a wonderfully wailing and moving Arab lament for Mokhtâr from his wife and the women of the Douar, the lament moves in Gaelic manner into a recall of ancestors – beginning with Ahmed, Mokhtâr's great-grandfather and the glorious horseman of the sanctified hosts of Abd el-Qader, as he leads his clan (like a Highland chieftain?) into spiritual war – which, as so often in Highland history, he loses – and in an ironic anticipation of Hay's own post-war illness, Ahmed retreats to lonely silence. The women are remembering the words of their forebears; now we hear from his son and Mokhtâr's grandfather, Omar the adventurer, the bold, who traversed the Sahara to bring home the riches of the other side of Africa – only to be exploited in his turn by Berber tribes who allow him only his life. I cannot begin to convey the sensuous and expansive sense of desert and the twists of Arab fate which Hay astonishingly masters in every detail, with total control of structure and theme. For after Warrior and Adventurer comes the ascetic and spiritual Obayd, Mokhtâr's father, again reminding the reader of the parallels in nations. After the richness of Obayd's very different seeking comes Mokhtâr's journey to the mouth of the mortar which will kill him – and end his traditions of warrior, adventurer, seeker after truth – traditions so evocative for Scotland also.

This first half is well over a thousand lines; we have slightly more than two hundred lines of Dùghall's Highland upbringing (reminiscent of Hay's in Tarbert), where Hay asks what makes us and what made Dùghall, setting him in the too often tragic history of the Gaels. We learn of his fishermen father and grandfather, their harmony with sea and land and season – and, from his mother, her fears for her wandering son, who has the Omar yearning. With her farewell blessing we leave Dùghall and the poem – although the moving 'Epilogue: Man and War' shows again how Hay had the complete structure of a quite magnificent epic and tragic poem in his mind. The poem was to have balanced Mokhtâr's journey to death with that of Dùghall; and, although a later short draft sequence of Dùghall's story survives, as he sails in grey ships in the U-boat-haunted Atlantic to Africa, where his predestined death awaits, we can only speculate as to how great the epic could have been. The heart of the poem is a meditation on the mystery of race, upbringing and values, with the profound differences between Mokhtâr and Dùghall somehow reconciled in the underlying similarities of respect for their forefathers, their traditions and their respective cultures, Arabic and Gaelic. The magnificent 'Epilogue: Man and War' draws the many rich strands of this ambitious poem to a powerful close – with strong parallels with the themes of 'Hallaig' (if closing with the more sombre affirmation that the dead live on in descendants).

> Saoghal fa leth mac-an-duine,
> domhan beò leis fhèin gach urra ...
> Cia mheud glùn a th' ann ar cumadh?

Chan innis sgeul, cha lorg cuimhn' iad,
's ath-bheirear iad uile cuideachd
san naoidhean, is a shinnsre cruinn ann …
Chithear a ghnùis 's e fhèin 'na uirigh;
faodar gur e a ghuth a chluinnear
is ogh' an ogha nach fhac' e 'bruidhinn.

A world apart is each son of man,
a living world in himself is every person …
How many generations go to shape us?
No story can tell and no memory trace them.
Yet they are all reborn together
in the little child, and his ancestry is united within him …
His face will be seen when he himself is in his grave,
and it may be that it is his voice that will be heard
when the grandson of the grandson he never saw is speaking.

Was dealing with war – and the fate of Dùghall – too hard for Hay? In the 'Epilogue' he seems to anticipate his own creative loss in the lines

Brisear an teud – stadar an ceilear –
nuair bu bhinne, àirde sheinn iad.
Sguirear 's gun am port ach leitheach.

The string is snapped, the singing stopped,
when the music sounded its sweetest.
They cease with the melody but half played.

And what we have of the poem concludes:

Mort nam marbh is mort nan naoidhean
nach do ghineadh – crioch dhà shaoghal.

Murder of the dead, murder of the children
never begotten – the end of two worlds.

With Hay, it seems to me that the pity of war and the paradox of Renaissance come together, singularly exemplifying the Scottish tragedy of Scotland's disproportionate war burden, and the twentieth century's lament for its children, whether at war or on return to damaged communities and cold houses. Yet, despite Hay's recurrent illness, *Wind on Loch Fyne* appeared in 1948 to fine reviews, MacDiarmid calling it 'the most distinguished volume of Scottish poems that has appeared for a quarter of a century'.[13] This later poetry is the more poignant for showing what Hay was still capable of. In especial, 'Seeker, Reaper' is a culmination (in ten movements sustained in a superbly vigorous Scots, Gaelic and Norse) of all Hay's wonderful poems of the sea, here giving his heroic boat human spirit and his own sea-breasting desire.

Hay is never less than a good poet; yet, as he says significantly, after the war he did 'quite a lot of writing, although scattered, which is often the post-war manner'.[14] He was annoyed by Maurice Lindsay's 1946 attack (in Lindsay's poem 'To Hugh MacDiarmid') on Gaelic and nostalgic poetic romanticism, the poem describing 'that contemptuous nonsense' of 'rotting shielings / and the dreary, crumbling dust of a vanished race'.[15]

It's true that after 1948 his poetry is more nostalgic, yet in, for example, 'The Walls of Balclutha' he still creates an ambitious long poem lamenting the decay of Highland community which in many ways anticipates the theme of 'Hallaig' (if lacking MacLean's astonishing compression and economy), yet insists angrily, if perhaps unconvincingly, on renewal in its ending: '"Was" will beget "will be" unwarped at last.' While indeed angry and deeply moved by the decline of Gaeldom, its traditions and poetry, Hay never admits that Gaelic culture is dying, as his poem of 1946, 'We Abide For Ever', insists. Acknowledging the blows of Culloden and Clearance, deploring foreign wars, yet

> We are the Gaels that centuries have not shaken;
> we are no broken ghosts, no vanished race.
> Our spirit cries in pride ...
>
> ... while light returns from darkness,
> with speech and melody we will abide.

As Michel Byrne points out, Hay's poems consistently believe in people and Scotland and the possibility of Gaelic Renaissance, and avoid cliché through their metrical subtleties and restraint. As for nostalgia, Hay said late in life (and this seems to me to be a classically simple statement of difference between Kailyard and truth):

> Time and time again in Gaelic and Scots and English I have written
> nostalgic poems, and either you mean it or you don't mean it. I have
> always meant it.[16]

Hay's case is the saddest of our three poets. Though living in Edinburgh, and in and out of hospital, throughout his life he idolised Tarbert as his spiritual home, only to find in his 1983 fulfilment of his long-cherished ambition to return there for the rest of his life that memory wasn't reality: Tarbert had changed, Gaelic and old friends had gone, fishing wasn't the same fishing, he could not find a house. He was respected but poor, and returned to Edinburgh and hospital again. Despite this, he tried to finish his most ambitious poem, but by now for him 'enough was enough', as his friend Angus Martin said, and he died in 1984 (with *Scotsman* tributes from fellow poets Sorley MacLean and Iain Crichton Smith).

We have to thank Michel Byrne and his fine work for re-asserting Hay as the fine poet, brilliant linguist and outstandingly decent man he was and is, with a poetry which physically encompasses and affirms Scotland, from the north to Edinburgh, the urban scene (often in the manner of his friend Robert Garioch) and the ordinary folk from the Borders to Kintyre, from Tarbert to Tinto, in Gaelic, Scots and English. Generous and committed to friends, and to ordinary people of many countries and beliefs, he deserves the same respect for courage in illness which Sorley MacLean celebrates in his magnificent elegy for his brother Calum.[17]

*

In 1978 Hay wrote four lines of exhortation to Sorley MacLean:

> Sorley MacLean over yonder,
> my advice to you, and it is no lie:
> shake your mane and start neighing.
> You are the master-poet, not I.[18]

This discussion cannot begin to do justice to the achievement – or the Gaelic – of Sorley MacLean, and, given the distinguished speakers to follow, I can only echo Crichton Smith's placing of his *Dàin do Eimhir* alongside MacDiarmid's *A Drunk Man Looks at the Thistle* (1926). Christopher Whyte, in his recent groundbreaking edition of the poem, considers 'The Cuillin' as 'a poem more cogent, unified and consistent than anything MacDiarmid was ever to achieve'.[19] What I would suggest is that of its two major themes, the first is of course that of the poet's guilt at failing to fight against fascism in Spain, and his agony at the cry of suffering Europe. Reading this and related poems in *O Choille gu Bearradh/From Wood to Ridge: Collected Poems* (1999) made me realise that the war poems of the 'Blàr/Battlefield 1942–1943' section, while most explicitly focused on desert battle, by no means contain the sum of MacLean's poetic deployment of war and its implications.[20]

Not only is the agony of Spain and the Asturian miners recurrent in the Eimhir cycle, together with 'Cornford and Julian Bell / and Garcia Lorca / always going round in my head' along with 'the madness / as brave as Dimitrov or as Connolly', or the rout of the Greeks; but violence and betrayal, from Deirdre of the Sorrows to Glasgow's John Maclean, thrust an obsessive motif of war to the front of the poem, an anger against aggressive imperialism summed up at the outbreak of war in his poem 'Cornford':

> Dè dhuinne ìmpireachd na Gearmailt
> no ìmpireachd Bhreatainn
> no ìmpireachd na Frainge,
> 's a h-uile tè dhiubh sgreataidh!

> *What to us the empire of Germany*
> *or the empire of Britain*
> *or the empire of France,*
> *and every one of them loathsome?*

The other major theme, moving agonisingly and profoundly through the feelings MacLean had for inspirational women, is that personal and relentless war between reason and emotion, duty and love, which flares endlessly in his poetry as a whole, one or the other side predominant, then giving way to guilt and anger regarding his own weakness. Thus the two themes are not separate: the horror of Europe and the power of ideal love are juxtaposed in a great cry of agony and dilemma. This is well-known territory, which I will not rehearse here, focusing rather on themes arising from my discussion of the pity of war and the paradox of Renaissance. MacLean's most explicit and finest poetry of war is found mainly in the grouping 'Blàr/Battlefield 1942–1943' in *From Wood to Ridge*. 'Going Westwards', 'Alasdair MacLeod', 'Move South', 'Heroes', 'Death Valley' and 'An Autumn Day' form a small group of explicit commentaries on the war in the desert leading up to El Alamein, where MacLean was seriously wounded. After this injury (on 2 November 1943), MacLean was sent home to recover. (It is striking that in letters to Douglas Young and others MacLean does not speak of his three injuries, but instead refers to the agony of his personal life at home.)

In these poems the poet finds no rancour in his heart against his hardy enemies in the desert, imprisoned like himself. A detached compassion pities the body of the German boy killed in 'Death Valley', and a puny Englishman of immense courage is wept for in 'Heroes' as a great warrior of England. These are great poems of lament for the brave dead, whoever they may be. Other and later poems show MacLean's awareness of the never-ending story of war. 'Palach' reveals change in his favourable attitude towards Russia, in recognising its cruelty to Czechoslovakia, and 'A' Bheinn air Chall'/'The Lost Mountain' connects Auschwitz with Vietnam and Ulster – but the heart of MacLean's feelings about *his* desert war are in 'Blàr/Battlefield'.

MacLean's war poetry is better known than that of Henderson and Hay. Rather than rehearse discussion of the familiar poems I have cited, let me dwell a little more on 'Dol an Iar'/'Going Westwards', since it's maybe less often cited than the others, and it seems to me to be the only 'war' poem to pull both of MacLean's conflicts together. It takes up once more the theme of guilt, as MacLean feels he goes to war in shame, far from love of country or woman. For our purposes, it is MacLean's context for his guilt which relates him clearly to Henderson and Hay, as he tells how he goes 'westwards in the Desert / with my shame on my shoulders'; his home island, as well as 'the bondage of Europe', is far from him, in Africa; so too Belsen and Dachau, the Clyde and Prague and Guernica. The concluding verses, with their sense of imprisonment in an inexorable duty to Gaeldom, ancestors and traditions of martial bravery, share much of Henderson's paradoxical fusion of humanity and aggression, together with their search for identity rooted in Scottish history and tradition – with a typically ironic sting regarding all those in the very last line in the adjective 'ruinous' and the final questioning:

Chan eil gamhlas 'na mo chridhe
ri saighdearan calma 'n Nàmhaid
ach an càirdeas a tha eadar
fir am prìosan air sgeir-thràghad ...

Ach 's e seo an spàirn nach seachnar,
éiginn ghoirt a' chinne-daonna,
's ged nach fuath liom armailt Roimeil,
tha sùil na h-eanchainn gun chlaonadh.

Agus biodh na bha mar bha e,
tha mi de dh'fhir mhór' a' Bhràighe,
de Chloinn Mhic Ghille Chaluim threubhaich,
de Mhathanaich Loch Aills nan geurlann
agus fir m' ainme – có bu tréine
nuair dh'fhadadh uabhar an léirchreach?

There is no rancour in my heart
against the hardy soldiers of the Enemy,
but the kinship there is among
men in prison on a tidal rock ...

But this is the struggle not to be avoided,
the sore extreme of human-kind,
and though I do not hate Rommel's army,
the brain's eye is not squinting.

And be what was as it was,
I am of the big men of Braes,
of the heroic Raasay MacLeods,

> *of the sharp-sword Mathesons of Lochalsh;*
> *and the men of my name – who were braver*
> *when their ruinous pride was kindled?*

Elsewhere, war, and MacLean's despair at seeing war as a recurrent part of the human condition (as in Henderson's 'Karnak' and Hay's 'Esta Selva Selvaggia'), pervade his poetry from *The Cuilinn* on, from its invocation of MacDiarmid and his intention: 'I would keep our noble Cuilinn / head on to the waves of Europe's battle'. It is not long before the wonderful evocation of surging ramparts begins to raise issues of conflict – 'clearing of tenants, exile, exploitation' – and, in the bewildering, ever-changing and phantasmagoric symbolism of the mountains it can seem that 'It was the Devil himself who built this rampart / to hide … chiefs and tacksmen plundering'. A ghost band of the Clearance factors, lawyers and landowners who 'dragged and plundered and drove' gathers in a Dance of Death, drawing in all those leaders of Europe and the world accountable, in MacLean's eyes, for similar cruelty and violence. Franco, 'the grey Pope of Rome', 'Wily Chamberlain' represent political corruption eternally struggling with disadvantaged brave men like Lenin, Marx, John Maclean in Glasgow, Dimitrov in Russia. And while with hindsight we may wonder at the inclusion amongst the brave figures of Mao Tse Tung and Stalin, there is no doubting the force of MacLean's anger and pity for the centuries of war and injustice, local and universal.

I'm returning to my theme of the intermingling of war and Renaissance, and to my paradox that some of our greatest poetry of the 'Scottish Renaissance' expresses, not rebirth, but decay and death. I can't resolve this paradox; but it seems to me that MacLean is a quite outstanding example of it, in his roll-call of heroes who fight or fought the good fight against the filthy swamp of corruption symbolised by the morass of Mararaulin, with its dead and ghosts from the fields of carnage. From the local example of the tragedy of the Gesto girl to the world-circling Clio, the Muse of history, MacLean's poem is a great cry of humanity against conflict and corruption, from the townships of Brae Eynort to the French Revolution and the Easter Rising in Dublin. And while the symbolism of the great Stallion of Skye argues for hope and 'a fresh red rose over a bruised maimed world', it seems to me, in the light of later poetry, that already this is more an act of will than belief. MacLean *wills* the Cuillin to stand as an emblem of hope for 'the free, the heroic, the great mind, the rugged heart of sorrow'. (Even MacLean's inspirer MacDiarmid had to finish his nightmare struggle in *A Drunk Man Looks at the Thistle* (1926) by taking the great debate of identity, Scotland and metaphysical truth to 'avizandum' – in legal terms, taking judgement out of court for further discussion.)

For after this, and increasingly, do fine extended poems such as 'The Woods of Raasay' and 'The Farther End' not suggest disillusion? 'The Woods of Raasay', beautiful in its tribute to MacLean's debt to their nurturing of his creativity, nevertheless, after continuing the theme of the *Eimhir* poems, asks bitter questions of the meaning of love, and how its loss 'has seen the Cuilinn wall knocked down, / brittle, broken, in a loathsome pit'. 'The Farther End' seems to me to indicate a debt to Muir, with its opening 'This is the ultimate place, / the lonely place without sight of hills', echoing Muir's many evocations of Bunyan-like spiritual desolation. Its familiar central question asks how the 'foolish and strong desire' of love took the poet to this limbo – 'Neither the tanks of your heredity / nor the big guns of your desire / nor the aeroplanes of your goodwill' were of any avail, since the poet, addressing himself, tells how he has ended with 'your Glen Etive a little pit / shrivelled, cold and wet'.[21]

And how much more disillusion must have followed with the breaking of Eimhir's loved one's image through deceit and falsehood, together with the loss of faith in communism? It's intriguing that section VII of *From Wood to Ridge*, '1945–72', begins with a Gaelic translation of the opening of *Paradise Lost*, followed by 'Culloden', which asks if that conflict 'brought the rotting in midwinter' of the Gaeldom of Scotland, bringing 'only the withered tree of misfortune'? I do not venture far into 'Hallaig', which I think is one of the world's greatest poems, but I do suggest that it is about locking in grief as private, since only private memory and grief – not to be cheapened by exposure – can survive the tragic loss of community, tradition, singing. Indeed, I suggest this poem as an outstanding example of the paradox of 'Renaissance'.

I finish with three wonderful poems which for me substantiate my claim that the magnificence of MacLean's poetry lies in their ruthless honesty, their stoic endurance – the quality which in 'Going Westwards', for all its shame and despair at false love and the horrors of Belsen and Guernica, has no rancour 'against the hardy soldiers of the Enemy' but pity for 'the innocent corpses of the Nazis', and which, in 'the struggle not to be avoided, / the sore extreme of human-kind', has no trace of final refuge in religion or pious hope but, with pride in ancestors alone, allows whatever is to happen to happen, all in the stark conclusion: 'be what was as it was, / I am of the big men of Braes'.

'The Lost Mountain' seems to me to go even further in its lament for the loss of both the affirmation of mountains and the consolation of woods, 'Because Vietnam and Ulster are / heaps on Auschwitz of the bones'. 'Heartbreak is about the mountains / and in the woods for all their beauty', now become 'a withered brittle comfort', 'Paradise without the paradise of his own people' – or the people of the world. I think too that I now understand a little more of that most difficult late poem, 'The Cave of Gold'. Am I right in finding MacLean himself, early and late, in that last profound unfinished poem, being both of the pipers who, weary of this world, seek (in an even darker mood than that of 'Hallaig') a more bitter truth and a kind of stoic ideal in personal darkness? When he asks of the first piper, 'strong, fortunate, happy, young', 'Who else would leave the land of MacLeod / if free from poor wretch's labour', the answer would seem to be MacLean himself: not through religious zeal, but through a stern questioning of truth and beauty, 'the band / that comes from the heart's smithy'. And is the second piper not MacLean after war and disillusion, 'the great horse of his aspirations / bridled and tethered by the past', 'the blue rampart / become a tough and flabby blue mould'? 'Two men in the Cave of Gold / meditating upon death', 'beguiled by two kinds of music'; 'My lack, my lack / with head and heart, / dim eye in the head / and no eye in the heart' concludes this wonderfully austere, if most difficult and dark, of philosophical and allegorical poems. We should not forget that the pipers are also warriors![22]

Finally, 'Screapadal', which is more explicit in its evocation not so much of the pity of war as of the threat of final and catastrophic war, with its jarring images of the basking shark giving way to the sleek black back of submarines, nuclear destruction and Nagasaki, and the threat of 'rocket, hydrogen and neutron bomb'. Clearly war and its aftermath have cast a long shadow over MacLean, bringing us closer to our own times. And I conclude by suggesting that in its heartfelt evocation of Screapadal – 'quite as beautiful as Hallaig' – its roll-call of betrayals, which have reduced the place to 'poisonous bracken' – this final example of clear-eyed, stoic sorrow stands at the end of *O Choille gu Bearradh* not just as a final example of the pity of war and the paradox of Renaissance, but as a startlingly relevant international condemnation.[23]

Notes

1   My arguments regarding 'Scottish Renaissance' are presented more fully than space allows here in 'Re-mapping Renaissance in Modern Scottish Literature' in *Beyond Scotland: new contexts for twentieth-century Scottish literature*, eds Gerard Carruthers, David Goldie and Alastair Renfrew, Amsterdam-New York: Rodopi, pp. 17–38.

2   I am indebted throughout to Michel Byrne's *Collected Poems and Songs of George Campbell Hay (Deòrsa Mac Iain Dheòrsa)* – two volumes, Edinburgh: Edinburgh University Press, 2000 – for his fine biography and scrupulous editing of Hay's poetry. See also his essay 'Tails o the Comet' in *Scotlit 26*, Glasgow: Association for Scottish Literary Studies, pp. 1–3.

3   *Four Points of a Saltire: The Poetry of Sorley MacLean, George Campbell Hay, William Neill, Stuart MacGregor*, Edinburgh: Reprographia, 1970, p. 8. Preface by Tom Scott.

4   Sorley MacLean, *Poems to Eimhir: Poems from* Dàin do Eimhir *Translated from Gaelic by Iain Crichton Smith*, London: Victor Gollancz, 1971, pp. 14–15: 'It is astonishing that a Highlander brought up in such a narrow world (though broadened by a liberal education at Edinburgh University) should not have succumbed in the furnace of Communist ideology, a love affair of great intensity, and a cause demanding decision of poets and artists. It is precisely this creative confusion which produced the poetry ... a union of the sophisticated and the primitive, of the intelligence and the passions, which is quite unique in Gaelic literature. It probably will not happen again in the conceivable future. That it should have happened at all seems little short of miraculous.'

5   Letter from MacLean to Young, 11 September 1941 (National Library of Scotland), quoted in *Sorley MacLean: Critical Essays*, eds Raymond Ross and Joy Hendry, Edinburgh: Scottish Academic Press, 1986, pp. 33–34: 'Why do I immediately sense a sort of political kinship with people as different as Muir and Grieve, but not with you, Davie, Deòrsa [Hay] etc. I think it is a class question. Neither you, nor Davie [George Elder Davie, philosopher and author of *The Democratic Intellect* (1960)] nor Deòrsa nor Robert MacIntyre [President of the SNP and first Nationalist MP in 1945] are really of my "class", and hence I have never immediately felt that intimate feeling of closeness politically with you ... though probably I should intellectually agree less with either Muir or Grieve on most questions than I would with you.'

6   Douglas Young, *Auntran Blads: An Outwale o Verses*, Glasgow: William MacLellan, 1943. MacDiarmid published Hay's poetic manifesto in his quarterly *The Voice of Scotland* in 1939; see Byrne, *Scotlit 26*, p. 2.

7   Timothy Neat, *Hamish Henderson*, Edinburgh: Birlinn, 2007 & 2009

8   Letter from MacLean to Young, 15 June 1943 (National Library of Scotland), quoted in Ross and Hendry, p. 34

9   Henderson's *Elegies for the Dead in Cyrenaica* was first published in 1948 by John Lehmann. After revision, a 1977 edition appeared, prefaced by Sorley MacLean and published by EUSPB, and another was published by Polygon in 1990. But all quotations here are from *Collected Poems and Songs*, Edinburgh: Curly Snake Publishing, 2000, edited by Raymond Ross.

10 Timothy Neat's ambitious biography decisively separates Henderson's pre-war and war experience, and the fine war poetry (Volume 1) from his post-war work as collector of traditional song and music for Edinburgh University's School of Scottish Studies, together with his huge range of cultural and political interests (Volume 2), accepting from the outset that 'by his mid thirties his personal artistic creativity was waning' (Preface, Vol. I, p. xiii).

11 See the third section, 'War', in '"Out of the Midst of Life": Recurrent Themes in Hay's Poetry', in Volume II of Byrne, pp. 90–92.

12 Ibid, p. 41

13 Ibid, p. 43

14 Ibid, p. 172

15 Lindsay's contempt for what he saw as a poetry lamenting the past is in his poem 'To MacDiarmid' in his edition of *Modern Scottish Poetry*, London: Faber and Faber, 1946, p. 134. The full offending verse 9 praises MacDiarmid: 'You have put that contemptuous nonsense back in its place, / and are no longer concerned with the rotting shielings / and the dreary, crumbling dust of a vanished race; / but with the steady hands and hearts that are willing / to cultivate the vast and desolate space / two hundred empty years have left behind, / you would cut all cancerous growth from the Scottish mind.'

As Byrne points out (Vol. II, 163), when Hay denies that the Gaels are 'broken ghosts', he refers to G. S. Fraser's 'To Hugh MacDiarmid' (Lindsay pp. 114–15), where Fraser refuses to 'revive the broken ghosts of Gael' – but protests that MacDiarmid's 'Keltic mythos shudders me with Fear'!

16 Byrne, Vol. II, 95. Hay's post-war nostalgia for his beloved Tarbert was to be disappointed. Yet the genuine desire to return had its practical side, comparable to Henderson's work with the School of Scottish Studies. Hay planned to use his war disability pension to find a place in Tarbert – 'I'm thinking of years recording the Gaelic of Kintyre, Knapdale, Cowal, Gigha, Islay, Colonsay, and Jura.' It's intriguing to note that he thought that when he went to Tarbert he would either sell his Edinburgh flat 'or else give it to Sabhal Mòr Ostaig for an Edinburgh HQ'!

17 'Elegy for Calum I. MacLean', in Sorley MacLean, *O Choille gu Bearradh/From Wood to Ridge: Collected Poems*, Manchester and Edinburgh: Carcanet Press/Birlinn, 1999, pp. 264–77

18 Byrne, Vol. I, p. 357. The exhortation 'start neighing' suggests that Hay had read of MacLean's heroic invocation to the Skye Stallion 'neighing on the Cuillin'.

19 MacGill-Eain, Somhairle, *An Cuilithionn 1939: The Cuillin 1939 and Unpublished Poems* edited by Christopher Whyte, Glasgow: Association for Scottish Literary Studies, 2011, p. 6

20 MacLean 1999, pp. 204–15

21 Ibid, pp. 194–97

22 Ibid, pp. 282–301

23 Ibid, pp. 304–13

2. Somhairle MacGill-Eain and the Imagination of Excess

ALAN TITLEY

When we look at any one of Somhairle's poems on the page, before we even engage with them, we see a cut and a shape and a form. We are aware that we are in the presence of a poet who appreciates 'the well-made thing', a poet whose work is 'not out of shape from toe to top'. We are aware of craftsmanship. And, as we know, discussion of poetry can often turn upon the axis of 'craftsmanship', on the one hand, and 'inspiration' on the other. We have one image of the poets, as our Scottish and Irish classical poets are said to have done, labouring in the dark with a stone upon their bellies, pumping their brains for encomium or panegyric – as we are told – and wrestling with the knotted knitting of their craft, piecing together verbal sudokus out of their stock of phrases and interlocking sounds. We have the other, more romantic image of the poet being visited by the divine afflatus, being borne on the wings of imagination and wonder by some outside force, if not necessarily assisted either by some opium or little shots of mescalin to fire the doors of perception.

Of course, those of us who have wrestled with writing of one kind or another know it is never either one thing or another, neither this nor that. There must be a muse – and Gaelic artists have called upon the muse, as Alasdair Mac Mhaighstir Alasdair was doing in his 'Guidhe no Ùrnaigh an Ùghdair don Cheòlraidh', or I believe Muireadhach Albanach Ó Dálaigh was doing five hundred years previously in 'Ling ar Mo Theanga, a Thríonóid'. But once you have got your muse, you have to start hammering away at it, as the muse doesn't do the writing for you.

There was a debate, quite a savage debate in its own terms, in Ireland in the 1920s and 1930s between two critical luminaries who were both university professors. In one corner there was Daniel Corkery, Professor of English in my own university of University College Cork, and in the other Monsignor Pádraig de Brún, a classical scholar who later became president of University College Galway, now National University of Ireland Galway. Corkery maintained that we did not need the classics of Greece and Rome, as Irish and Gaelic literature had its own classicism; but, on the other hand, seemed to argue in his own writings, particularly in *The Hidden Ireland*, that we were fundamentally romantic. De Brún, in contrast, insisted that we needed the craft and example and coldheadedness that the European classics gave us, and followed this by translating both *The Odyssey* and *The Divine Comedy* into Irish. The debate, which was about many things but was also about whether literature should be classic or romantic, like all debates of yesteryear seems reasonably pointless with the passing of time.

In a similar vein, I have heard it debated, although not maybe quite as explicitly as I put it now, whether Somhairle is more of a classical or a romantic poet. These are interesting debates in the categorisation, the pinning down and the stuffing of a writer, but they are not always illuminative. Even if you are happy with the label, and can defend it with pistols at dawn, your beloved category does not exhaust the possibilities of the writer.

The critic's search for a frame is always more illuminating of the critic than it is of the writer, and yet we have to use some kind of quasi-rationalist language in order to talk about literature. We find the same kind of framing debate in much of contemporary Gaelic and Irish literature, where writers are ranked along a judgement rack on how traditionalist or modernist they may be. The great thing about Somhairle is that he gobbles all this stuff up. He is both determinedly modernist and proudly traditionalist at the same time. He can be romantic or classical, depending on which spyglass you are looking through. My concern in this short paper is to bypass these categories, but not entirely, and to link him with the only damn useful thing that a poet has, and which he cannot live without, and that is his imagination.

The imagination is not just some kind of ghostly presence, of course – one which hovers about and whispers in your ear. It is fed with all kinds of food and fodder, from a writer's past and reading and inclinations and beautiful prejudices. For all that, a writer is not wholly responsible for the kind of imagination he or she has. It is part of temperament, a kind of hunger or craving of the mind, a rambling of understanding. As one cannot add a cubit to one's height (it might be a good idea) by wishing, so someone cannot possess a different imagination other than the given one. It is as much given to you as your limbs, your digits, the shape of your nose. It is your artistic DNA. It is your artistic personality.

But if anything can feed and jizz up and enfructify the imagination, it is the language the writer is given, or chooses to write in. I have no doubt that Somhairle would have been a poet, some kind of poet, no matter where he came into the world; but he would not have been Somhairle MacGill-Eain if he had not been born into the Gaelic world. His English translations of his own poetry are often excellent, and, as we know, they are often poems in their own right, but they inhabit an entirely different world from that of his originals. It is something I cannot prove, just as you cannot prove more or less anything about literature, but I sense that James Joyce would not have been James Joyce if it had not been for the English language; just as critics say that Rabindrinath Tagore does not transfer from Hindi; or, as my Russian spies tell me, that Chekhov is not the Victorian dramatist in Russian he appears to be in English; or that, when John Millington Synge's writings, which are based on the rhythms and idioms of Irish, are sent back into that language, they no longer appear exotic, or colourful, or weird. In fact, we can often see this difference when bilingual writers use both their languages. Seán Ó Ríordáin's few English poems are quaint, almost Edwardian, in the worst sense of that word and of the many Edwards, while his Irish is as sharp as a warlock's tongue, as cutting as surgery. Máirtín Ó Cadhain, who wrote a great deal of polemical stuff in English as well as in Irish, displays the same blasting personality, and his English has much of the zest and zing of his Irish, but it has no echoes. And echoes are one of the chambers in which aural writing sings.

So, there is nothing new in my saying that MacGill-Eain is an outgrowth of the Gaelic world and the Gaelic language. Along with the best of writers, his poems are a commentary on the past as well as a statement of the present. The Gaelic tradition was an ant-heap of intertextuality before the word was ever invented. It was not a 'spot-the-allusion' game, but a chequerboard where a move at one end influenced everything else – because that is simply the way things are. Tradition is its own Book of Kells, its own Persian carpet where one thread finds a meandering loop runnelling to the corner of its world.

He has again and again admitted his indebtedness to Gaelic song, going so far as to say that if he had been a singer he would have written no poems, but if he had been a singer he would have tried to create original melodies. He again avers that the great songs made the first great artistic impact on him, and that all Gaelic poets are aware of song and of sung poetry. And that he has been banging on about this for more than thirty years. Despite this, however, we cannot simply trace direct influences and make bald assertions that this line is derived from that, and that this image is stolen from the other. This kind of Sherlock Holmesian deductionism is a reductionism too far. It is the carrying around in the head and in the heart and in the ears that is most important. And so I am not going to try to add 'a' to 'b', but rather to throw all the letters into the pot, knowing that they join up somehow.

It was Iain Mac a' Ghobhainn who said, 'His greatest poem is "Hallaig"; a strange moving poem not amenable to reason but emerging, I believe, from a racial consciousness uncorrupted by strategies of the mind'. Whether we agree with this or not – and I think that most of his poetry was governed by strategies of the mind – I do think that a great deal of the best poetry of the world is 'not amenable to reason'. Otherwise it would not be poetry but a legal document, or a dull constitution, or a recipe for bread, or a driving instruction manual. It is because we get a buzz from poetry, that it raises us up, that it gets to us where other parts of language do not reach, that we read it and hear it.

And we have his own words for it. In his essay on 'Old Songs and New Poetry', MacGill-Eain states that 'all poetry is romantic in one sense or another'. And, if this is not enough, as the word 'romantic' is a broad church with many hovels and hiding-places, he goes further in his essay on Màiri Mhòr nan Òran, where he writes with regard to 'Nuair Bha Mi Òg': 'No poem of nostalgia has more of the "objective correlative", more of a strange counterpoint of joy and sorrow, and the language has as much consistency as is possible in poetry that is in any way Dionysian (and all poetry is Dionysian) and not just a laboured distillation in the top of the head.'

There is a lot of revelation in that, and not just about Màiri Mhòr. Leaving aside the ugly phrase 'objective correlative' – and it is as ugly a phrase as you will find to struggle to describe something that is necessary in all art – the revealing phrase is that 'all poetry is Dionysian'. I wanted to jump up and clap and shout hosannas when I read that. At the most profound level – and actually it is not a level at all, nor is it profound; at the highest reaches poetry is up there and floating about. For some reason we dig down for meaning, when we should actually be taking off. We talk about 'unearthing' a problem, or removing layers, or penetrating into the thick of things. These are all agricultural metaphors which might be suitable for people who want to stay in one place and be stuck in the mud. But why the fear of flying? Poetry does not dig, or plough, or harrow, or grub about; it should soar and lift and wing and untie the mortal threads. It should, as another great poet once said, 'float like a butterfly and sting like a bee'. It is the Dionysian which is the ferment which gives MacGill-Eain's this permanent lift-off. And if you think I am mixing and mangling my metaphors, then, yes, I am, as metaphors are there begging to be mixed and mangled and mushed.

John MacInnes's phrase that he is 'a romantic who uses strict classical forms' must be tempered by his assertion that he is a writer who often uses 'a positively Shakespearean excess of language'. This from his essay 'A Radically Traditional Voice'. In a further essay, 'Language, Metre and Diction', MacInnes refers to MacGill-Eain's being 'positively cavalier in his attitude to language'. This, of course, is the mark of Dionysius, the Rabelaisian gift, the joy in the use of language just for its own sake.

There was once an Irish scholar who said with regard to old Irish lyrics, and indeed to some poetry of the early medieval period, as I recall the phrase, 'that the half-said thing to them is dearest'. This harmless aphorism was often used as a twig to beat the wild bush of the imagination of excess. But, of course, that imagination of excess runs deep through Irish and Scottish Gaelic poetry.

John MacKenzie, the editor of that wonderful collection *Sar-Obair nam Bard Gaelach: or, the Beauties of Gaelic Poetry and Lives of the Highland Bards,* refers to Alasdair Mac Mhaighstir Alasdair's 'Òran an t-Samhraidh' as using 'a redundancy ... of epithets', and it is not difficult to see why. As I am sure that a mathematical criticism would be more highly valued by those who like to count and to measure, I was tempted to do an adjective inventory of a number of Irish and Gaelic songs to see which of them contained the most, but I ran out of pencil fairly quickly. What are we to make of

> Am mìos lusanach, mealach,
> Feurach, failleanach, blàth,
> 'S e gu gucagach, duilleach,
> Luachrach, dìtheanach, lurach,
> Beachach, seilleanach, dearcach,

Ciuthrach, dealtach, trom, tlàth,
'S i mar chùirneanan daoimein,
'Bhratach bhoillsgeil air làr!

Just words heaped on words, we think. Probably as much as we would make of his 'Allt an t-Siùcair', or of Donnchadh Bàn Mac an t-Saoir's 'Òran Coire a' Cheathaich', which seems to me to be as fine an example of this exuberance as you can find:

Tha mala ghruamach den bhiolair uaine
Mun h-uile fuaran a th' anns an fhonn,
Is doire shealbhag aig bun nan garbhchlach,
'S an grinneal gainmhich gu meanbh-gheal pronn;
'Na ghlugan plumbach air ghoil gun aon teas,
Ach coilich bùirn tighinn à grunnd eas lom,
Gach sruthan uasal 'na chuailean cùl-ghorm
A' ruith 'na spùta 's 'na lùba steoll.

I could go on, as he did, because it is only one of eighteen verses of similar twisting vines. He must have enjoyed composing it, as his listeners must surely have rejoiced in the sheer bravado of the piece.

It has its own beauty, but there is much more than description going on here. The poet is, let us be clear, showing off. This is the poet displaying his talents. This is the poet doing what the peacock's tail is. It is the dance of the bird of paradise, the hovering of the spatula tail hummingbird, the mandible of the stag beetle, the flashing of the weedy sea dragon, it is the juggling of the juggler in the circus, it is the footballer who dribbles past his opponent and then turns around and does it again. It is, as I say, display. It is the showing up of talent, the saying of 'Yes, I can!' and the doing of it.

In all the critical theory debates that took place during the last fifteen or twenty years, where people clobbered one another over structuralism, or post-modernism, or Marxism, or post-colonialism, or feminism, or more seriously those of us who claimed to have no theory at all, there was never a demonstration or a presentation of Darwinian critical theory. Although most critical theory has happily been consigned to the dustbin of old ideas along with phlogiston and the flat earth, there might be some value in kicking a Darwinian theory around, for what it's worth. And within Darwinian theory there is a corner which argues that one thing that is admired within the animal and the human species is this display of skill, of talent, of colour, of not just being dull and functional and boring.

I suggest that this is a vital factor within all poetry and art, and, therefore, within Gaelic and Irish poetry also. It is remarkable that more or less contemporaneously with Alasdair Mac Mhaighstir Alasdair and Donnchadh Bàn Mac an t-Saoir we have Irish poets doing the same thing. A poet such as Eoghan Rua Ó Súilleabháin wanted to write and to sing Jacobite poetry, but had the problem that the Jacobite cause was more or less shot by the time he grew up. This did not stop him, however, and in poems such as 'Im Leabain Aréir' or 'Mo Léan le Lua agus M'atuirse', it's as if he is fighting the Jacobite wars again and winning them, just as American films of the 1980s with Chuck Connors or whoever refought the Vietnam war on screen and this time they won.

Even if you don't have any Irish, you get the same impression from the rhythm alone in his 'Mo Léan le Lua', yet another vision poem in which he hopes that the rotten Stuarts might return to defeat the rotten Hanoverians, and in which the language far exceeds the practical realities:

> ... is gach lonna-bhile borbchruthaigh tréanchumais d'fhás
> De bhrollastoc na sona-chona do phréamhaigh ón Spáinn
> Go cantlach faonlag easpaitheach
> Faoi ghall smacht ghéar ag Danaraibh,
> An camsprot claon do shealbhaigh
> A saorbhailte stáit.

And so on for seven long wonderful verses of fifteen lines each, repeating one another in rolling waves of eloquence.

In a similar fashion, Tadhg Gaelach Ó Súilleabháin, a generation later and no relation of Eoghan Rua, wrote poetry of highly technical accomplishment where the technical is in fact the accomplishment and the accomplishment is purely technical. Tadhg Gaelach had the honour of being the first Irish poet to be published in printed book form – a bit like Alasdair Mac Mhaighstir Alasdair in Scotland – but there the similarity in lifestyle ends, whatever about the style of their poetry. Mac Mhaighstir

Alasdair wrote some particularly rough and erotic poetry and was not renowned for his piety, and Eoghan Rua Ó Súilleabháin lived life as a rake, being murdered in a pub brawl when somebody smashed his head in with a spade; but Tadhg Gaelach ended his days wearing out the boards of his local church in Waterford by constant praying on his knees. This did not stop him living an earlier dissolute life when he wrote some of his best poetry. One of these, 'Ar Maidin Inné Dom Is Déarach a Bhíos-sa', was described by the great lexicographer Patrick Dineen as 'hardly surpassed in Irish literature for exuberance of epithets bordering on the synonymous'. We have heard its like before from our other poets as it warms up from the second verse on:

> Ba ghleanmhar dréimireach néamharach fraínseach
> A carnfholt claona 'n-a slaodaibh ag síneadh
> Go bachallach péarlach go réilteach go soillseach
> Go camarsach craobhach go néamharach aoibhinn
> Ag feacadh 's ag filleadh 's ag sileadh 'n-a deóidh
> 'Na mbeartaibh 'n-a sruithibh 'n-a muirear go feóir
> Go haltaibh go huile go frithir i gcomhad
> Go slamarach cumarach umarach órdha
> 'N-a sraithibh ag tuitim go himeallach ómrach.

Too much of this does the modern mind in, but the modern mind has been seduced by the banalities of the middle style between ordinary speech and high eloquence.

It is as if, in the eighteenth century, in Scotland and in Ireland, there was an explosion of language as an expression of linguistic spirit, a language which was freed from the tight corset and chastity belt of the classical language, and allowed to roam and to soar and to grow and to let fly. Among his inheritances, this was one of the great inheritances that belonged to Somhairle MacGill-Eain, and one which he had no other choice but to allow it to inhabit his imagination.

We see it in many of his poems, but perhaps nowhere more vividly than in 'Coilltean Ratharsair'. I think that the wild dogs and wolves of his imagination are let loose here more than anywhere else. I say this because there is a sense in which I haven't the least clue as to what this poem means.

I have some clue as to what it is about, because it is about just about every-thing – about nature, about the fall, about love, about the impossibility of perfection, about art, about the world, the universe and everything. I am extremely beholden to Máire Ní Annracháin's close and subtle and persua-sive reading of the poem in *Aisling agus Tóir*, and it has been always illuminating to me. But we all read in different ways, and there was also a sense in which I didn't want to understand the poem at all. I just wanted to walk through it, as I have walked through the woods of Ratharsair. I wanted to experience the poem, as I experienced the woods, and this is what you do, leaving aside all the other philosophical and personal issues which are faced and wrestled with in its depths and twists. And the excess of the woods, the excess of the wonder of the woods, is precisely mirrored in the tangle and glory of the poem.

And I asked myself: if you wanted to write a poem just about a wood, what would you do? – and, yes, I know this is not just about a wood, but let that be for now: would it be a wood like Andrew Marvell's where 'flowers and trees do close / to weave the garlands of repose'? Or Siegfried Sassoon's one replete with 'the chant and whisper of the glade', or Thomas Hardy's dreams of 'sylvan peace / offered with harrowed ease', or Wordsworth's groves of 'primrose tufts', or Anne Bronte's sheltered bower of 'green and glossy leaves / all glistening in the sunshine fair / and list the rustling of their boughs / so softly whispering through the air'? It might be your way, but it certainly is not Somhairle MacGill-Eain's. Because his wood is a wild place, where the fierce burst of the language outruns whatever he is trying to say, particularly in the opening of the poem.

Máire Ní Annracháin is correct is saying that the second part, where there is a change of gear, a change of tuning, is an attempt to control the anarchy of the first – 'cheapfá go raibh iarracht á déanamh cosc a chur le leathnú na hainrialach' ('you would think an attempt was being made to put a stop to the spread of anarchy') – and he does partially succeed in doing this, but the anarchy, or at least the irregularity, the knobbliness, returns at various points before the end. But even with that, the energy is in the language itself, the excess is in the green shoots of the words. If anyone believes any more in all that Freudian stuff, there is plenty here about rising sap and thrusting trees and snakes in the long grass to keep you busy in the hunting of the snark and the snaring of the symbol.

I don't think that the best of Somhairle MacGill-Eain's poetry requires any more than a willingness to be wooed by language – in the case of 'Coilltean Ratharsair', to get lost in the woods. He has already said that 'the auditory is the primary sensuousness of poetry', and the 'auditory', as well as the tactile and the tastebuddyness and the shape and the feel and the touch and the glow of words, are all and everything in poetry. Especially in the poetry of someone who composes out of an imagination of excess.

3. 'Coilltean Ratharsair': Temptation in the Woods

PETER MACKAY

In courtly love poetry, the respectability of the poetic gaze is always at risk of slipping, the idealised version of the beloved only a drop of the mask from revealing the rot and maggot in the bloom. Idealisation is both product of and flight from a realisation of earthly, physical decay; and desire, if it ever reached its object, would destroy it, strip flesh from the bone.[1] Much of Sorley MacLean's early poetry – most obviously the *Dàin do Eimhir* – is written in complex engagement with the *amour courtois*; and in his work desire often brings with it a sense of danger. In 'Gleann Aoighre' ('Glen Eyre'), for example, both 'miann' (desire) and 'àrdan' (pride) are self-defeating, restless forces, making the speaker realise 'gu robh balla eadar aoibhneas / agus mo chroit bhig neo-chaomhail' ('that there was a wall between joy / and my harsh little croft'),[2] and aware that the nature of desire means that his 'joy' will never be attainable:

> Agus ged dh'fhanainn far an robh mi
> gun shaothair agus fuachd nam mullach,
> nach tuiteadh mo mhiann, an t-ubhal
> dearg, abaich, cùbhraidh, 'na mo làmhan,
> agus nach ruigteadh e le sàr-strì
> no le àrdan tuilleadh.

> *And though I stayed where I was*
> *without the toil and cold of the tops,*
> *that my desire, the red ripe fragrant apple,*
> *would not fall into my hands,*
> *and that it was not to be reached with surpassing effort*
> *or with pride any more.*

In 'Coin is Madaidhean-allaidh' ('Dogs and Wolves'), meanwhile, there is the clear understanding that 'coin chiùine caothaich na bàrdachd' ('the mild

41

mad dogs of poetry') will devour 'àilleachd' or beauty if they are successful in their hunt.[3]

This sense that desire is self-destructive or self-defeating – and that poetry *is* desire – is developed most fully in 'Coilltean Ratharsair' ('The Woods of Raasay'). A complex rumination on the role and purpose of poetry located in a psycho-dramatic landscape, 'Coilltean Ratharsair' presents poetry as a quest for knowledge that is necessarily self-defeating. I will argue that this allows the poem to be read as touching on the ethics of poetic representation and utterance, particularly through the incorporation of the myth of Artemis and Actaeon. Towards the end of 'Coilltean Ratharsair' the narrator's communion with the woods has been ruptured by desire, pride and burgeoning sexual awareness. Paradise lost, the narrator catches sight of the goddess Artemis/Diana:

> Chunnaic mi an triùir gu siùbhlach,
> an triùir bhan-dia chuimir rùiste:
> b' aithne dhomh Actaeon brùite
> le triùir fheargach ga sgiùrsadh.

> Chunnaic mi an triùir sa choille,
> an triùir gheal rùiste loinneil,
> an triùir 'nan aiteal mum choinneamh,
> an triùir dho-labhairt an coinneamh.

> *I saw the three in their swift course,*
> *the three shapely naked goddesses,*
> *I recognised the bruised Actaeon*
> *harried by the three angry ones.*

> *I saw the three in the woods,*
> *the three white naked graceful ones,*
> *the three a glimmer before me,*
> *the three unspeakable in meeting.*[4]

This is just a glimpse of Artemis: she is not named or, indeed, alone. Instead of a single goddess there are 'an triùir bhan-dia chuimir rùiste … triùir fheargach' ('the three shapely naked goddesses ... the three angry ones'). There are many examples of 'triadic deities' (gods or goddesses appearing with two accomplices) in classical literature: Hera, Athene and Aphrodite; the Charites; the Fates; or 'Diana Nemorensis' (Diana of the Wood), who is associated with Egeria and Virbius. There are also many examples of 'triune' goddesses, goddesses who have three distinct manifestations – this was the case with Artemis, who appeared as divine huntress, moon goddess and goddess of the underworld (Hecate), and had responsibility for three areas associated with these manifestations: the hunt, the moon and chastity. From 'Coilltean Ratharsair' it is unclear quite who these goddesses are (or how they are constituted), except for the 'recognition' of Actaeon, a recognition that associates the narrator with Actaeon's crime against Artemis.

In the classical myth, Actaeon-the-hunter happens upon Artemis-the-huntress-goddess while she is bathing. As punishment, the goddess turns Actaeon into a stag; he is then pursued and torn apart by his own hunting pack.[5] There are different elements to Actaeon's crime and punishment. On one level it is a crime against chastity: it is an intrusion into the private, a gaining of knowledge that is explicitly sexual. Thus, in *Being and Nothingness*, Sartre reinterprets the Actaeon myth – as he develops Heidegger's critique of knowledge as violence – to argue for the connection between knowledge and sex: for Sartre, the 'Actaeon Complex' is the 'totality of images which show that knowing is a form of appropriative volition with overtones of sexuality.'[6] On another level, Actaeon's is an intrusion into the realm and rights of the divine; certainly, in Lacan's use of the myth to criticise 'The Freudian Thing' what is important is the fact that Actaeon breaks the barrier between the human and the godly.[7] This intrusion is, again, ambiguous, and can be seen as a hubristic crime, rightly punished, or can be related to Prometheus's theft of fire from the gods (another incursion into divine 'knowledge'). As Robert Pogue Harrison – writing from an eco-critical perspective – suggests, the breach of the divine can be seen as helping us deconstruct our preconceptions of how we structure our world through language and symbols:

> The story has an unmistakable psychological effect upon the reader, for while Actaeon is literally de-anthropomorphized, the stag that

> he turns into becomes humanized. Now that Actaeon has become a
> stag we are able to suffer its fate as it if were a human being. The
> distinctions collapse. Like Actaeon, we are made to see that the forms
> of the world are transient, illusory and reversible.[8]

Without undergoing Actaeon's fate, that is, we learn to see through the
transience of the structures of thought that would separate us from animals,
and the 'natural' – or, indeed, the 'divine'.

On the level of most interest to me here, however, Actaeon's can be seen
as a crime of speech or utterance. In Callimachus's telling of the myth,[9]
Artemis does not turn Actaeon into a stag immediately she discovers him,
but when he attempts to call out to his hounds; in Ovid's version, when
Actaeon tries to call to his dogs – 'Actaeon ego sum' ('I am Actaeon') – he
can no longer master human speech.[10] In both, that is, speech is disallowed
or punished. As Cynthia Nazarian comments, 'the Ovidian myth includes
both an interdiction on speech – Diana's transformation of Actaeon so that
he cannot tell what he has seen – and simultaneously a command to do just
that, in her defiant imperative "Speak, if you can"';[11] in the Callimachian
myth, it is the speech-act itself that is the crime. In 'Coilltean Ratharsair'
there is an allusion to this element of the myth. The goddesses are described
as 'do-labhairt' ('unspeakable'); this has implications for the poem itself, and
for the narrator's relationship to Actaeon. When the narrator claims 'b' aithne
dhomh Actaeon brùite' ('I recognised the bruised Actaeon'), he implies that
their 'crimes' might be the same: both see the goddess naked in the forest
and speak (or try to speak) of what they have seen (although the narrator
has more success in rendering the goddesses 'speakable'). Through this
recognition, 'Coilltean Ratharsair' itself becomes identified with Actaeon's
crime, as a form of coercive, sexual knowing that has to be punished.

This punishment can be connected to the poem's central narrative, the
fall from Paradise that the poem's narrator undergoes.[12] By following shifts
in metrical patterns, the poem can be broken into three sections; these can
be glossed as paradise, fall and realisation of the fall. In the first section, the
narrator has an untarnished, complete relationship with the eponymous
woods of Raasay. The second section introduces the poem's other symbolic
landscapes: Sgùrr nan Gillean (the Peak of the Young Men), which – like
the hills in 'Gleann Aoighre' – symbolises desire that is destructive and

insatiable; and the Clàrach, the stretch of water that separates Raasay and Skye, and where the narrator is attracted by his desire (for the Sgùrr). In this vacillating, uncertain landscape the speaker is – for the first time – separated from the woods and able to see – from outside – the cycle in which the people of Raasay return at their death to 'tàmh an fhuinn' ('the repose of the earth');[13] as a result, however, the speaker has also forever lost the certainty of his childlike relationship with the wood. Thus, in the final section the narrator steps outside the confines of the poem's psychodramatic landscape to ask directly of the reader what point there is in believing that one thing was 'coileanta / àlainn so-ruighinn' ('complete, / beautiful, accessible'), and, even more explicitly, 'Dè fàth bhith 'toirt do nighinn / gaol mar ghormadh speur ...?' ('What is the meaning of giving a woman / love like the growing blue of the skies ...?'),[14] when love can never – by necessity – be fulfilled, and the desired object will be destroyed by the act of desiring it.

Throughout this structure, the narrator's 'fall' is linked to developing sexual awareness. The desire that leads the narrator out of the woods is clearly sexual: his identification with the forest is broken at first by the introduction of new 'helmets' – which combine the masculine and the military – 'gam chiùrradh le buaireadh, / clogadan àrdain / gam mhàbadh le luasgan' ('hurting me with temptation, / helmets of pride / maiming me with unrest').[15] The introduction of 'àrdan', MacLean's favourite word for 'pride' and 'haughtiness', is also significant – although in MacLean's poetry 'àrdan' is generally positively related to ambition, it can also suggest the pride that was the cause of Satan's ruin. The characteristics of Sgùrr nan Gillean in the second section take the physical embodiment of masculine development a stage further: the mountain is described (in opposing mythological terms) as 'a' bheithir / cholgarra' ('the warlike fire-dragon') and ''n t-aon-chòrnach ... foistinneach' ('the reposeful unicorn'). The narrator is made aware, in other words, of sexual potency, and a violence associated with sexuality – 'gath a' chràdhghal anns an t-sùgradh' ('the venom of the cry of pain in the love-making')[16] – which had been presaged by the earlier imagery of the 'helmets'. In the final section the cause of this sexual unrest is clearly located in the forest:

> Bu choille Ratharsair an tè
> a liubhair pòg mheala rèidh,

a' phòg nach fòghnadh don chrè,
a' phòg chuir luasgan sa chlèibh.

The wood of Raasay was the one
that gave the smooth honeyed kiss,
the kiss that would not suffice the clay,
the kiss that put unrest in the body.[17]

This passage also identifies the woods of Raasay directly with the goddesses. The wood then becomes 'Tè a liubhair na pògan / nach do shàsaich an tòrachd' ('One who gave the kisses / that did not satisfy the pursuit');[18] the wood/goddess is then both cause of, and punisher of, the narrator's sexual knowledge.

Among what is lost, as a result of this newly gained sexual knowledge, is a way of speaking. In the final section, the relationship between the narrator and the wood becomes inverted: it is the wood that now speaks like a child, and is described as 'm' ionam, labharag: / mo chiall cagarain, / mo leanabh cadalach' ('my dear prattler, / my whispered reason, / my sleeping child').[19] The notion of the 'prattling' wood is repeated and developed in a later stanza:

Coille Ratharsair an labharag,
coille bhrìodail, coille chagarain,
coille aotrom ri taobh nam marannan,
coille uaine an suain neo-chadalach.

The wood of Raasay is the talking one,
the prattling whispering wood,
the wood light beside the seas,
the green wood in a sleepless slumber.[20]

This form of speech – childish, prattling, whispering – is one the speaker can no longer access; the separation of poet and landscape is in part caused by the development of speech, but speech itself is of no use to resolve the schisms between them. The speaker is caught, once more, in the paradoxes with which the *Dàin do Eimhir* are riven: he needs to know what it means to attempt to give voice to a 'gaol do-labhairt' ('unspeakable love')[21] that will fail because it is 'unspeakable'; he needs to know what point there is in worshipping the Cuillins when his desire (the pull of Sgùrr nan Gillean) and his attempt to 'speak his love' has itself destroyed the paradise from which he started out.

The poem gives no answer to these paradoxes. Instead, the final stanzas offer the aftermath of the realisation of his fall: a description of what it means to live in a fallen world that contains constant reminders of the paradise lost. Both the Cuillins and the woods of Raasay have lost their perfection, their numinous, luminous glory: the Cuillins have been knocked down 'an sloc sgreataidh' ('in a loathsome pit'); the wood is home now to 'Mìltean nathraichean 'na lùisreadh' ('Thousands of adders in her rich growth').[22] There is, however, still nobility to the woods and mountains even in their fallen state. The misery out of which the Cuillins grow adds to their heroism, just as poetry and music gain their beauty from the torn reason out of which they are born, while the wood itself remains 'seud beothanta anns an doille' ('the lively jewel in blindness').[23] What is gone forever, however, is knowledge of the human heart, and the peace that this produced. While 'slighe an t-snodhaich' ('the way of the sap') is known,

> Chan eil eòlas, chan eil eòlas
> air crìch dheireannaich gach tòrachd
> no air seòltachd nan lùban
> leis an caill i a cùrsa.

> *There is no knowledge, no knowledge,*
> *of the final end of each pursuit,*
> *nor of the subtlety of the bends*
> *with which it loses its course.*[24]

Unlike that of Adam and Eve, this is not a fall into knowledge. Rather, the hunt leads to the repeated negation of knowledge: 'chan eil eòl air an t-slighe ... chan eil eòlas, chan eil eòlas' ('there is no knowledge of the course ... there is no knowledge, there is no knowledge').[25] Grasping after knowledge precipitates the Fall; after the Fall knowledge is impossible.

This is the moral of the poem's central, catastrophic narrative. There is, however, also another Artemisian narrative hidden in the woods of Raasay leading us in a quite different direction, if we follow the goddesses rather than Actaeon. The goddesses offer another possible way of representing or standing for the wood, despite – or precisely because of – their unspeakableness. As their punishment of Actaeon makes clear, the goddesses guard and protect the divinity of the forest as much as their own divinity: they are both target of the narrator's hunt and 'hunters' who themselves forever bring unrest into the speaker's life. As such, the goddesses suggest another myth relating to Artemis/Diana which had currency in the early twentieth century, and which complicates any interpretation of the story of Actaeon and Artemis. In the following passage, James Frazer introduces the central drama of his *The Golden Bough*:

> In this sacred grove there grew a certain tree round which at any time of the day, and probably far into the night, a grim figure might be seen to prowl. In his hand he carried a drawn sword, and he kept peering warily about him as if at every instant he expected to be set upon by an enemy. He was a priest and a murderer; and the man for whom he looked was sooner or later to murder him and hold the priesthood in his stead. Such was the rule of the sanctuary. A candidate for the priesthood could only succeed to office by slaying the priest, and having slain him, he retained office till he was himself slain by a stronger or a craftier.[26]

The 'sacred grove' is the temple to (the triune goddess) Diana Nemorensis, located at Nemi in the Alban hills of Italy. The 'priest' of the wood lives in a strangely self-destructive and self-denying relationship with the forest. He is condemned to give his life in defence of the grove, having only come into his role himself by murdering the previous incumbent. The forest stands in metonymically for the goddess, and the priest-murderer has the vocation of protecting and – to some extent – representing the goddess. The priest-murderer is Actaeon-turned-Artemis, intruder-turned-protector of the sacred grove: at some point, however, the cycle will turn and the priest himself be killed, and lose his quasi-divinity.

The narrative of the fall is linear, following a pattern of pride, search for knowledge, crime, fall; it is a one-off event, a singular, irreversible rupture, after which there can be 'no knowledge of the human heart', no access to

Truth whether it be poetic, historical, philosophical, psychological or religious. The myth of the sacred grove at Nemi, on the other hand, presents a circular, repetitive pattern. Just as another rough beast will always slouch to Bethlehem to be born, there will always be another prospective 'priest-king' making the quest to the sacred grove at Nemi, to kill the holder of the post and to take on the role (of guarantor of the seasons and of fertility). This archetypal cycle of crime, sacrifice and renewal lies behind MacLean's poem, at least at one remove, and can be related to the cyclical, repetitive pattern of the rhythm of 'Coilltean Ratharsair'. The poem's insistent repetitive assonance is unavoidable if it is read aloud: consider this passage, from early in the poem, which draws on the musical effects to try and evoke complex natural processes, in a similar way to Donnchadh Bàn Mac an t-Saoir in his 'Moladh Beinn Dòbhrain':

> A' choille san sgarthanaich
> dùsgadh sa chamhanaich:
> a' choille le langanaich
> brùchdadh gu tabhanaich:
> a' choille le dùblachadh
> crùnluaith chabhagaich:
> a' choille 's i mùirneach
> ri sùgradh nam marannan.

> *The divided wood*
> *wakening at dawn,*
> *the wood with deer-belling*
> *bursting to baying:*
> *the wood with doubling*
> *of hurrying 'Crunluath',*
> *the wood delighted*
> *with the love-making of the sea.*[27]

The repetition of word, syllable, vowel and consonant – loosely evocative of the strictures of the *dán díreach* – creates a swirling, cyclic pattern, a helical repetition over time, a rhythmical perning in a gyre. By introducing the possibility that the catastrophic linear narrative of the Fall is, in fact, part of a cyclical or helical process, the poem keeps hope of regeneration open, despite the prospect of inevitable destruction.

This is a tempting reading – perhaps too tempting – given the historical context of the poem's composition. MacLean was careful in later years to append the year in which he wrote it – 1940 – so that its wartime composition could not be elided (this was not a particularly common practice for MacLean, as a glance through *O Choille gu Bearradh*, the collected works that the poet himself authorised, will show). In this precise dating, 'Coilltean Ratharsair' has a companion piece in MacLean's translation of the opening of *Paradise Lost* (ending on 'and justify the ways of God to men'), which was completed in 1945: both clearly depend on narratives of the Fall, and the catastrophic outcome of following unchecked desire. Read within this context, 'Coilltean Ratharsair' is a 'coming-of-the-war' poem, in which the natural idyll is destroyed by a rise of martial imagery and passionate desire; as such, it has comparator texts in MacNeice's 'The Closing Album' and *Autumn Journal,* or Ezra Pound's earlier 'The Coming of War: Actaeon', which adopts the Actaeon myth to present the Great War as a form of retribution against Actaeon's transgression of the divine:

> High forms
> With the movement of gods,
> Perilous aspect;
> And one said:
> 'This is Actaeon.'
> Actaeon of golden greaves!
> Over fair meadows,
> Over the cool face of that field,
> Unstill, ever moving
> Hosts of an ancient people,
> The silent cortège.[28]

Pound's use of the myth is more pointed than Edith Wharton's 1909 'Artemis to Actaeon', which does not transcend a Romantic and neo-Classical focus on nudity, nature, transgression and transformation – it is important, however, that 'Coilltean Ratharsair' ends on the individual's confusion and uncertainty, rather than on Pound's pan-historical, sanitised version of noble loss and mourning (with its air of *noblesse oblige*).

The prospect of war was more immediate for MacLean than for Pound, who did not fight in the Great War. MacLean was called up on 26 September 1940, and would be severely injured at the battle of El Alamein; throughout late 1939 and 1940 his imagined impending participation in the war gave an edge to his poetry and a keen sense of loss, both historical and futural. As with the work of Neruda, much of MacLean's 'most compelling poetry stems from an acute sense of loss and deprivation'.[29] This is perhaps most obvious in his poems of the 1950s, such as 'Sruth Tràghaidh' and 'Hallaig', that create a (nostalgic) remove from the landscapes they describe as they envisage and interrogate cultural loss. 'Sruth Tràghaidh' is a nightmarish, gothic rewriting of Yeats's 'The Lake Isle of Innisfree', with the poet on city streets imagining himself back to the countryside; characteristically, Yeats's poem uses myth to energise the present, while MacLean's draws on myth to picture a culture becoming attenuated and passing away. 'Hallaig', meanwhile, creates a doubled relationship to cultural loss: it evokes this loss precisely in an attempt to hold it off, to provide some means of historical continuity.[30] But a sense of loss also pervades MacLean's work in the late 1930s and early 1940s, coming into focus most clearly, perhaps, in 'An Cuilithionn'. And I would argue that 'Coilltean Ratharsair' – like 'Hallaig' – has a doubled relationship to loss; the narrator is at one and the same time the criminal who breaks continuity with nature (through the transgression into sexual knowledge) and also the one who guarantees the sanctity of the woods, fulfilling the role of the priest-king who will sacrifice himself at some point to save the grove. In 'Coilltean Ratharsair' these narratives co-exist; the same event is, from one perspective, an individual tragedy, the fall from paradise; from another it is a necessary part of a cycle (the cycle of growth and decay in the woods of Raasay). And it is the lack of cohesion between the two narratives, the emotional chaos that they wreak, and the desire, pride and anxiety that fills that gap between the falling individual and the cycles of history, that give 'Coilltean Ratharsair' much of its mystery and resonance.

The two myths of Artemis suggested in 'Coilltean Ratharsair' also present a dilemma present in any mimetic or representative writing: the risk that all writing is a form of coercive (sexual) knowledge, which tries to take possession of some ineffable other; the risk that representing or 'speaking for' can slip from witnessing into (violent) Sartrean appropriation. The quest for the golden bough and the glimpsing of the naked Artemis are transgressions into the divine; indeed, even to write of, and so represent, Artemis's nudity is a crime. To avoid such a transgression, one would have to accept, with Emmanuel Levinas, an 'ethical' 'sense of responsibility to the other, to forms of alterity which are outside the self',[31] and especially a realisation that the other is fundamentally unknowable (or unrecognisable). In other words, all poetry can hope for is incomplete gestures, a pointing towards truths that can never be reached: open, ethical fragments of 'knowledge'. In this light, the end of 'Coilltean Ratharsair' – with its exclamation that 'Chan eil eòlas, chan eil eòlas / air crìch dheireannaich gach tòrachd' ('There is no knowledge, no knowledge, / of the final end of each pursuit') – can be read not just as the lack of knowledge and certainty caused by a fall from paradise, but also as an *ethical* refusal to 'know', to appropriate, to claim poetically. The wood is ultimately unknowable and any attempt to describe it must necessarily fail. In this reading, Artemis cannot legitimately and completely be represented; instead, the best that can (and should) be hoped for is a fleeting glimpse of the goddess glimmering in the wood.

Notes

1   Cf. Slavoz Žižek, *The Metastases of Enjoyment: Six Essays on Women and Causality*, London: Verso, 2005, p. 91. Žižek comments that 'the Lady in courtly love has nothing to do with actual women, how she stands for the man's narcissistic projection which involves the mortification of the flesh-and-blood woman' – a projection that is for Žižek derived from a masochistic impulse.

2   Sorley MacLean, *Caoir Gheal Leumraich/A White Leaping Flame*, Edinburgh: Polygon 2011, pp. 24–25

3   Ibid, pp. 132–33

4   Ibid, pp. 62–63

5   Cf. Jenny March, *Cassell's Dictionary of Classical Mythology*, London: Cassell, 1998, p. 32.

6   Jean-Paul Sartre, *Being and Nothingness*, trans. Hazel E. Barnes, London: Routledge, 2000 [1943], p. 629. Cf. Timothy Clark, *The Cambridge Introduction to Literature and the Environment*, Cambridge: Cambridge University Press, 2011, pp. 55–61, and Martin Heidegger, *Pathmarks*, ed. William MacNeill 1967, Cambridge: Cambridge University Press, 1998, p. 147.

7   See Marie-Rose Logan, 'Antique Myth and Modern Mind: Jacques Lacan's version of Actaeon and the fictions of surrealism', *Journal of Modern Literature*, June 2002.

8   Robert Pogue Harrison, *Forests: The Shadow of Civilization*, Chicago: University of Chicago Press, 1992, p. 26

9   Callimachus, *The Fifth Hymn*, ed. A.W. Bulloch, Cambridge: Cambridge University Press, 1985, pp. 107–18

10   Ovid, *Metamorphoses*, ed. Frank Justus Miller, University of Michigan: Loeb Classical Library, 1977 [Heinemann, 1916], 3.230

11   Cynthia Nazarian, '*Actaeon ego sum*: Ovidian Dismemberment and Lyric Voice in Petrarch and Maurice Scève', in Alison Keith and Stephen Rupp, eds, *Metamorphosis: The Changing Face of Ovid in Medieval and Early Modern Europe*, Toronto: Centre for Reformation and Renaissance Studies, 2005, p. 219

12   Cf. Máire Ní Annracháin, *Aisling agus Tóir: An Slánú i bhFilíocht Shomhairle MhicGill-Eain*, Maynooth: An Sagart, 1992, pp. 40–83.

13   MacLean, *Caoir*, pp. 62–63

14   Ibid, pp. 64–65

15   Ibid, pp. 60–61

16   Ibid, pp. 62–63

17   Ibid, pp. 64–65

18   Ibid, pp. 64–65

19   Ibid, pp. 62–63. 'Ciall', which whispers here, can refer to 'love' as well as 'sense' or 'reason'; it certainly, however, denotes affection rather than sexual desire.

20   Ibid, pp. 64–65

21   Ibid, pp. 66–67

22   Ibid, pp. 66–67

23   Ibid, pp. 68–69

24   Ibid, pp. 68–69

25   Ibid, pp. 68–69

26   James Frazer, *The Golden Bough*, London: MacMillan, 1920 [1890], pp. 8–9. Frazer's influence on twentieth-century poetry came largely through the mediation first of T. S. Eliot's 1922 *The Waste Land* (and then of Robert Graves's 1948 *The White Goddess*); MacLean was well versed in the work of Eliot, if not of Frazer, from his university syllabus, while Graves's work obviously post-dates 'Coilltean Ratharsair'.

27   MacLean, *Caoir*, pp. 58–59. The translation obviously loses the music of the original; MacLean can be heard reading the poem on numerous recordings, perhaps most notably *Barran agus Asbhuain* (Dublin: Claddagh, 1973). The phonic repetitions in the poem continue throughout – the last two stanzas (eight lines in all) feature the syllable 'eòl' five times, and the related 'òr' once.

28   Cf. Louis MacNeice, *Collected Poems*, London: Faber, 2007, pp. 178–82 and 99–164; Ezra Pound, *Lustra*, London: Elkin Matthews, 1916, p. 42.

29   John Felstiner, *Translating Neruda: The Way to Macchu Picchu*, Stanford: Stanford University Press, 1980, p. 48

30   Cf. Peter Mackay, *Sorley MacLean*, Aberdeen: RIISS, 2010, pp. 137–43.

31   Eugene O'Brien, *Searches for Answers*, London, Dublin and Sterling, Virginia: Pluto Press, 1993

4. The Sorley MacLean–Douglas Young Correspondence: New Approaches to the Archive

EMMA DYMOCK

Emily Dickinson said that 'a Letter always feels to me like immortality because it is the mind alone without corporeal friend. Indebted in our talk to attitude and accent, there seems a spectral power in thought that walks alone.'[1] This idea of spectral power would have been very familiar to Sorley MacLean, who seems to have been well aware of the power of ghosts in much of his work, and who wrote in his long, political poem, 'An Cuilithionn':

> Cò seo, cò seo oidhche 'n spioraid?
> Chan eil ach tannasg lom cridhe,
> manadh leis fhèin a' falbh a' smaointinn,
> cliabh feòil-rùiste air an aonach.

> *Who is this, who is this in the night of the spirit?*
> *It is only the naked ghost of a heart,*
> *a spectre going alone in thought,*
> *a skeleton naked of flesh on the mountain.*[2]

In the autumn of 2008 I began to make regular visits to the National Library of Scotland to transcribe the correspondence between Sorley MacLean and the nationalist and Scottish Renaissance figure, Douglas Young. Letters have the power to transport the reader to a different era – to take the reader out of their own time and to place them into the past of the writer. For that reason, the spectre of these letters remains with the reader long after the manuscripts have been returned to the stacks. Temma Berg has written that 'researchers become haunted by the spectral presences they call forth. They want to ask more and more questions of the ghosts they have raised.'[3] I first came across these letters while conducting research for my PhD thesis. The letters between the two men proved to be very useful in my particular field of research, which involved a study of 'An Cuilithionn'.[4]

My work focused on MacLean's view of the state of mankind from a socialist perspective. Many of the letters between MacLean and Young involved discussions centring on 'An Cuilithionn' or, at least, themes which coincided with the perspective of this poem, and I do not think I would have achieved the richness of insight into MacLean's thoughts and ideals, outside of MacLean's poetry, without the aid of these letters.

The purpose of this paper is to introduce these letters and perhaps to highlight some of their potential. At the present time, the Sorley MacLean–Douglas Young correspondence is in the latter stages of being prepared for publication with commentary and notes. While the letters have never been published before in their entirety, this is not the first time that their worth has been noted. Scholars of Gaelic literature and language such as Christopher Whyte and Michel Byrne have used parts of these letters to date MacLean's poems and to piece together the publishing process of some of MacLean's work and the work of others including George Campbell Hay.[5] These letters have been referred to in a number of conference papers and articles, but always in order to prove a specific point in relation to MacLean's poetry.[6] It is perhaps time to address the issues and matters which arise in the correspondence in their own right rather than as a support text or as verification or consolidation of other work or biographical details of MacLean, Young, or even their wider circle of friends who are mentioned in the correspondence.

The letters themselves are split into two separate holdings in the National Library of Scotland: MS29501 has the correspondence from Young to MacLean and Acc 6419 Box 38b has the other side of the story, the letters from MacLean to Young. During the transcription process, the letters have been put into chronological order so that the more complete 'story' or narrative element of the correspondence can be better viewed and understood. This would normally be quite a straightforward task but has been complicated by a number of factors, mostly influenced by the time in which the majority of the letters were composed. It is understandable that the effect of the Second World War on the authors of these letters and the wider effect of the war on their posting and delivery would impinge on how the correspondence would be received and answered. Firstly, it should be noted that there are gaps in the correspondence – the collection is incomplete and may remain this way due to certain letters being lost because of outside circumstances. (MacLean, in particular, was in many locations between 1939 and the mid-1940s and letters may have been lost in transit.) Secondly, there is the fact that many of the letters were sent when MacLean was stationed away from home from 1940 onwards. Some had gone missing or were very slow in being delivered and turned up months later, meaning that Young had already written a few more letters before he answered MacLean's questions from previous letters. It may also be the case that some of the letters never reached their destination. After all, Douglas Young was a fervent nationalist who was imprisoned for his non-participation in the Second World War and the issue of censorship on the letters should not be discounted. On the other hand, the chronology and preservation of the correspondence was aided, in particular, by Douglas Young, who made copies of many of the letters he sent to MacLean. This act of preservation, consolidated also by MacLean, who wrote on the top of some of the letters the date on which he received them, raises questions regarding the self-consciousness of both MacLean and Young, who clearly understood the importance of what they were writing and were mindful of the possible future significance of the letters in relation to Gaelic and Scottish literature and their responsibilities and role in the preservation and continuation of the language. For example, there is much discussion in the letters about the publication of Gaelic poetry and the need for the establishment of a new Gaelic dictionary.[7]

There are one hundred letters in the collection, dating from as early as 1940 to as late as 1972. However, the majority are dated during the years of the Second World War. These letters are definitely the most detailed. Not only was this a period of intense discussion regarding politics and literature, it was also the time when both men were unlikely to be able to have any other means of communication with each other (especially with MacLean being abroad for a great deal of the time). As the years go on (from 1946 to 1972) more 'holes' start to appear in the correspondence. Any gaps in the later correspondence are probably due to the fact that by this time the two men had other means of communication. Also, they were older and having families of their own. While this in itself would not have diminished the intensity of their ideals, it may be that they simply did not have the luxury of writing their thoughts down as often because of their busy lives.

The correspondence covers a number of different spheres and during the research conducted on the correspondence it has been beneficial to separate the issues discussed by MacLean and Young into three separate categories as follows:

The Historical Sphere: This includes important insights of MacLean into the experience of a Scottish left-wing radical and the complexity of the political choices which faced those in this position during the period; MacLean's descriptions of British army life, his routine as a soldier and his experiences of war; Douglas Young's political commitment to Scottish nationalism and the difficulties he encountered.

The Gaelic–Scots Literary Sphere: This covers the literary influences on Sorley MacLean and his views on the Gaelic language; Douglas Young's views of the Scots language as a medium for both poetry and literary/ historical pamphlets; the detailed history of the publication of MacLean's work during the 1940s; contemporary views of MacLean's poetry and the English translations that were intended to accompany the Gaelic originals.

The Philosophical–Political Sphere: This includes the intellectual climate in which the literati of the 1930s and 1940s moved, as suggested by Young and MacLean's perspectives on the complexity of pacifism; concepts of 'Gaeldom' and its relationship to communism and nationalism; the intellectual debate regarding Russia and its place in the Second World War and opinions on the British Government; Young's literary and political influence on Gaelic/Scottish writers such as MacLean and George Campbell Hay; Young's continuously evolving role as an arbiter and orchestrator of the Renaissance.

*

The remainder of this paper will focus on some specific points regarding the use of the letters as a study aid and a resource, using as a reference point MacLean's political standpoint and how he argues this out in the letters. While there are many issues arising from the various spheres above which would be of significance to those interested in the life and literature of Sorley MacLean, one of the richest seams by far in the correspondence is the political discussion. One of the most important features, especially in the earlier letters, is MacLean's justification for taking part in the Second World War and Young's justification for not. For a social or political historian,

the divergence in beliefs between two friends as evidenced in the correspondence is a true window into the minds of literary men of conscience in
1940s Scotland. Their views may not have been that of the majority, but the
fact that such views even existed and have been catalogued is a useful
addition to the social history of twentieth-century Scotland. In a letter from
Catterick Camp, Yorkshire, on 1 October 1940, MacLean, who had been
recently stationed there, argues out his case to Young:

> As for my conscience, well! Am I being a traitor to Scotland and
> more so to the class struggle? Am I just in the army because I haven't
> the courage to object? All I can say is that I have such an instinctive
> loathing and fear of Nazism … that I cannot accept for myself the
> option of refusing to resist it even with the co-operation of English
> imperialist capitalism. My reading of it may be wrong as you say.[8]

MacLean's hatred of fascism can be viewed here (corresponding with his
poetic output slightly prior to this period). He feels fascism must be obliter-
ated at all costs, even if he is forced to surrender some of his socialist principles
in the process. It is interesting to note that young men such as MacLean who
had come through the university system and had been given the opportunity
to widen their knowledge of philosophy and politics (MacLean's discussions
during his university days with his friends George Davie and James Caird
are good examples of this[9]) had formulated ideas and were now finding their
standpoints put to the test. In an earlier letter dated 24 September 1940
Douglas Young wrote to MacLean from Ardlogie, Leuchars, that:

> I am filled with fury and disgust that you should tamely surrender
> your coolin-ascending philabeg-swinging legs to be encased in H.M.
> shit-coloured breeks and thus trot up and down the muddy plains
> of Yorkshire at the bawling of a Sassenach sergeant. The only good
> thing I can see about it is that, when and if you come back, you will
> be a fervent patriot.[10]

Beyond the jocular teasing of this letter some fundamental points can be
identified. Young obviously views MacLean's heritage as being of major
importance and he sees nationalism as an ultimate goal. On the other hand,

while MacLean's sense of his Gaelic identity is always strong in his poetry,[11] his decision to join the army as a way of stopping fascism in its tracks is far more in keeping with the sort of poetry he was writing up to 1939.[12] Young's stance in the war was different because he put his sense of nationalism at the forefront of his ideals. It is obvious from the letters that Young was not alone in his experiences. The atmosphere of suspicion and distrust is very obvious in at least one instance. On 11 February 1941 Young writes to MacLean about what he should do with the poetry that MacLean has left with him for safe-keeping:

> I am anxious, doubtless unnecessarily, but I have a Fife canniness, to have these things put in order against the eventuality of an utter chaos in which we might all go to hell. I shall tonight give Macdonald[13] your own book of MSS to keep; he is an accurate scholar, to judge from his edition of the Gaelic Homer, and would edit it properly if it was left to him. When my bound copy of yourself and Deorsa is fully corrected and amplified, I thought of committing it to John MacKechnie, although he is liable to have his papers searched by the police (his Iain Lom was purloined and some valuable researches lost); or J. L. Campbell, whom I once knew slightly and have corresponded with; or Carmichael Watson, whom I don't actually know. It is hard to know the best course. I myself am still at large, though the khaki-coloured communications grow more frequent and peremptory.[14]

Thus it can be seen Young was not only helping MacLean in his work but having to take into consideration the climate of censorship at the same time (so all three of the spheres interact here – the political, historical and Gaelic/Scots literary spheres). Young was right to be worried about where he left MacLean's poetry, since a few months after this letter was written raids were carried out on the homes of nationalist radicals throughout Scotland. Those targeted on 3 May 1941 included Arthur Donaldson, Rev. John MacKechnie, Douglas Young and the Hays.[15]

These are random examples of political standpoints taken from a large body of correspondence, and to understand the real significance of these letters it is necessary to view them as a complete collection (however incomplete this collection actually proves to be). When viewed in this way it is clear that the correspondence contains within itself the best example we have of autobiographical writing by Sorley MacLean. In many collections of letters, the 'glue' that holds the whole collection together is often the famous literary or historical figure who has penned most of the letters in the collection or on whose place in literary history it is hoped more light can be shed. It is tempting to view Sorley MacLean as the 'glue' in this collection. He has penned the largest number of surviving letters and his poetic output can be read in conjunction with the letters in many places. However, to take this view would be to simplify the situation to a great extent. It would mean eliminating what is most precious to the collection – the idea that each man is 'performing' for the other in the letters that are written, and the performance is more often than not from a political stand-point rather than from a literary one. The collection acts as a window into the lives of two literary men rather than just one, and, perhaps more impor-tantly, demonstrates the relationship that existed between them and how this affected literary affairs in Scotland during this period. Douglas Young's views and concerns have a balancing effect on the correspondence as a whole and are integral to the collection and should not be sidelined. This collection may indeed provide Scottish literary studies with a clearer picture of Douglas Young and the part that he played in the lives of other poets and political figures.

It is clear that the issues of using letters as a study aid are far more complicated than is at first apparent on a surface level. While the letters and the men who wrote them are real, the language of letters can never be a proper window into the way these men would have spoken in everyday 'real' life. The language of letters is not the equivalent of speech and much depends on the conditioning of written norms, different types of letter, topics and the relationship between the writer and the addressee. When these factors are taken into consideration our understanding of the devel-oping friendship between MacLean and Young becomes clearer. Changes in register can be detected from the tentative earliest letters to the full-blown letters of the later war years when both men were debating politics in earnest. When Douglas Young writes in an early letter on 26 June 1940 that 'my judgement may be biased here by the fact that I know you personally (though not so well as I hope to yet)',[16] one cannot help but wonder if he means to get to know the 'man' MacLean or MacLean as the 'writer of letters', or, indeed, both. MacLean and Young were known to each other before the beginning of these letters and yet a relationship of a different nature develops when they are writing to each other rather than speaking face to face. MacLean and Young both seem to set a great deal of store by letter writing, and a relaxation of writing style and an opening up of opinions can be sensed as the letters continue. This is where the most interesting political discussions and debates come into play. While the friendship between the two men was no doubt flourishing, it is the development of the friendship between writer(s) and addressee(s) in the shape of MacLean and Young that the correspondence charts.

From the correspondence both MacLean and Young's written mannerisms, habits and eccentricities can be viewed. While, however, a great amount of information can be gleaned from the letters, what is left unsaid can likewise indicate much about the writers. It should be remembered that these letters are written in English and one can only wonder what would have differed in the written relationship between MacLean and Young if MacLean, as a native speaker of Gaelic, had been able to write to Young in Gaelic and be understood by him. Register and tone would almost certainly differ if any possible Gaelic letters by MacLean were to be compared alongside his English ones. The register would perhaps be altered but MacLean's letters to family (even if they were not in his mother-tongue) would inevitably be more familiar (but might yield less politically motivated information), simply on account of to whom they were addressed. There is also the issue of 'distance' in relation to the reality of class issues and MacLean's words in a letter dated 11 September 1941 are a case in point.

> Why do I immediately sense a sort of political kinship with people as different as Muir and Grieve but not with you, Davie, Deòrsa etc. I think it is a class question. Neither you nor Davie nor Deòrsa nor Robert MacIntyre are really of my 'class' and hence I have never immediately felt that intimate feeling of closeness politically with you as I have felt in one meeting with Muir and Grieve ...[17]

This particular comment is an indicator of acute self-consciousness on the part of MacLean. Throughout many of the letters MacLean goes to some lengths to prove his credentials as a member of the working class, and a need to prove himself as part of the same 'group' as his political heroes, including James Connolly and John Maclean, may have been part of his wider political identity.[18] This conscious portrayal of self and the need to push a particular aspect of oneself to the forefront is part of a much greater issue in epistolary theory. In 'Portrait of the Artist as a Bad Character', Cynthia Ozick points out the dangers of treating letters and diaries as undisputed truth, highlighting the instability of the letter-form.[19] This brings to mind a letter from MacLean to Young dated 9 November 1941 in which he writes:

> When I see you again I'll tell you of this matter properly but don't mention anything of it to anyone, even to John, and I should like no one but yourself to see this particular letter. It is a matter which concerned primarily not me but someone else, hence my reticence.[20]

He would rather discuss this personal matter involving 'Eimhir' when he sees Young face to face rather than write it down, thus suggesting that the very act of putting pen to paper is dangerous and incriminating in some way. Therefore, the MacLean–Young correspondence can never tell the whole story because on some occasions the writer deliberately leaves a part of himself out of the text. It is, of course, his prerogative to do so. A poststructuralist would argue that this is not an unusual occurrence. Truth remains elusive in any text, and rather than taking the view that the writer of a letter cannot be trusted because that writer is in a state of constant flux, it may be more beneficial to treat each letter as a fragment of truth – a moment in time which must be contextualised. In this way MacLean's views on Russia and communism do not appear flippant or changeable but rather the transitory thoughts of a man who is coming to terms with a time of political upheaval.

In conclusion, the MacLean–Young correspondence will yield many treasures if it is approached in a sensitive manner. The letters can be seen as a political tool of strong communist, socialist and nationalist rhetoric, as can be evidenced in some of the examples provided earlier in this paper. Some of the more protracted discussions are actually extended monologues. However, what gives the correspondence its added power is the human experience behind the rhetoric. Especially during the wartime letters there is the sense that each letter could be the last and so there is an urgency to commit to paper certain thoughts and ideas. In specific instances the letter-writing process is hindered by a sandstorm in the desert while MacLean is on active duty there, and also a lack of paper (at one point MacLean has to make the choice to write to his family rather than write a longer letter about his poetry to Young).[21]

Jacques Derrida's description in *Archive Fever* of the utopian dream of the archivist who comes across 'an archive without archive'[22] is a tempting prospect, as it would mean a completely authentic and immediate encounter with the past. However, this dream is impossible. There will always be more letters, journals and literature to alter our views of the past. Douglas Young and Sorley MacLean were both keen correspondents, keeping in contact with a number of people at any one time, and a single collection of letters can offer only one dimension to a much wider picture. While a writer can never be completely understood, Derrida notes that 'the place of the one who writes must always be sought even if it is not fixed'. In recent years the Scottish literary scene of the 1930s, 1940s and beyond has begun to be researched in more detail. Beth Junor's *Scarcely Ever Out Of My Thought: The Letters of Valda Trevlyn Grieve to Christopher Murray Grieve (Hugh MacDiarmid)* has emphasised the less 'public', women's perspective of the Scottish Renaissance and its figurehead, and Susan Wilson's *Correspondence Between Hugh MacDiarmid and Sorley MacLean* and John Manson's *Dear Grieve*[23] are also good examples of how the archive is being utilised. Thus, the work on the MacLean–Young correspondence is only one path of many on a journey which will eventually lead to a better appreciation of the lives and legacy of a circle of literary friends, of which Sorley MacLean was certainly one of its strongest Gaelic voices.

Notes

1   Quoted in Temma Berg, *The Lives and Letters of an Eighteenth-Century Circle of Acquaintance*, Hampshire: Ashgate, 2006, p. 2.

2   Sorley MacLean, *Caoir Gheal Leumraich/White Leaping Flame: Collected Poems*, Christopher Whyte and Emma Dymock, eds, Edinburgh: Polygon, 2011, pp. 412–13

3   Berg, p. 7

4   Emma Dymock, 'The Quest for Identity in Sorley MacLean's "An Cuilithionn": Journeying into Politics and Beyond': unpublished PhD thesis, University of Edinburgh, 2008

5   See for example Christopher Whyte's edition of MacLean's *Dàin do Eimhir/Poems to Eimhir*, Glasgow: Association for Scottish Literary Studies, 2002, and Michel Byrne's edition of *Collected Poems and Songs of George Campbell Hay (Deòrsa Mac Iain Dheòrsa)*, Edinburgh: Edinburgh University Press, 2003.

6   As far back as 1986, the MacLean–Young correspondence was being referred to in e.g. Joy Hendry, 'Sorley MacLean: The Man and his Work' in *Sorley MacLean: Critical Essays*, eds Raymond J. Ross and Joy Hendry, Edinburgh: Scottish Academic Press, 1986, pp. 9–38. On 31 October 2009, I made extensive use of the MacLean–Young correspondence in a conference paper, delivered to the 'Global Nations?' Research Institute of Irish and Scottish Studies conference, University of Aberdeen, entitled '"The Mad Delirium of War": Placing Sorley MacLean's War Poems in a Socio-Political Context'.

7   In a letter to Young on 27 May 1943, MacLean writes that 'The hospital routine breaks up one's day very much and one gets little time to settle down. There is so much I want to do, to learn Greek, to learn Old Irish and to study Gaelic metrics exhaustively, to start a systematic movement of collaborations to supply Gaelic with a full scientific, philosophical and technical vocabulary, from the parts of car or aeroplane engines to Logical Positivism, or even the latest 'catch-words' of the aesthete play-boys. I think it fitting that Gaelic should have such even if it is never to be used. But I can't decide whether the way is to use native compounds or derive directly from Greek and Latin. At any rate, quite an imposing number of words could be added in a few years by, say, a hundred collaborators. They would have their work checked and corrected by a committee of men of known ability in Gaelic philology …': Acc 6419, Box 38b, National Library of Scotland.

8   Acc 6419, Box 38b, National Library of Scotland

9   'At that time our discussions would range widely over politics, both national and international. These were the days of Hitler, "the brute and brigand at the head of Europe", and of the dreary, pusillanimous Chamberlain government. We were both affected by the myths of 1916 and 1917 and were both interested in and sympathetic to Irish nationalism … As for literature, we ranged widely over Greek, Latin, French, English and Scottish poetry. Coming to modern times we talked about Yeats, Eliot, Valéry, Pound, Lawrence, MacDiarmid, and the emerging MacSpaunday group': J. B. Caird, 'Sorley MacLean: a Personal View' in *Sorley MacLean: Critical Essays*, eds Raymond J. Ross and Joy Hendry, Edinburgh: Scottish Academic Press, 1986, pp. 39–43 (40).

10 MS 29540, National Library of Scotland, f. 43

11 See, for example, 'Dol an Iar', in which MacLean clearly sets out his Gaelic and family history in the last stanza of the poem, despite the apparent internationalist tone of the rest of the poem – 'Agus biodh na bha mar bha e, / tha mi de dh'fhir mhòr' a' Bhràighe, / de Chloinn Mhic Ghille Chaluim threubhaich, / de Mhathanaich Loch Aills nan geurlann, / agus fir m' ainme – cò bu trèine / nuair dh'fhadadh uabhar an lèirchreach?' ('And be what was as it was, / I am of the big men of Braes, / of the heroic Raasay MacLeods, / of the sharp-sword Mathesons of Lochalsh; / and the men of my name – who were braver / when their ruinous pride was kindled?'): *Caoir*, 2011, pp. 200–01.

12 MacLean's *Dàin do Eimhir*, in particular, discusses the threat of fascism in Europe: *Caoir*, 2011, pp. 96–171. Other poems which exhibit his social conscience and a socialist philosophy are 'Ban-Ghàidheal' ('A Highland Woman') and 'Calbharaigh' ('Calvary'): *Caoir*, pp. 16–17 & pp. 20–21.

13 John MacDonald (1886–1970). Born Milifiach, Inverness-shire. Lecturer, then Reader in Celtic, University of Aberdeen, 1922–56. Edited the poems of Ewan MacLachlan (1773–1822), including his translation of Books 1–7 of the *Iliad*, in 1937.

14 MS 29540, National Library of Scotland, f. 60

15 Byrne, 2003, p. 469

16 MS 29540, National Library of Scotland, f. 18

17 Acc 6419, Box 38b, National Library of Scotland

18 One example of this is in a letter dated 2 May 1943 in which MacLean expresses his hope that his long poem 'An Cuilithionn' ('The Cuillin') will not just be available in a handsome edition for a readership with money to spend on books but as an affordable pamphlet for his intended readership of crofters: 'So my opinion now is, let the "Dàin" go as they are, but I must take some care to get the "rant" out at a crofter's price, but of that later'. He also wrote to Young on 20 April 1943 that 'As to your 'note on the making [of "An Cuilithionn"], the only points I noted that might need adjusting are that you exaggerate the "difficulty" of my Gaelic. Indeed I use hardly more than a dozen words at most that won't be at once understood by a crofter of average intelligence and knowledge of Gaelic': Acc 6419, Box 38b, National Library of Scotland.

19 Cynthia Ozick, 'Portrait of the Artist as a Bad Character' in *A Cynthia Ozick Reader*, ed. Elaine M. Kauvar, Bloomington and Indianapolis: Indiana University Press, 1996, pp. 311–13 (p. 313)

20 Acc 6419, Box 38b, National Library of Scotland

21 On 30 March 1942 MacLean wrote to Young: 'There is a sandstorm from which I am protected by thin canvas on one side, but it blows round the corners. Today I have a free afternoon. The Major is away and I am using his tent, which is facing the right way; my own happens today to be facing the sandstorm. Apart from sand the climate is ideal as yet for one who has only to mind a wireless-set; the nights are still pretty cold but we are pretty well provided for against it.' Later that year (27 October) MacLean wrote to Young: 'I sent you a longish letter about a fortnight ago which I hope you get. Nowadays it is awfully difficult to get airgraph forms and letter-card forms and those few I get I have to use telling my people I am still alive etc., and so I have to fall back on the long letter which takes about two months, I believe': Acc 6419, Box 38b, National Library of Scotland.

22 Jacques Derrida, *Archive Fever: A Freudian Impression*, trans. by Eric Prenowitz, London: University of Chicago Press, 1996, p. 98

23 Beth Junor (ed.), *Scarcely Ever Out of My Thoughts: The Letters of Valda Trevlyn Grieve to Christopher Murray Grieve (Hugh MacDiarmid)*, Edinburgh: Word Power Books, 2007; Susan Wilson (ed.), *The Correspondence Between Hugh MacDiarmid and Sorley MacLean: An Annotated Edition*, Edinburgh: Edinburgh University Press, 2010; John Manson (ed.), *Dear Grieve: Letters to Hugh MacDiarmid (C. M. Grieve)*, Glasgow: Kennedy and Boyd, 2011

Bibliography

Berg, Temma, *The Lives and Letters of an Eighteenth-Century Circle of Acquaintance*, Hampshire: Ashgate, 2006

Caird, J. B, 'Sorley MacLean: a Personal View' in *Sorley MacLean: Critical Essays*, Raymond J. Ross and Joy Hendry, eds, Edinburgh: Scottish Academic Press, 1986

Derrida, Jacques, *Archive Fever: A Freudian Impression*, trans. by Eric Prenowitz, London: University of Chicago Press, 1996

Dymock, Emma, 'The Quest for Identity in Sorley MacLean's "An Cuilithionn": Journeying into Politics and Beyond': unpublished PhD thesis, University of Edinburgh, 2008

Hay, George Campbell, *Collected Poems and Songs of George Campbell Hay (Deòrsa Mac Iain Dheòrsa)*, Michel Byrne, ed., Edinburgh: Edinburgh University Press, 2003

Hendry, Joy. 'Sorley MacLean: The Man and his Work' in *Sorley MacLean: Critical Essays*, Raymond J. Ross and Joy Hendry, eds, Edinburgh: Scottish Academic Press, 1986

Junor, Beth, ed., *Scarcely Ever Out of My Thoughts: The Letters of Valda Trevlyn Grieve to Christopher Murray Grieve (Hugh MacDiarmid)*, Edinburgh: Word Power Books, 2007

MacLean, Sorley, *Dàin do Eimhir/Poems to Eimhir*, Christopher Whyte, ed., Glasgow: Association for Scottish Literary Studies, 2002

MacLean, Sorley, *Caoir Gheal Leumraich/White Leaping Flame: Collected Poems*, Christopher Whyte and Emma Dymock, eds, Edinburgh: Polygon, 2011

Manson, John, ed., *Dear Grieve: Letters to Hugh MacDiarmid (C. M. Grieve)*, Glasgow: Kennedy and Boyd, 2011

Ozick, Cynthia, 'Portrait of the Artist as a Bad Character' in *A Cynthia Ozick Reader*, Elaine M. Kauva, ed., Bloomington and Indianapolis: Indiana University Press, 1996

Wilson, Susan, ed., *The Correspondence Between Hugh MacDiarmid and Sorley MacLean: An Annotated Edition*, Edinburgh: Edinburgh University Press, 2010

Manuscripts

Letters from Sorley MacLean to Douglas Young: Acc 6419, Box 38b, National Library of Scotland

Letters from Douglas Young to Sorley MacLean, MS 29540, National Library of Scotland

5. Sorley MacLean and the Modern Panegyric

TIMOTHY NEAT

On 11 August 1985 Sorley MacLean gave the keynote address at the celebrations surrounding the unveiling of the Hugh MacDiarmid Memorial Sculpture in Langholm, Dumfriesshire. MacLean labelled his talk minimally: 'Address at Langholm – 11 August 1985' and it remains almost unknown. It was, however, a significant speech: important for what it says about MacDiarmid and a startling affirmation of the continuing power of the panegyric. First we should hear MacLean's words; then I shall give brief facts about the memorial project and contextualise MacLean's speech.

Sorley MacLean: 'Address at Langholm – 11 August 1985'

It is a great honour for me to be asked to speak here 'in honour of Hugh MacDiarmid', but it is also an honour I accept with much misgiving and diffidence, remembering the great address delivered at Christopher's funeral by Norman MacCaig.

In conversation during MacDiarmid's lifetime I more than once referred to him as the best living poet in Europe, and I have said as much, though not in the same words, in print. It is not that I have ever set myself up as a judge of the poetry of Europe. For one thing I could not set myself up as a fit judge of the poetry written even in Wales and Ireland because I do not know Welsh at all and do not know Irish Gaelic well enough to be a judge of its poetry. And there is no other European language that I know well enough to be a judge of its poetry. Therefore, to say or have said that MacDiarmid was the best poet of his time in Europe means only that I could not imagine a better poet than the poet of *Sangschaw, Penny Wheep, A Drunk Man Looks at the Thistle* and many more things that were written by MacDiarmid. So I let it stand and say again: 'MacDiarmid was the best poet of his time in Europe.'

No poet or artist can be judged except by thinking of his best poetry or art, and that is as true of MacDiarmid as of others. There is enough of his best to be astonishing. A great number of his lyrics are to the ear and the mind, and even to the neuro-physical perception, the words of a man sending back messages from a forward observation post on the frontiers of consciousness, and they are words that can set a human situation against the great universe with resonances and rhythms for which the first Scots word I can think of is 'uncanny' and the English word 'magical'. And his messages are such that the high frequencies of his sensitivities are transformed in language to what I and many more recognise as truth and profundity, the kind of truth that Matthew Arnold called 'high seriousness'; and often that 'high seriousness' is, as it were, implicit, said and understood without being explicitly said.

It is not only in the soaring, irradiating, sometimes coldly passionate lyric that Hugh MacDiarmid, your Christopher Murray Grieve, was supreme and as original as any art can be. I cannot imagine any other long poem as original and as great as his *A Drunk Man Looks at the Thistle*. In it the great symbolist movement of European literature has a breadth, variety and an inevitable organic unity in diversity that makes other long symbolist poems seem factitious and laboured and contrived. I am sure there is nothing like it anywhere else; that it is the last word in originality and in its whole effect supreme.

Hugh MacDiarmid, or if you would prefer it, Christopher Murray Grieve, had a sensibility that was and is beyond words, and with that a courage and spiritual ambition that made him live a life of material poverty in order to have no trammels on his visionary spirituality. He was the kind of man who was at once a philosophical materialist and a moral idealist of idealists, and to me at any rate that is the most admirable of men.

Grieve himself said that 'a Scottish poet maun assume / the burden o' his people's doom,' and the burden of one nation's 'doom' is the burden of the doom of all peoples; and of that Grieve was mostly, if not always, aware, for he had the accidental inconsistencies inevitable in one who sought to be where extremes meet. I consider those inconsistencies accidental, not at all essential. It seems to me that his accidental inconsistencies were by-products of his spiritual ambition, one result of which was the attempt to do the impossible in poetry. But such spiritual ambition is a glorious thing, and MacDiarmid's failures are glorious failures. Matthew Arnold said of Byron:

> When Byron's eyes were closed in death
> We bowed our heads and held our breath.
> He taught us little, but our soul
> Had felt him like the thunder's roll.

Of Christopher Murray Grieve, or Hugh MacDiarmid, I would say that 'our soul [has] felt him like the thunder's roll' and that he taught my generation, and I daresay many of this generation too, not a little, but mountains and mountains of things about the human spirit.

The project to create the Hugh MacDiarmid Memorial Sculpture began its long gestation in the Eskdale Hotel, Langholm, following MacDiarmid's funeral on the afternoon of 13 September 1978. Seven years later, on 11 August 1985, the completed Memorial (a sculpture in the form of a great open book, set in the landscape, on Whita Hill, above Langholm) was unveiled by MacDiarmid's wife, Valda Trevlyn Grieve. The sculptor was Jake Harvey of Maxton, by Kelso, Roxburghshire. Because of a violent storm, all the speeches – including MacLean's address – took place in the dance hall of the Eskdale Hotel, just yards from where the idea of a sculptural Memorial first began to germinate.

The whole project was organised by the Scottish Sculpture Trust, a charitable body, of which I was convenor from 1981 to 1986. It became a seven-year campaign that developed in a strangely symbiotic relationship with the making of two of my films, *Hallaig: The Poetry and Landscape of Sorley MacLean* and *Tig! For the Morn's the Fair Day! – The Langholm Common Riding, 1979*. This is not the place to discuss the interrelationship of these three projects, but, when Jake Harvey's sculpture was finally on site, Sorley MacLean seemed the obvious person to lead the tributes to MacDiarmid. With only the slightest hesitation, he rose to his task with the responsibility of genius – and delivered his great panegyric.

If the word panegyric is used at all these days, it tends to be used scholastically, or derogatively. It rhymes with eulogy, hagiography, and the demeaning bitchiness of our age! But Sorley's address shows us why the panegyric – the word, the idea, the tradition – retains an ancient validity – at least in some parts of the world. The *Oxford English Dictionary* also remains loyal to the panegyric, describing it as:

a) A public eulogy fit for a public assembly or festival.
b) A public speech or writing in praise of some person, thing, or achievement; a laudatory discourse, a formal or elaborate encomium or eulogy.

Sorley's address exactly fits that description. The dictionary then describes how, in 1814, the German historian Winkelmann 'fell in love with the sculpted relics of ancient art, and undertook to describe them panegyrically': a sense of love – shared pride, shared kinship – has always fuelled the panegyric impulse. Certainly, these emotions and values are intensely alive in MacLean's address.

The *OED* also states that Stukeley in England, in 1737, was described in these words: 'Here was in British times the great panegyre of the Druids, the mid-summer meeting of all the country round'– a panegyre being a celebration of a people, at home, on their native heath. Again, Sorley's address fits the dictionary definition and links both speaker and subject to a tradition that both MacDiarmid and MacLean were, consciously, part of. The dictionary also describes how, 'in 1603, Ben Johnson subtitled one of his historical essays, "A panegyre upon the happy entrance of James, our sovereign, to his first high session of Parliament" ...' Historically, James VI was the royal fulcrum on whom British renaissance modernism and old Celtic, druidic tradition rested, and as a modern poet Sorley MacLean stood astride a similar Scottish fulcrum in his day. He was a makar whose intensity, surreal conjunctions and dramatic gravitas (not least in his oral delivery) can rightly be described as druidic. MacLean was a culture-carrier (tailor-made on Raasay!) to carry the ancient panegyric tradition into contemporary society – and literature.

Certainly, those who heard MacLean's 'Address at Langholm' will remember it, not just for what was said, but for how it was spoken. MacLean read his speech (because he knew every word was important) but spoke with a measure and authority – occasionally a sense of mischief – that was unforgettable. He spoke without a microphone. He spoke to about three hundred people. Many in his audience had drunk a fair bit but, once the bard began to speak, one might have heard a pin drop. Here was history concertina-ed. Here was one great poet addressing another and endorsing traditions that go back to the pre-Christian era.

The extent to which MacLean's address was the high point of a great day is hinted at in the following notes made by Janet Law, from Auchterarder, daughter of the poet T. S. Law:

> *Scotland, Sunday, 11 August 1985* – Shrouded in cloud, beaten by blasts of wind, drenched by this summer's predictably heavy rain – an impressive gathering of already soaking wet poets, artists and not-the-literati have conveyed themselves by bus and car up the bleak and narrow Whita Yett road behind Langholm. Congestion threatening near the Memorial, wrapped in two saltires. 'He would have had it this way!' The weather and the problems with planning permission making the occasion one for determination in adversity – a peculiarly Scottish Pleasure ... Political demonstrations and live theatre have a lot in common. The transient engendering of a sense of precariousness and urgency, as well as a feeling of participation ... Unfortunately, the red flag which had been planned as an inner wrapping to the saltires – to be revealed before the sculpture itself was revealed – had to be removed to spare the blushes of certain locals. Red roses and fireworks shooting out red smoke did not compensate for the loss ... Do we need these symbols? Could there have been a better occasion for them?
>
> Now the Memorial stands revealed – a symbolic interpretation in tangible form of MacDiarmid's poetry ... The saltires stripped away, the sculpture bared, the malt whisky and rainwater, camera crew up to their knees in glaur, loudspeakers not working but highly dangerous. Timothy Neat, miraculously almost audible above the wind – adjourning the event to a local hostelry ... On the way home, one of the youngest generation there: 'What was the best part of the day for you?' 'The Speaker,' she says (she must remember sounds

more than pictures). 'Which one?' 'The one Sorley.' When the Unveiling Party arrived at the local hostelry – the Eskdale Hotel – the Carnival of Scottish life suddenly assumed a more Lenten form. Everyone was droukit – including Valda's dog, much frightened by the thunder! And, scurrying into the warmth of the hotel, they met an immovable object – the management. No dogs allowed! Rules is rules! Help for Heroes does not extend to the wives and dogs of poets – be they alive or be they dead, be they hungry and unfed! The path of Valda Grieve was barred and, refusing to be parted from her dog, she, the day's Guest of Honour, heard not one word of the speeches made in honour of the man she had rescued from imminent oblivion half a century earlier – Scotland's greatest Scots/English poet, Hugh MacDiarmid.

The first speaker was Alex McCrindle, an old friend of MacDiarmid's, a communist and actor; he spoke for the Communist Party and the absent Valda. Then up spake Willie Wolfe – for the Scottish National Party. Local MacDiarmid enthusiast Wattie Bell spoke for the Langholm Community. Arthur Elliott and Arabella Harvey recited MacDiarmid's poetry. Hamish Henderson gave honour to the sculptor, Jake Harvey. Finally, Sorley MacLean delivered his panegyric ...

In the Fifties, the Irish painter Jack Yeats (whom MacDiarmid knew) informed John Berger: 'You can plan an event but, if it turns out as planned, it won't be an event!' The day of the unveiling of the MacDiarmid Memorial in Langholm was an event – of the first order! It did MacDiarmid justice. It gave three hundred MacDiarmid enthusiasts a wild day out. And it gave MacLean a stage on which he could retune one of the Gaelic world's defining art forms, the panegyric – a form despised by many academics but beloved by the crowd and the politically committed. Academia can be self-regarding, reductive and 'doun-takin'; over-wary of commitment and suspicious of love. MacLean's 'Address at Langholm' was a product of love: his love for MacDiarmid, for poetry, for Scotland, for Gaelic tradition and the communist ideal. In this new Gaelic University these subjects of MacLean's love should be honoured and treated with high seriousness.

In conclusion, I will now read the letter Sorley MacLean wrote from Braes, on 22 December 1985, to accompany a handwritten copy of the Langholm address. It shows another side to the poet we honour at this conference – his down to earth simplicity, his generosity, his helpfulness and concision. MacLean was a man who embodied many aspects of the culture and virtues of the Gael. I salute him.

Dear Tim,

I enclose an exact copy of what I said at Langholm, no corrections or improvements. Also I am enclosing a cheque for £50, viz equivalent of 100 Canadian dollars for use of the film [*Hallaig*], which went down very well. Also there is a translation of two quatrains sung by Catriona on Norman son of Norman, my MacLean great-great-grandfather. There is too the very brief version of the words of 'Mackintosh's Lament' – as we had them. There are long versions in Volume V of *Carmina Gadelica*, which I will copy out and send you.

Yours,
Sam

6. Guth Shomhairle

JOHN PURSER

Sorley's voice is much imitated, and the measured pace of his speech, never mind his readings, mimicked and even satirised. I am guilty myself. I am told that Norman MacCaig pointedly looked at his watch when Sorley was reading.[1] Seamus Heaney wrote:

> Everyone imitated Sorley's accent, everything highly pitched and atremble; so, when you met him, you were meeting with the real performance – and he was no disappointment. Country people, when I was growing up, stood up when they were going to recite, and they formally recited. I took it to be that Sorley was a product of an oral culture; and, if you are going to recite, you make a job of it![2]

Precisely. The art of rhetoric was not wholly dead – indeed, was still fundamental to a good sermon. And, of course, the Gaels are used to singing psalms many times more slowly than they are sung in English. There was even a tradition of reading or reciting a Fenian *Laoidh* to induce sleep.[3] Sorley reading 'A Chiall 's a Ghràidh' is typical of his manner. He, and many another poet of his generation and earlier, would vary the pitch of the voice; and many a poet, Gaelic and otherwise, would publish his poems as 'Songs'. A fascinating parallel can be heard in the voice of another bard from Skye – Calum Ruadh – as heard in Torkild Knudson's remarkable recording of Calum Ruadh's 'Fairy Song', in which Knudson placed two ways of delivery together.[4]

Essential to the delivery of poetry is comprehension. Bardic verse was not designed so much for the ceilidh house as the big hall. It required some degree of projection and time also for the audience to pick up the references, applaud, or otherwise respond. Modern poets rarely allow time for the audience to react.

Bardic poetry was composed long before the microphone, but by the nineteenth century poets were performing in large theatres, which called for even greater projection and a slower pace. The pace, one might say, of *pìobaireachd*. It was also, like *pìobaireachd*, designed to function rhythmically, rhymingly and with assonance and alliteration – sound values akin to music. Here is what W. B. Yeats had to say about it in a 1932 BBC recording:

> I am going to read my poems with great emphasis upon the rhythm, and that may seem strange if you are not used to it. I remember the great English poet, William Morris, coming in a rage out of some lecture hall, where somebody had recited a passage out of his 'Seagulls of Ulster':
>
> 'It gave me a devil of a lot of trouble,' said Morris, 'to get that thing into verse.'
>
> It gave *me* [says Yeats] the devil of a lot of trouble to get into verse the poems that I am going to read. That is why I will *not* read them as if they were prose.

And here is Sorley, whom I remember as keeping his chin up like a good singer:

> If I have time to do it, I brood over something until a rhythm comes, as a more or less tight rope to cross the abyss of silence. I go on it, as far as I can see, unconsciously. Nowadays I shun 'free verse' because so very little of it in others satisfies me and because its rope is so often so slack as to be loose bits of Chopped Prose, even if courtesy gives them the name of rhythm. I could not be primarily a Gael without a very deep-seated conviction that the auditory is the primary sensuousness of poetry.[5]

The theme of music in poetry and, in particular, in relation to 'An Cuilithionn'/ 'The Cuillin', was picked up in William Crosbie's cover design for *Dàin do Eimhir*. The artist has stitched one of the four cello strings through the Cuillin, in the background, and I strongly suspect that Crosbie had read drafts of 'The Cuillin' through his connection with MacLellan.

There are many references to music in MacLean's work and, in particular, to MacCrimmon *pìobaireachd* such as *Maol Donn* and *Cumha na Cloinne*. These iconic works inhabit the poetry in a way which brings together landscape and music, exploring both outer and inner realities. MacLean commented shrewdly on music, and on his own relationship with it. Here he writes:

> Even to this day, I sometimes think that if I had been a singer I would have written no verse ... very early in life I came to be obsessed with the lyric, first of all because of my unusually rich Gaelic background; with the lyric in the Greek sense of a marriage of poetry and music, and then, because I was not a musician, with the lyric in the Shelleyan and Blakeian sense of a short or shortish poem suggesting song even if it could never be sung, a concentration running or flying away from anything that could be called *sermo pedestris*.[6]

Scotland has a great lyric tradition, and MacDiarmid's lyrics, very many of which were wonderfully set to music by his teacher, Francis George Scott, were much admired by MacLean. But the introduction to 'An Cuilithionn' acknowledges MacDiarmid in a broader manner, extending lyricism into cosmic drama:

> A Chrìstein MhicGréidhir, MhicDhiarmaid,
> na robh agamsa an iarmad
> a sgrìobhadh o bhàrrlach trian bheag
> d' aigne gheur dhomhainn fhiadhaich,
> gun cuirinn-sa an Cuilithionn iargalt
> 'na theine-sionnachain san iarmailt
> 's gun toirinn as an Eilean éigheach
> a dheanadh iolach dàin 's na speuran.

> *Christopher Grieve, MacDiarmid,*
> *had I the remnant*
> *scraped from the dregs of a small third part*
> *of your sharp profound wild spirit,*
> *I would put the awesome Cuillin*
> *in phosphorescence in the firmament,*
> *and I would make the island shout*
> *with a cry of fate in the skies.*

The rich assonance of those lines evokes a lyric strength that extends beyond song into lay and epic.

Perhaps the musicality of Shelley in particular, coupled with his eccentric version of radical republican socialism, had its appeal for MacLean. The verse drama *Prometheus Unbound*, with Prometheus tied to a rock high in the Caucasus mountains, and exposed to the elements while addressing and being addressed by gods, spirits of the planets and mythical figures, is not without its parallels in MacLean's 'An Cuilithionn'.

> Thuirt Shelley gun do chlisg am mullach
> Caucasach ri pian a' churaidh,
> agus chunnaic mise leumraich
> air sliabh a' Chuilithinn le éibhneas
> ri faicinn Dimitrov 'na aonar
> a' toirt air an spiorad dhaonda
> leum as a chochull le faoisgneadh
> gu stad analach an t-saoghail.
> Anns an stad ud bhàsaich diathan
> aosda bùirdeasach crìona;
> thuit iad bho na mullaichean caola
> sìos gu glomharan le glaodhaich.

> *Shelley said that the Caucasian summit*
> *started at the hero's pain,*
> *and I saw a leaping*
> *of the Cuillin mountain for joy*
> *to see Dimitrov alone*
> *making the human spirit*
> *leap out of his shell, unhusked,*
> *to stop the breath of the world.*
> *In that stoppage died*
> *ancient paltry bourgeois gods:*
> *they fell from the narrow ridges*
> *down to abysses, shrieking.*[7]

MacLean, like Shelley, uses the musicality of his verse with a strong sense of underlying parallels with Greek lyric drama in the form of 'the marriage of poetry and music'. For Shelley, that marriage was stimulated in particular by Aeschylus's *Prometheus Bound*, though we should not forget the possible influence of the Jacobean masque, especially in the work of that second-generation Scot, Ben Jonson. I do not have space here to pursue the political and other elements which are common to *Prometheus Unbound* and 'An Cuilithionn', never mind the fact that the masque flourished in a Jacobean court, not an Elizabethan one, except to point out what I have published elsewhere: that there was a possible relationship between Gaelic declamation and the development of opera in Italy – never mind in these islands.[8] There is much to be researched and discussed here.

But for a quintessential Gael such as Sorley, the precedent of his own culture was already profoundly embedded in his whole understanding of bardic delivery, and Aeschylus and Shelley can only have acted as reinforcements to that understanding, rather than being any sort of *fons et origo*. However, the sound of the *fons et origo* in the voice of the scholar of ancient Greek music, Stelios Psaroudakes, can be heard in his delivery of a passage of Greek drama in as close to the style as we can get. What is interesting about this is that it is not unfamiliar to those who have heard Sorley at his most dramatic, and it is worth listening to Angus MacLellan intoning 'Òran na Comhachaig' in his nineties, in the same context. One could readily intone the Shelley passage to MacLellan's melodic outline. There is a case to be made for a treatment of 'An Cuilithionn' in a quasi-operatic manner such as Carl Orff uses so effectively in his version of Aeschylus's *Prometheus Bound* which is remarkably close to the performance of Stelios Psaroudakes.[9]

Song was, of course, fundamental for MacLean. Terence McCaughey has pointed out the direct influence of a song from Benbecula for a drowned man on Sorley's lament for his brother, 'Cumha Chaluim Iain MhicGill-Eain'.[10] MacLean himself has written extensively on song as a major part of his upbringing and inheritance, and, for instance, discusses the contrasting merits of the song melodies for one of the laments for Iain Garbh – 'Seall a mach an e 'n là e' – preferring J. C. M. Campbell's tune to his own Raasay one.[11]

MacLean's introduction to 'An Cuilithionn' concludes with a reference to one of his greatest predecessors, Alasdair Mac Mhaighstir Alasdair:

Agus, a Dhòmhnallaich ghlòrmhoir,
na robh agam trian do threòir-sa,
chumainn ar Clàr-Sgìthe òirdhearc
ceann-caol ri tuinn àr na h-Eòrpa.

And, glorious MacDonald,
if I had a third of your might,
I would keep our noble Cuillin
head on to the waves of Europe's battle.

Well, Mac Mhaighstir Alasdair was head-on to everything and, amongst other things, is the composer of the first known poem based upon the form of a *pìobaireachd*.

It was Emma Dymock who first made, to me, the intriguing suggestion that 'An Cuilithionn' might be based upon a similar formal notion. Given that MacLean printed only what he thought 'tolerable' of the poem, we cannot make any very precise connection between it and *pìobaireachd*: but there are certainly suggestive parallels – some of them made by Sorley himself in the poem – and so what follows here springs from Emma's own insight, and from comments made by Christopher Whyte.[12]

Air Sgurr Dubh an Dà Bheinn
thàinig guth gu m' chluais a' seinn,
Pàdraig Mór 's a cheòl a' caoineadh
uile chlann a' chinne-daonna.
Agus feasgar air a' Ghàrsbheinn
bha ceòl eile ann a thàinig,
'Maol Donn' agus ùrlar sàth-ghaoil
a' bristeadh cridhe nam fonn àlainn.

On Sgurr Dubh of the Two Hills
a voice came to my ear singing,
Patrick Mor and his music mourning
all the children of mankind;
and an evening on the Garsven
there was another music that came,

> *'Maol Donn' and its theme of love-fullness*
> *breaking the hearts of lovely tunes.*[13]

This passage comes from Part II, and contrasts a *pìobaireachd* of beautiful but desolate lament – Patrick Mor's *Cumha na Cloinne* (*The Lament for the Children*) it has to be – and *Maol Donn*, to which are attached various legends, including the suggestion that it is a MacCrimmon *pìobaireachd*.[14] Whatever the truth behind this music, MacLean describes it perfectly. *Maol Donn* indeed has *sàth-ghaol*, is full of love, and is a great favourite with pipers.

It was also a favourite with the Scottish modernist composer Erik Chisholm, whose *Pibroch Piano Concerto*'s opening movement is based upon *Maol Donn*. The context of the first public performance of the Chisholm could scarcely have been more apposite to Sorley MacLean's own use of *Maol Donn* in the context of war and human brutality, writing as he was in the late 30s, for Chisholm first performed the work in Glasgow in 1940.

I do not know whether Erik Chisholm had read anything of Sorley's, including 'The Cuillin' in manuscript or typescript, but it is highly likely that he did. He already knew Sorley's publisher William MacLellan well, and MacLellan even danced the part of Ogma the Wise in Chisholm's very Celtic ballet *The Earth Shapers* (Glasgow 1941), with sets and costumes designed by William Crosbie, who, of course, illustrated Sorley's *Dàin do Eimhir*. The programme cover was designed by Crosbie and entitled *Clàr-Cuimhneachais*. Chisholm was a left-wing socialist with strong pacifist leanings and an admiration for the Soviet Union which he sustained well into the 1950s. He had stood up for Crosbie's refusal to kill a fellow human being under orders, but Chisholm himself was spared from confronting the authorities through his failure to pass the medical on account of his poor eyesight.[15]

Chisholm also set *Cumha na Cloinne* – though his setting is incomplete, it is instructive to hear his very modernist treatment of this classic, with its deeply disturbing undercurrents and passionate protest. We do not know when this was composed, but it is safe to say that it comes from the period of the Second World War.

Returning to *Maol Donn*: in 'An Cuilithionn', MacLean hears this *pìob-aireachd* in the evening on the Gàrsbheinn. Having climbed these mountains myself, I cannot propose a direct connection between the tunes and the summits upon which they are heard – except to point out that the Gàrsbheinn is the last and southernmost mountain of the ridge. From there one does indeed look out towards Barra, and it is perhaps that prospect, following the sun south and west, that allows the poet's mind to travel across the ocean and back to the west coast of Skye and face once more the sorrow of his people, for the view to Barra must include Rubha an Dùnain:

> 'S ag éirigh bho roid Rubha 'n Dùnain
> anns na tlàman geura cùbhraidh
> gaol is bròn tuath na dùthcha …

> *Rising from the bog-myrtle of Rubha 'n Dunain*
> *in sharp fragrant wafts*
> *the love and grief of the peasants of the land …*[16]

Rubha an Dùnain had, of course, been cleared. But it had also once been the home of Frances Tolmie, she who collected and annotated so many vital songs, of which a number came from Rubha an Dùnain.

But in the final section of MacLean's poem, the music heard is not a lament, but an incitement:

> Latha dhomh sa' Chuilithionn chreagach,
> chuala mi phìob mhor 'ga spreigeadh,
> nuallan cinne-daonna freagairt,
> an eanchainn 's an cridhe leagte.

> Chualas iolach air na sléibhtean,
> gàir shaorsa an t-sluaigh ag éirigh.

> *I was one day in the rocky Cuillin,*
> *I heard the great pipes incited,*
> *the roar of mankind in answer,*
> *brain and heart in harmony.*

> *A cry was heard on the hills,*
> *the people's shout of liberty rising.*[17]

I wish Sorley could have heard the Harlaw *Brosnachadh* composed by Niall Mòr MacMhuirich as sung by Ailean Dòmhnallach to the *ùrlar* of *Cogadh no Sìth – War or Peace*. Courage and desperation, despair and hope, go hand in hand, as they do in MacLean's verse.[18]

In another example of the marriage of *pìobaireachd* with verse, Mac Mhaighstir Alasdair concludes 'Moladh Mòraig' with a *crùnluadh*. Likewise, MacLean changes the rhythm and increases the repetition in the beautiful concluding 'Có seo …' section. I defy anyone – even the ghost of Sorley – to deliver this slowly. It would become ludicrously portentous when it is tremendously excited – because this IS the climax.

MacLean has a clear idea of how poetry and music should match each other at such a point, particularly in relation to Rob Donn:

> Rob Donn poses a question: how can such relaxed poetry be great? Even 'Iseabail NicAoidh', a pibroch poem, is relaxed, and in the last *crùnluadh* especially the relaxation is at strange variance with the expertise of the stylised metre.[19]

At first I thought Sorley was criticising Rob Donn. But on further thought I think perhaps he is marvelling. Rob Donn's subject-matter – the attractions of the girl on her own, herding cattle – has no need of tension, and the techniques employed are extremely effective.[20] Elsewhere MacLean, writing in the context of 'Realism in Gaelic Poetry', says of this same song:

> It has great grace and virtuosity of technique imposed on matter very mundanely realistic.[21]

But for myself, I will have no pretty girl, be she tending cows or washing clothes, reduced to mere mundane realism. It is MacLean's great achievement to have married realism and idealism, the brutal realities of Clearance and War, with the mythological realities of the aspiring human spirit. In that aspiration, he uses the music of verse, and reminds us of some of the finest music of his own culture, to take us beyond the restrictions of words. There is no realism in music. Just its own reality, and therein lies the greatest strength of MacLean's epic – that it shouts and sings from the mountains.

Notes

1 Personal communication from Stewart Conn
2 Seamus Heaney in interview with Dennis O'Driscoll, in *The Dark Horse*, Winter/Spring 2011, p. 12
3 Purser, J., *Scotland's Music*, Edinburgh: Mainstream, 2007, p. 147
4 *Scottish Tradition 7: Calum Ruadh: Bard of Skye*, London: Tangent TNGM 128; Edinburgh: Greentrax CDTRAX 9007, Track 10a
5 MacLean, S., 'My Relationship with the Muse', in *Chapman* No. 17, 1976, reproduced in MacGill-eain, S., W. Gillies, ed., *Ris a' Bhruthaich*, Stornoway: Acair, 1985, p. 13
6 Ibid, p. 9
7 MacLean, S., 'An Cuilithionn', Earrann VII, in *O Choille Gu Bearradh*, Manchester and Edinburgh: Carcanet/Birlinn, 1999, pp. 120–21. A relevant passage in the Shelley is in Act I, lines 91–92.
8 *Scotland's Music*, pp. 150–51
9 Private recording made at the International Study Group of Music Archaeology, Michaelstein, 19–26 September 2004
10 McCaughey, T., 'Somhairle MacGill-eain', in Craig, C., ed., *The History of Scottish Literature*, Volume 4, Aberdeen: Aberdeen University Press, 1987 and 1989, p. 155
11 MacLean, S., 'Obscure and Anonymous Gaelic Poems', in *The Seventeenth Century in the Highlands*, Inverness: Inverness Field Club, 1986, pp. 98–100
12 Whyte, C., 'Sorley MacLean's 'An Cuilithionn', in McLeod, Fraser and Gunderloch, eds, *Cànan & Cultar/Language & Culture: Rannsachadh na Gàidhlig 3*, Edinburgh: Dunedin Academic Press, 2006, pp. 123–26
13 *O Choille Gu Bearradh*, pp. 78–79
14 Mackenzie, B., 'History and Folklore Surrounding This Music': CD liner notes for *Donald MacPherson – Living Legend*, siubhal.com, pp. 9–10
15 Purser, J., *Erik Chisholm, Scottish Modernist 1904–1965 – Chasing A Restless Muse*, Woodbridge: Boydell and Brewer, 2009, Chapter 5, esp. pp. 87–88 and 95
16 *O Choille Gu Bearradh*, pp. 78–79
17 Ibid, pp. 124–25
18 Recorded on *Harlaw – Scotland 1411*: Tulloch Music tm 505, Disc 1, Track 2
19 MacLean, S., 'Some Thoughts About Gaelic Poetry', in *Transactions of the Gaelic Society of Inverness*, Vol. LII 1980–1982, reproduced in MacGill-eain, S., *Ris a' Bhruthaich*, Stornoway: Acair, 1985, p. 131
20 Gunn, A. and MacFarlane, C., eds, *Orain agus Dàin le Rob Donn MacAoidh*, Glasgow: John MacKay, 1899, pp. 88–89
21 MacLean, S., 'Realism in Gaelic Poetry', in *Transactions of the Gaelic Society of Inverness*, Vol. XXXVII 1934–1936, reproduced in *Ris a' Bhruthaich*, Stornoway: Acair, 1985, pp. 36–37

7. The film *Hallaig: The Poetry and Landscape of Sorley MacLean*

TIMOTHY NEAT

This film was completed in the Alva Film Workshop, Clackmannanshire, in 1984, and what follows is the Director's statement, which introduced a showing of the film at the conference.

The film *Hallaig* provides us with a documentary record of Sorley MacLean in his prime. Sorley himself was closely involved in its evolution over a period of six years (1978–1984). A lack of institutional belief in MacLean as a film subject made funds very difficult to come by. Years of struggle meant, however, that Sorley and I spent a lot of time together – in Skye, on Raasay, in Fife, in Edinburgh – and we became close friends and geographical accuracy became part of our concept.

Money finally arrived from the EU Minority Languages Fund and from the Scottish Film Production Fund, and the sync sound sequences were filmed in Skye in February 1984. All interviews with MacLean were recorded in Gaelic and English. The film was then completed in English (with extensive Gaelic sections), there still not being enough money for the completion of the purely Gaelic version we had planned. Following the success of the English–Gaelic version, the Gaelic Department of BBC Scotland, in Glasgow, agreed to complete this Gaelic version. All the film footage and sound recordings were then given to the BBC and the film was re-edited by the late Alasdair Duncan. It was consequently broadcast as a one-hour Gaelic film in 1986. It is this Gaelic version that will be shown at Sabhal Mòr Ostaig. I would like to make it clear that I, as Director (indeed the film-maker), was excluded from this editorial process. I have viewed this Gaelic version only once, when it was first broadcast. What do I think of it? I think one or two sequences work better than in the original film, but this Gaelic version of *Hallaig* is not the film I would have directed. It might be interesting for students, in future years, to compare and contrast the two versions ...

We do not have time for analysis here, but the English version of *Hallaig* did stimulate interesting responses from two champions of the Celtic world – Nessa Doran and Seamus Heaney. They wrote letters that I hope will not be seen as mere egotism on my part, but as thoughts that throw light on MacLean, on Gaelic values and the fellowship of artists.

(1) Letters from Nessa Doran

Nessa Doran (Ní Shéaghdha), a leading Irish scholar, is the woman who inspired Sorley's early love poetry. These letters, written in age, show all the charm, passion and timeless grandeur that set the young MacLean ablaze.

17 December 1984

Dear Timothy,

I thank you for the photocopies of reviews etc. But I thank you more for your letter which is an 'Ode' to Sorley. Your pen is as lyrical as your eye (vision) on camera. It gave me insight into the mind of an artist.

I do hope that when the film sojourns for viewing to all countries and quarters it will be as deservedly well received as it was that night in Edinburgh. I would not have missed that occasion for the world!

I did my best to give an appreciative account of the film to my son-in-law, Muiris Mac Conghail. He is very anxious to see it. His major effort – the film on the Blaskets – is getting its first viewing on RTE the first Sunday in January (lasting 2 hours!). I am going to a preview some days before that.

Bless you for all your nice letters and phone-calls to me. Keep in touch – a Happy Christmas and New Year.

Nessa

10 January 1985

Dear Tim,

You are indeed very faithful to me – I certainly don't deserve it from you. Your 'bits and pieces', as you call them, are not bits and pieces to me but a panoramic view of an artist named Timothy Neat. I know you better now from my reading of them all – including those on Serge Hovey! No wonder your film of Sorley was such a success.

And yes, RTE are showing your film 'Hallaig' on a Tuesday slot 7:30–8:30 next month (Muiris tells me and he will let me know in time which Tuesday). Let me know if you get reviews of RTE matters – otherwise I will hopefully gather them for you (with Muiris' help – as I don't buy all kinds of papers and magazines). I am most definitely looking forward to seeing it again – the better I will appreciate other features of it this time. I showed Muiris your card in which you commented on the RTE copy of your film – but he thought everything in that respect all right. I have asked my son Daivi to video it at the time of showing so that I can see it again and again (in my house) as time goes on.

Of further interest: I met Prof. Breandán Ó Madagáin, University College Galway, before Christmas and he told me that the Faculty of Irish (staff and students) had a treat of their lifetime when a film on Somhairle was shown in the College! They are very interested in Somhairle in Galway. And, by the way, he is performing there 12/16 March for the Galway Festival of Arts. I hope to travel there to hear him. He has had a successful tour (his third I think) of Canada. And his grand-children are increasing which means a lot to him.

I thank you again, dear Timothy, keep in touch – I like it.
Love,
Nessa

(2) Letters from Seamus Heaney

Seamus Heaney – whose presence and words give the English version of the film *Hallaig* such authority – writes letters almost equally revealing.

Seamus Heaney, Dublin 4, 23 September 1984
Dear Tim,

When I got back from the US in June, there was still a drop of that excellent malt you brought with you in January and I downed it, without toothache, and with happy memories of your visit. I was sorry to be so afflicted at the time, but glad that something good came out of it, not only the film, but the pleasure of the weekend's company.

I hope the showing went well for you on Wednesday. As you know, I was then in Sligo, having met the bard the previous weekend and attended another of his authentic and confirming readings. A great gift he has, in addition to the art, is the way his presence fortifies one's own sense of the worth and power of the artistic enterprise in general. I always come away from meeting him with my trust in poetry itself and in my own cultural donnés strengthened.

Anyhow, Tim, this is just a greeting and a thanks for your kindness in keeping me informed about the film. Don't worry if you have to cut out any more of my contribution in order to shorten it for TV distribution. All I wanted to do was to be of service to the whole enterprise.

Every good wish in the new academic year and with the rest of the *Hallaig* business. Máire and the children send their regards. Slainte!

Seamus

Dublin, 24 October 1984

Dear Tim,

In other circumstances, I would not have missed next Tuesday's event but my mother died last week and we are a bit at sixes and sevens. If there is any opportunity to do so naturally, please express to the gathered group my regret that I cannot be with you and Sorley to celebrate the film, and my sense of gratitude at being allowed to associate myself with the poet and the poetry in *Hallaig*. I'm proud to have been included because, to change Yeats' pronoun, '*He* is foremost of those I would hear praised'.

Máire sends her fondest wishes, as do I too. Some day we'll see you on your native heath, but just now I'm not in the mood to go pleasuring myself abroad among the people of art. I hope you'll understand.

Fondly,
Seamus

P.S. Thank you for keeping me informed, and take pride and pleasure in what you've done. I only hope you get proper thanks for it – though it does not always follow! S.

25 August 1985

Tim,

Many thanks for your invitation to Langholm on Sunday. I wish I could be there but do not think I can make it. Much love to Valda. And Sorley. And Norman. And yourself. And all hands. Seamus

This message was written on the back of a postcard of a painting by George Bellows of a boxing match entitled 'Introducing John L. Sullivan, 1923'. Heaney's references are to the unveiling of the Hugh MacDiarmid Memorial Sculpture in Langholm (11 August 1985), at which Sorley MacLean made the keynote address (see Chapter 5).

*

After Hallaig *had been shown, Timothy Neat sought to stimulate academic inquiry into the connections that might exist between the poetry of Sorley MacLean and the poetry of Samuel Taylor Coleridge.*

Certainly MacLean admired some of Coleridge's poetry. Was MacLean intrigued by Coleridge's name? The title of MacLean's collected poems, *O Choille gu Bearradh/From Wood to Ridge*, carries echoes of Coleridge's English/Celtic name? Is this coincidence, synchronicity or homage?

Does the 'vertigos' element in the mountain poetry of MacLean echo Coleridge's observations of the mountains? For example, during his walk over Helvellyn to meet the Wordsworths in the summer of 1800, Coleridge made notes that anticipate certain approaches that MacLean will make in 'The Cuillin' and 'The Woods of Raasay':

Am now at the Top of Helvellin – a pyramid of stones – Ullswater, Thirlemere, Bassenthwaite, Wyndermere, a tarn in Patterdale. On my right two tarns, that near Grasmere a most beautiful one, in a flat meadow. Travelling along the ridge I came to other side of those precipices and down below me on my left – no – no! No words can convey any idea of this prodigious wilderness. That precipice was fine on this side but its ridge, sharp as a jagged knife, level so long, then ascending boldly – what a frightful bulge I stand on, and to my right how the crag which corresponds to the other, how it plunges down, like a waterfall, reaches a level of steepness, and again plunges! – The moon is above Fairfield almost at the full! – now descending over a perilous peat-moss then down a Hill of stones all dark, and darkling I climbed stone after stone down a half dry Torrent and came out at the Raise Gap. And O! my God! How *did* that opposite precipice look – in the moonshine – its name Stile Crags.

On page 278 of Vol. I of Richard Holmes's biography of Coleridge, the poet describes his study, in Greta Hall, as having a spectacular view of the fells – 'A whole camp of giants' tents' – Derwent Water and Borrowdale to the south-west, Bassenthwaite to the north-west ... His bedroom looked north towards Helvellyn:

My Glass being opposite to the Window, I seldom shaved without cutting myself. Some Mountain or Peak is rising out of the Mist, or some slanting Column of misty Sunlight is sailing across me; so that I offer up soap and blood daily, as an Eye-servant of the Goddess of Nature.

Coleridge himself, the most Celtic of the English poets, was certainly influenced by Scotland and Scotland's balladic poetry. Holmes writes:

He was Christianed after his godfather, a local worthy, Mr Samuel Taylor, and was always known in the family as 'Sam', a name he grew to dislike with a poignant intensity. Like many a youngest child he was petted and indulged, and almost his earliest memory was of being specially carried out by his nurse to hear a strolling musician playing ballads in the moonlight, during the harvest festivities.

> To hear our old musician, blind and grey,
> (Whom stretching from my nurse's arms I kissed,)

His Scottish tunes and warlike marches played,
By moonshine, on the balmy summer-night ...[1]

With regard to 'Hallaig', generally accepted as MacLean's greatest single poem, Coleridge's poem 'The Knight's Tomb' is of interest:

Where is the grave of Sir Arthur O'Kellyn?
Where may the grave of that good man be? –
By the side of a spring, on the breast of Helvellyn,
Under the twigs of a young birch tree!
The oak that in summer was sweet to hear,
And rustled its leaves in the fall of the year,
And whistled and roar'd in the winter alone,
Is gone, – and the birch in its stead is grown. –
The knight's bones are dust,
And his good sword rust; –
His soul is with the saints, I trust.[2]

If one views MacLean's Hallaig community as embodying similar values to those of Coleridge's single knight (the personification of a medieval community), a number of connections can be drawn between the two poems. Somhairle's is longer and more ambitious but there are similarities in the narrative sequence, the imagery, as well as the vision that draws time past, present and future mesmerically together. Both poems contain 'druidic' echoes and an Old Testament/New Testament sense of moral progression. In both poems, suggestions of social disharmony and war are contrasted with nature's great evolutionary cycle and the hope of human spiritual renewal. There is also a love of youth, of the beauty of birch trees, and the beauty that art layers on beauty in both poems.

Notes

1   From 'Lines Composed in a Concert Room', *The Poems of Samuel Taylor Coleridge*, Ernest Hartley Coleridge, ed., London: Oxford University Press, 1964, p. 324
2   Ibid, 'The Knight's Tomb', p. 432

8. A Necessary Common Ground: Sorley MacLean's Poetry and its Significance for Visual Art[1]

MURDO MACDONALD

Consider the image by William Crosbie on the dust jacket of the first edition of Sorley MacLean's *Dàin do Eimhir agus Dàin Eile*, published by William MacLellan in 1943. The image is used as a frontispiece in some volumes. It is one of the most interesting works made with respect to the Scottish Gàidhealtachd by any Scottish artist of the mid-twentieth century. It shows a pillar-like standing stone against the backdrop of a serrated mountain ridge, the strings of a fiddle linking earth and sky. One sees in it not just a reflection of Sorley MacLean's poetry but an indication of the place that his poetry occupies locally, nationally and internationally, for it is quite clear that Crosbie had absorbed the lessons of European modernism, just as had MacLean. Along with that modernist knowledge Crosbie possessed the quality of intuition that enables a perceptive visual artist to be driven not simply by his own skill but by the passions of the writer with whom he is collaborating. He has picked up not just on the poet's words but on MacLean's trajectory as a poet, both as a representative of the Gàidhealtachd and as a great European. One cannot look at Crosbie's image without thinking of MacLean's work as a whole, including his sequence 'An Cuilithionn'/'The Cuillin', not just because of the presence of the Cuillin ridge in the image, but because Crosbie seems to conjure images from that ridge, which is what MacLean does in his poetry. Thanks to a new edition of 'The Cuillin', the first in book form, it is now possible to fully appreciate that work.[2] In using this particular image by Crosbie for the cover of the book the publisher William MacLellan clearly understood the significance of the Cuillin for Sorley MacLean and the significance of Crosbie's visual response. There have been many outstanding responses by visual artists to MacLean's work in the years since 1943, among them those of Will Maclean and Donald Urquhart, yet this very first response to *Dàin do Eimhir*, and the set of images of which it is part, still holds its own.

The standing stone that connects earth to sky in the composition is resonant with Sorley MacLean's line, which reads 'Thog mi an calbh seo / air beinn fhalbhaich na tìme' – in translation, 'I raised this pillar / on the shifting mountain of time' (*Dàin do Eimhir* XIX) – and here Crosbie is tapping into a theme in Scottish art that extends from Alexander Runciman in the eighteenth century to Calum Colvin in the twenty-first century. Such prehistoric reference is often used to imply the cultural continuity and endurance of the Gàidhealtachd, and indeed of Scotland as a whole. Although prehistoric standing stones date from about five thousand years ago and therefore considerably predate the Highlands as a Gaelic-speaking area, as Ronnie Black (Raghnall MacilleDhuibh) has pointed out, they frequently form points of reference in Gaelic stories. A print by John Duncan of *Ossian*, which dates from perhaps about 1910, echoes this, for the bard is backed by Calanais-like stones.[3] Standing stones are frequently associated with Fionn's warriors, who, as Black notes, 'are always described as giants, and the existence of standing stones in the area was always a good excuse for telling stories about them'. They thus exist at the heart of the Gaelic oral tradition as cues for stories; indeed, again as Black points out, in Coll two standing stones are called *Sgialaichean*, that is to say 'Tale-Tellers'.[4] By use of such a stone Crosbie has thus, following his artist's intuition, identified Sorley MacLean as one who tells the tales that need to be told. In passing, I also note Crosbie's startlingly effective cover for another MacLellan publication, the first issue of *Poetry Scotland*, published like *Dàin do Eimhir* in 1943. There he evokes the tale of the sea rover Mac Iain Gheàrr, who, as the cover information notes, harried the west coast of Scotland and to confuse pursuit had his ship painted white on one side and black on the other.[5] There is much else one could say about William Crosbie in the context of the culture of the Gàidhealtachd, and a start has been made to this by John Purser in his paper 'The Celtic Ballet: Ballet, Baton and Brush in Search of Peace in Time of War'.[6]

Sorley MacLean's fellow poet Douglas Young played a crucial role in the publication of *Dàin do Eimhir*, and he makes specific reference to the importance of the visual dimension. In his preface he notes that the publisher was 'remembering the glorious Celtic tradition of illustration' and that he 'wished to have the book embellished by a first-rate leading young Scots artist'. The importance of that comment is that it recognises both the need to reclaim a visual tradition and the role that William MacLellan was playing in that reclamation. Young (after an initially unfavourable reaction!) is emphatic: 'It may be that five centuries hence [Crosbie's images] will be rated with the designs in the Book of Kells'. That may be hyperbole, but it is a good use of it, for what Young writes is important. He is drawing attention to the significance of Crosbie's work by associating it with one of the most important works of medieval European art, which is at the same time a key early example in the long history of visual responses to literature in Scotland. By mentioning the Book of Kells, an illuminated manuscript thought to have been begun in Iona in the late eighth or early ninth century, he stakes a claim to that history not just for William Crosbie but for Sorley MacLean and, indeed, for William MacLellan, and he is, of course, absolutely right to do so.

In the context that Young creates for us, that of reclaiming Scottish cultural history, it is worth remarking upon the persistence in Scotland of the type of Celtic design that one finds in the Book of Kells. This type of design, with its characteristic interlace, can be found again in the West Highland School of Sculpture in the fourteenth and fifteenth centuries, and it can be found later still in the decoration of musical instruments and weapons in the sixteenth, seventeenth and eighteenth centuries. It is then taken up in the nineteenth century by the artists of the Celtic Revival, and through that route it comes to us today. The unusual persistence of this type of design was noted as early as 1851 by Daniel Wilson in his pioneering *Archaeology and Prehistoric Annals of Scotland*; indeed, Wilson can be credited as an early advocate of the notion of Celtic art as a category in its own right. Wilson's perception here was no doubt aided by the fact that he was himself an excellent artist – indeed, his first profession was as an engraver. The claim of Celtic art was bolstered by Owen Jones, who placed it in a global context in his *Grammar of Ornament*, published in 1856. A third figure is important here: the great Gaelic scholar John Francis Campbell of Islay, who cites Jones in the fourth volume of his *Popular Tales of the West Highlands*, published in 1862. It can be noted that the first editions of the books of both Wilson and Campbell have early examples of Celtic Revival covers, both most probably the work of the respective authors: like Wilson, Campbell was an accomplished artist, if not a professional. This continuity of Celtic Revival design extends seamlessly, via the designs of the titles of Patrick Geddes's Celtic Library and the decorations by Mary Carmichael for *Carmina Gadelica*, to the milieu of the publication of *Dàin do Eimhir*. Indeed, the most distinguished Celtic Revival artist at the time of the publication of *Dàin do Eimhir* was George Bain, whose influential explorations of Celtic art were also published by William MacLellan. George Bain is an interesting figure: like most of the MacLellan circle, he united a local, a national and an international vision. An example of his internationalism is his correspondence on traditional art matters with Patrick Geddes's friend, Ananda Coomaraswamy, the pioneering historian of Indian art who was at that time director of the Oriental collections at the Museum of Fine Arts in Boston. Building on the visual analyses of scholars like Romilly Allen and artists like John Duncan, Bain engaged in the geometrical analysis of Celtic knotwork, beginning with the interlace on Pictish stones, and proceeding in due course to the illuminated manuscripts of Iona and Northumbria. He began publishing his work in booklet form in the 1940s and in 1951 came his definitive *Celtic Art: The Methods of Construction*. Like *Dàin do Eimhir* as published by MacLellan, that book was a work of art in its own right. It was the point of origin for all subsequent work, much as Romilly Allen had been for Bain himself. It remains the classic statement. Bain often utilised his knowledge for book and magazine covers designed for MacLellan publications. These include the Gaelic and English magazine *Alba*, published in 1948. Bain also made numerous illustrations for Douglas Young's book of poetry in Scots, *A Braird of Thristles*, published in 1947. The dust jacket is of particular interest because in its detail one can see Bain making a visual hypothesis about the relationship between Celtic knotwork and tartan. Thanks in large part to the work of Susan Seright, much of Bain's work has been preserved at Groam House Museum in Rosemarkie near Inverness.[7]

You will note that the distinction between what one might want to call 'modernist' and what one might want to call 'Celtic Revivalist' is becoming blurred to the point of disappearance here. This is far easier to pick up from the visual record than it is from the literary. Bain's illumination of Douglas Young's poem in memory of the Perth poet William Souter, first published in *A Braird of Thristles*, is a case in point. It appeared again, printed in a maroon ink, in another MacLellan publication, the edition of *Scottish Art and Letters* which marked the PEN Conference held at the Edinburgh Festival in 1950. The cover of that special edition of *Scottish Art and Letters* was by J. D. Fergusson, who further undermines the Celtic/modern distinction with a tartan-inspired design which would have been quite at home in the Bauhaus. Soon after, Fergusson was to make his unique contribution to this late period of the Celtic Revival through his use of Ogham script and other Celtic references in his decorations for Hugh MacDiarmid's *In Memoriam James Joyce*, published in 1955, again by William MacLellan.

This close association of modernism and Celtic Revivalism gives me an opportunity to reflect on the relationship between the twentieth-century Scots Renaissance of Hugh MacDiarmid and Sorley MacLean on the one hand and, on the other, the earlier Celtic Revival of Patrick Geddes and his milieu of the 1890s. These movements are often portrayed as in opposition to one another, the one modernist and forward-looking and the other nostalgic and backward-looking, but in fact they are continuous and complementary. In terms of intellectual continuity MacDiarmid's admiration for Geddes is made clear in *The Company I've Kept*. Indeed, the use of the phrase 'Scots Renascence' can be traced back to Patrick Geddes himself as the title of one of his essays published in 1895 in his Celtic revival magazine, *The Evergreen*. But there were, of course, tensions. Sorley MacLean's contempt for the Celtic Revival *Hebridean Love Lilts* of Geddes's collaborator Marjory Kennedy-Fraser is well known. He refers to, for example, 'Mrs Kennedy-Fraser's travesties of Gaelic songs'.[8] But this draws attention to an interesting issue. As John Purser has pointed out, Kennedy-Fraser's work was just one example of what other composers were doing with folk material throughout Europe.[9] Indeed, this was a practice that Scotland had helped to pioneer through George Thomson's work with Robert Burns's songs a century earlier; an example is Thomson's commissioning of Beethoven's outstanding setting of 'The Lovely Lass of Inverness'. Thus the problem that Sorley MacLean faced was not Kennedy-Fraser's work as such, but the fact that her songs were one of the very few accepted outlets for Gaelic culture at the time. MacLean's critique was made in the 1930s, a period when Gaelic culture was still enduring the full force of the anti-Gaelic provisions-by-omission of the Education Act of 1872. As John MacInnes has commented, 'The processes of ethnocide work at many levels and in many guises, but they are most conspicuous in the domain of formal education'.[10] It is instructive to note that it is only since 2005 that any legal protection for Gaelic has existed. The heart of MacLean's concern was that to encounter the Gàidhealtachd only through Kennedy-Fraser is not really to encounter it at all. The value of Kennedy-Fraser's contribution in its own right as European art song was not the issue.[11]

That point can be applied not just to Kennedy-Fraser but to the way we still encounter so much of Scottish culture through stereotype rather than through knowledge. Just as to encounter the Gàidhealtachd only through Kennedy-Fraser is not really to encounter it at all, to encounter the Gàidhealtachd (and indeed Scotland as a whole) through Landseer's *Monarch of the Glen* is, again, not really to encounter it at all. Landseer's skill as an animal painter can no more stand in for the culture of a people than can a set of art songs. Such mismatch of stereotype and reality was explored with perception and verve in John McGrath's *The Cheviot, the Stag and the Black, Black Oil* in the 1970s.[12] But, although both Kennedy-Fraser and Landseer lead easily to stereotyping, that stereotyping only becomes a problem when the stereotype is the only source of information available – that is to say, when all other sources of information are impoverished or denied. When that is the case stereotypes begin to function in a negative way.[13] Then ignorance rules, or, to put it another way, the ignorant rule. As long as our universities, schools and galleries treat Scottish culture as tokenistic and subsidiary rather than as central to our international identity and well-being, such ignorance will be maintained.

Consider for example the decision by the National Galleries of Scotland to mount an exhibition of Landseer and the Highlands as the first Scottish-related exhibition in the Royal Scottish Academy building after its refurbishment.[14] That evoked from one Gaelic-speaking critic the memorable comment: 'rarely does an exhibition make my blood boil ...' and in the same review: 'The Clearances are pushed under the carpet while captions enthuse about the intermarriage of this "noted beauty" with that "dashing" duke, and their consequent official title. The highlander's house is consistently described as a "bothie", preserving Victorian sentimentality along with its spelling. ... People have joked for years that the National Galleries are stuck in Victorian times. This, finally, is the proof.'[15]

That is to the point. The employment of stereotypes at the expense of international context will continue as long as the leadership class of our institutions – galleries, universities etc. – remains content in its ignorance of Scotland, except in the most superficial sense. That might seem to be an argument in favour of Scottish independence; in fact it is just an argument against ignorance. But if the only way of addressing such ignorance is political independence, so be it. If we need a further example to explore such active maintenance of ignorance, it can be found easily enough. The persistence of the over-valuing of Landseer is complemented by the persistence of the suppression of information about James Macpherson's *Ossian*, a work consistently ignored by the cultural establishment both with respect to its influence on English literature and with respect to its importance to the visual art of Europe.[16] It is a further indication of our ignorance that so many of us still find it easy to dismiss *Ossian*, reflecting in our own attitudes an endorsement of the atrocities perpetrated on our own culture in the wake of Culloden, for it is in the tragedy of that battle that one finds the origins of *Ossian*. Those atrocities still mark Scotland today, most prominently through continuing attempts to thwart the survival of the Gaelic language. Macpherson tried to legitimise his own Gaelic culture by presenting *Ossian* in the forms and language of the oppressor, and this English-language book written by a Gael became one of the foundation works of modern European literature. That its importance has never been admitted by the gatekeepers of English Literature is perhaps the final irony of Culloden. Even the anglicising of the culture of the Gael is still rejected by the victor and dishonest debate predicated on the active maintenance of ignorance continues. This despite the fact that, as Fiona Stafford has pointed out, all the information required to assess Macpherson's achievement has been in the public domain for a long time.[17] Indeed, most of it is not only public but was actually published over two hundred years ago in the Highland Society of Scotland report of 1805.[18] But to be two hundred years out of date seems to be a minor point when anti-Highland prejudice is in play. Publishing in 2003, fifteen years after Stafford's text, Dafydd Moore comments that 'references frequently seem specifically designed to obscure, not reveal, *Ossian*'s place in the Romantic pantheon'.[19] Moore's comprehensive analysis of the dishonest treatment of Macpherson within academia should be the last word on the subject, but because what we are dealing with here is cultural politics, not objective analysis, it will not be. The paradox with respect to *Ossian* is that, despite the weight of evidence to the contrary, Macpherson's work is still treated by otherwise credible commentators as though it were of no importance.[20] So the irony is that the very work that helped to rehabilitate the Gàidhealtachd after Culloden has become swept along in the general tide of cultural clearance of the Gàidhealtachd. That only applies within Anglocentric academia. European views, and the views of European or Scottish-studies orientated academics in the UK and North America, tend to be quite different.[21] So: the cultural politics continue around Macpherson today and Culloden is refought in texts and lack of texts about a text. For the present paper the images included in the 1805 report are of particular importance, for they are precursors of the establishment of Celtic art as a category. The initial letters reproduced as the frontispiece were used in due course in both John Francis Campbell's *Popular Tales of the West Highlands* and in Alexander Carmichael's *Carmina Gadelica*.[22]

Carmina Gadelica was published in 1900 and it is not only a key point of reference for Gaelic scholarship, it is also a key work of Scottish Arts and Crafts book design. Its decorative initials are the work of Alexander Carmichael's wife Mary. She drew on a number of sources of Celtic illuminated initials, including the tenth-century Book of Deer; indeed, that work provides some of her most direct visual references. Other sources can be found in manuscripts in the National Library of Scotland.[23] It is of interest to note that, if there was a William MacLellan equivalent for the Celtic Revival of the 1890s, it was the key figure behind the production of *Carmina Gadelica*, Walter Blaikie, the director of the Edinburgh printers T. & A. Constable. Blaikie's achievement is extraordinary. Like MacLellan half a century later, he facilitated the interaction of Scottish visual art and literature. As well as the first edition of *Carmina Gadelica*, his projects include Patrick Geddes's *Evergreen* and the *Centenary Burns* – complete with a Celtic Revival cover by John Duncan.

That Celtic Revival publishing effort of which *Carmina Gadelica* was part finds its echo not just in William MacLellan's work with Douglas Young, George Bain, William Crosbie and Sorley MacLean, but in much more recent publishing. I refer specifically to the remarkable book and international touring exhibition, *An Leabhar Mòr/The Great Book of Gaelic*, commissioned by Pròiseact nan Ealan and published in 2002.[24] By referring frequently to much earlier Celtic material it shares something of its ethos with *Carmina Gadelica*, but its visual reference is to the art of our own day.

In it one hundred contemporary artists from Scotland and Ireland responded to one hundred poems in Scottish Gaelic and Irish both ancient and modern. Their responses were skilfully mediated by typographers and calligraphers.[25] In a key image, Sorley MacLean's 'Hallaig' is evoked by Donald Urquhart – in a direct manner – by using water collected in the deserted township itself to create a simple rectangle of washed out colour. The work is thus part of the place itself rather than simply a representation of it or a reflection on it. So Urquhart's contribution is land art rather than watercolour. The composition of that 'Hallaig' work has now been echoed in Urquhart's work from 2009, in which he explored the Gaelic alphabet and its relation to nature.[26]

As I implied earlier, Will Maclean must also be considered here, for he has transformed the level of contemporary work made by Highland artists, and at Hallaig itself we find the source of one of his key works, *Inner Sound*, made in 1984. It shows the broken, boarded window of a deserted croft-house. Beyond that window is the conning tower of a submarine. Maclean thus juxtaposes those two fundamental and interconnected elements of the history of the Highlands: clearance and militarism. And he does it in the context of Sorley MacLean's poetry, for the boarded window specifies 'Hallaig'. Sorley MacLean writes: 'Tha bùird is tàirnean air an uinneig / trom faca mi an Àird an Iar' – 'The window is nailed and boarded / through which I saw the West'.[27] But Will MacLean's work specifies not just 'Hallaig' but its great companion work, 'Screapadal'.

Thogadh ròn a cheann / agus cearban a sheòl, / ach an-diugh anns an linnidh / togaidh long-fo-thuinn a turraid / agus a druim dubh slìom / a' maoidheadh an nì a dhèanadh / smùr de choille, de lèanagan 's de chreagan, / a dh'fhàgadh Sgreapadal gun bhòidhche / mar a dh'fhàgadh e gun daoine.

A seal would lift its head / and a basking-shark its sail, / but today in the sea-sound / a submarine lifts its turret / and its black sleek back / threatening the thing that would make / dross of wood, of meadows and of rocks, / that would leave Screapadal without beauty / just as it was left without people.[28]

The *Inner Sound* of Maclean's title is the stretch of water between Raasay and Applecross, a major submarine testing area, with which in his days as a fisherman he would have been very familiar. Through the image of the submarine from Sorley MacLean's 'Screapadal', Will Maclean links the ideology of clearance with the ideology of war. The point is reinforced in the exploration of the poem in Timothy Neat's 1984 film about the poetry and landscape of Sorley MacLean.[29] In that film drawings by Will Maclean of basking-sharks transforming into submarines are in balance with both the words of the poet and the filming of the land-and-seascape of the poet's life.

In 1992, introducing Duncan Macmillan's book on the work of Will Maclean, Sorley MacLean wrote that 'never has a common ground between art and poetry been more necessary than it is today, but that necessity is timeless and universal'.[30] It is from those words that I have made my title 'A Necessary Common Ground'. That necessary common ground refers equally to the time of the Book of Kells and to our own present. That necessary common ground harks back to the significance of William MacLellan's approach to publishing in the mid-twentieth century, and, indeed, to the approach of Walter Blaikie half a century before that. That necessary common ground became the foundation upon which was built the remarkable achievement of *An Leabhar Mòr/The Great Book of Gaelic*.

The thought I want to conclude with is this. Would the art of *An Leabhar Mòr* even exist without the cultural activism of Sorley MacLean? It would certainly have been part of a lesser work. The issue now is to take the example of Sorley MacLean's cultural activism into the future. To do so we must continue to attend as he did to that necessary common ground of art and poetry.

Notes

1   In this paper I have drawn both on my presentation 'From *Carmina Gadelica* to *Dàin do Eimhir*: The Visual Tradition', for *Ainmeil thar Cheudan* in June 2011, and on material from my Andrew Tannahill Lecture, given on October 1, 2009 at the National Library of Scotland, with the title of 'Scottish Literature and Visual Art: A Caledonian Synergy'.
2   MacGill-Eain, S., Whyte, C., ed., *An Cuilithionn 1939/The Cuillin 1939 & Unpublished Poems*, Glasgow: Association for Scottish Literary Studies, 2011
3   Collection of the Royal Scottish Academy
4   Raghnall MacilleDhuibh, 'Standing stones: Tall tales', *West Highland Free Press*, 17 August, 2007, p. 19

5   Cover note, *Poetry Scotland*, No. 1, Glasgow: MacLellan, 1943

6   Purser, J., 'The Celtic Ballet: Ballet, Baton and Brush in Search of Peace in Time of War', *Journal of the Scottish Society for Art History*, No. 13, 2008–2009 (2009), pp. 7–15; see also Purser, J., *Erik Chisholm, Scottish Modernist*, Woodbridge: Boydell & Brewer, 2010.

7   See, e.g., Seright, S. E., *George Bain: Master of Celtic Art*, Rosemarkie: Groam House Museum, 2007. Note also (for reflections on different styles of visualising Pictish designs prior to the work of George Bain) Ritchie, J. N. G., *Recording Early Christian Monuments in Scotland*, Rosemarkie: Groam House Museum, 1998.

8   Quoted from an essay, 'Realism in Gaelic Poetry', published in 1934 by the Gaelic Society of Inverness. There MacLean also describes John Duncan's work as 'exceedingly strange' to Gaelic eyes, and notes that W. B. Yeats has been, from the same perspective, 'utterly discredited … as being completely un-Irish and un-Celtic'. Republished in Mac Gill-eain, S., W. Gillies, ed., *Ris a' Bhruthaich: Criticism and Prose Writings*, Stornoway: Acair, 1985. I quote from pp. 19 and 20. See also MacLean's 'Aspects of Gaelic Poetry' in the same volume, pp. 75–82, in particular p. 77.

9   Purser, J., *Scotland's Music*, 2nd ed., Edinburgh: Mainstream, 2007, especially p. 285

10   MacInnes, J., 'The Gaelic Continuum in Scotland', in R. O'Driscoll, ed., *The Celtic Consciousness*, Scranton: George Braziller, 1982, pp. 269–81; 269

11   For a reassessment see Ahlander, P., 'Introduction' to Kennedy-Fraser, M., *A Life of Song*, Isle of Lewis: The Islands Book Trust, 2011, pp. v–xxxiii.

12   McGrath, J., *The Cheviot, the Stag and the Black, Black Oil*, Breakish: West Highland Publishing, 1974

13   For more on this see Macdonald, M., 'Finding Scottish Art', in Norquay, G. & Smyth, G., eds, *Across the Margins: Cultural Identity and Change in the Atlantic Archipelago*, Manchester: Manchester University Press, 2002, pp. 171–84

14   *The Monarch of the Glen: Landseer in the Highlands*, National Galleries of Scotland, April–July 2005

15   Black, C., *Sunday Herald*, 24 April 2005: review of *The Monarch of the Glen: Landseer in the Highlands*

16   For a comprehensive illustrated account see Hohl, H. & Toussaint, H., *Ossian*, catalogue of exhibition at Grand Palais, Paris, and Kunsthalle, Hamburg; Paris: Ministère des affaires culturelles: Éditions des musées nationaux, 1974. See also Macdonald, M., 'Ossian and Art: Scotland into Europe via Rome', in H. Gaskill, ed., *The Reception of Ossian in Europe*, Vol. V, Athlone Critical Traditions Series, London: Thoemmes, 2004, pp. 393–404; and Macdonald, M., 'Art and the Scottish Highlands: An Ossianic Perspective', in Ogée, F. and M. Geracht, eds, *Interfaces, Image, Texte, Language*, No. 27, *Ossian Then and Now*, Paris: Université Paris 7, Denis Diderot, and Worcester, Mass.: College of the Holy Cross, 2008, pp. 75–88.

17   Stafford, F., *The Sublime Savage: A Study of James Macpherson and the Poems of Ossian*, Edinburgh: Edinburgh University Press, 1988, p. 3

18   MacKenzie, H., ed., *Report of the Committee of the Highland Society of Scotland Appointed to Inquire into the Nature and Authenticity of the Poems of Ossian*, Edinburgh: Archibald Constable, 1805

19   Moore, D. R., 2003, 'The critical response to Ossian's Romantic bequest', in Carruthers, G., and Rawes, A., eds, *English Romanticism and the Celtic World*, Cambridge: Cambridge University Press, 2003, pp. 38–53; 38

20 This ignorance is worthy of study in its own right. As recently as 1995 one finds the phrase 'such Icelandic tales as the poems of Ossian': Anscombe, I., 'A Sense of Place: Knox, Manx Nationalism and the Celtic Revival', in Martin, S. A., ed., *Archibald Knox*, London: Academy, 1995, pp. 68–76; 72. The point is not the mistake by the individual author but the level of general ignorance with respect to *Ossian* that it indicates.

21 The Icelandic academic Gauti Kristmannsson is a case in point. In a perceptive review of his work, Howard Gaskill notes that Kristmannsson 'makes the most of the perspective of the detached but knowledgeable outsider to launch some very telling points about the way in which discussion has been, and still tends to be, blighted by national prejudice. He is particularly severe on Hugh Trevor-Roper, in whose essay "The Invention of Tradition: The Highland Tradition of Scotland" he finds the most unpleasant expression of "racist ideology" based on paradigms which "were all invented in the furious nationalist wars that engulfed the Ossianic poems from the start"': Gaskill, H., 'Review of *Literary Diplomacy* by Gauti Kristmannsson', *Translation and Literature*, 16, 2007, pp. 104–12.

22 See Macdonald, M., 2009, 'The Visual Preconditions of Celtic Revival Art in Scotland', *Journal of the Scottish Society for Art History*, Vol. 13, 'Highlands' issue, 2008–2009, 16–21.

23 See Macdonald, M., 'The Visual Dimension of *Carmina Gadelica*', in Stiùbhart, D. U., ed., *The Life and Legacy of Alexander Carmichael*, Isle of Lewis: The Islands Book Trust, 2008, pp. 135–45.

24 Maclean, M. & Dorgan, T., eds, *An Leabhar Mòr / The Great Book of Gaelic*, Edinburgh: Canongate, 2002. Published in a new edition by O'Brien Press, Dublin, in 2009.

25 For example, Calum Angus Mackay responded to poetry by Duncan Bàn Macintyre, Kate Whiteford to the work of Murdo MacFarlane, Mhairi Killin to Meg Bateman, Will Maclean to Aonghas MacNeacail.

26 Urquhart consulted John MacInnes about that work, an indication of the continuing influence of that Gaelic scholar on contemporary art since his links with Richard Demarco in the 1970s. Re this work by Urquhart, see also Macdonald, M., 'Seeing Colour and Shape in the Gàidhealtachd: An Ecology of Mind?', *Scottish Affairs*, No. 73, 2010.

27 These lines led to the project title *Window to the West*:

> Tha bùird is tàirnean air an uinneig / trom faca mi an Àird an Iar / 's tha mo ghaol aig Allt Hallaig / 'na craoibh bheithe, 's bha i riamh …

> *The window is nailed and boarded / through which I saw the West /and my love is at the Burn of Hallaig, / a birch tree, and she has always been …*

28 A verse from 'Screapadal', which appears on pp. 322 and 323 of Somhairle MacGill-Eain, *Caoir Gheal Leumraich/White Leaping Flame*, Edinburgh: Polygon, 2011. For earlier poetry associated with the land struggle see Meek, D. E., ed., *Tuath is Tighearna/Tenants and Landlords*, Glasgow: Scottish Gaelic Texts Society, 1995.

29 Neat, T. (film), *Hallaig: The Poetry and Landscape of Sorley MacLean*, 1984

30 MacLean, S., introduction to Macmillan, D., *Symbols of Survival: The Art of Will Maclean*, Edinburgh: Mainstream, 1992

9. Mion-mhothachadh ann am Bàrdachd Shomhairle MhicGill-Eain

MAOILIOS CAIMBEUL

In this essay Myles Campbell investigates the sensibilty of MacLean as a poet and how his world-view emerged from that sensibility. It is apparent that many strands contributed to MacLean's weltanschauung: *among them love in its widest sense, the suffering of humankind, the history of his people and of the world, his upbringing in a tradition-bearing family, Presbyterian religion and politics. Campbell briefly compares MacLean's world-view with that of some traditional Gaelic poets of the twentieth century and identifies what makes him radically different from them. His is a new voice in Gaelic poetry, a humanist and existential voice that rejects traditional religious beliefs. New strands exemplify this, for example, the politics of international socialism, European sceptical philosophy and the influence of English and European poetry. Finally, Campbell compares the Christian philosophy of MacLean's contemporary, Derek Prince, with the Gaelic poet's humanist position and notes that there was one strand missing from the world-view of the latter: that which would integrate the spiritual – and indeed supernatural – experiences of humankind with the naturalistic.*

San aiste seo bidh mi a' beachdachadh air mion-mhothachadh (no *sensibility*) ann am bàrdachd Shomhairle MhicGill-Eain agus mar a dh'fhaodas am mion-mhothachadh a tha aig neach a bhith ciallachadh gu bheil sealladh farsaing agus domhainn aige, no aice, air an t-saoghal. Sin ri ràdh, a' *weltanschauung* a th' aig duine. Dè, ma-thà, a' *weltanschauung* a bh' aig MacGill-Eain? Bidh mi a' dèanamh coimeas aithghearr eadar an sealladh saoghail aigesan agus sealladh saoghail bhàrd Gàidhlig eile. Anns a' cho-dhùnadh, bidh mi a' dèanamh coimeas eadar *weltanschauung* MhicGill-Eain agus *weltanschauung* Crìosdail, gu h-àraidh mar a tha sin air a riochdachadh ann am feallsanachd agus dòigh-beatha Dherek Prince nach maireann, duine a bha na sgoilear ann an Oilthigh Chambridge anns na Tritheadan nuair a bha Somhairle ann an Dùn Èideann.

Bu toigh leam an toiseach dìreach facal a ràdh mu na tha air a chiall-achadh le mion-mhothachadh agus mar a dh'fhaodas sin buaidh a thoirt air an t-sealladh a th' aig duine air an t-saoghal. Chan e rud cumhang a tha sa mhothachadh seo ged a tha an ro-leasachan 'mion' air a chleachdadh. Bha mi a' feuchainn ri facal fhaighinn airson an rud ris an canar *sensibility* anns a' Bheurla. Faodaidh e a bhith a' gabhail a-steach iomadh nì: mar a tha neach a' faireachdainn mu dheidhinn an t-saoghail agus nan rudan a tha neach a' creidsinn mu dheidhinn – a' toirt leis nithean cultarach agus poil-itigeach agus spioradail, moraltachd, dòighean smaoineachaidh agus mar sin air adhart.

Tha mi a' creidsinn gur e am mion-mhothachadh domhainn agus farsaing a bh' aig MacGill-Eain a tha ga dhèanamh sònraichte am measg nam bàrd Gàidhlig, ann an linn sam bith. Chan eil bàrd eile ann a tha a' tighinn faisg air. Ma chleachdas sinn ròpa mar shamhla air a' mhion-mhothachadh seo, chì sinn gu bheil iomadh dual anns an ròpa.

A' chiad dual, 's e gaol. Tha dìoghras a' ghaoil sa bhàrdachd. Agus tha mi ciallachadh gaol agus gràdh san t-seagh as fharsainge: chan e dìreach gaol do bhoireannach ach dhan chinne-daonna, agus an gaol cuideachd aig a bheil a cheann-uidhe anns an t-sìorraidheachd. Nuair a chanas e ann an Dàn do Eimhir XLI:

> Chaidh mo ghaol ort thar bàrdachd,
> thar mac-meanmna, thar àrdain,
> thar sùgraidh, thar mànrain,
> thar ealain, thar ceòl-gàire,
> thar èibhneis, thar àilleachd,
> thar dòlais, thar àmhghair,
> thar cèille, thar nàdair,
> thar an t-saoghail mhòir bhàrcaich.[1]

tha fhios againn gu bheil e ga chiallachadh! Agus tha fhios againn nach e gaol feòlmhor air a bheil e a-mach. Tha sin nas soilleire buileach ann an Dàn do Eimhir LVII, far a bheil e ag ràdh:

A thràth de thìm, nuair dh'fhalbhas
do rèim mar an allacheo,
dè am breannachadh ùr-laist'
don diùchd t' fhalbhan?[2]

Tha e soilleir gu bheil an t-aodann a tha ga 'thathaich' san dàn sin na shamhla
air iarrtas nas maireannaiche na tìm.

Ach ged a tha doimhneachd agus farsaingeachd sa ghaol seo, ann an
àiteachan eile tha na faireachdainnean agus na smuaintean cho pearsanta
's as urrainn iad a bhith. 'S e pong ùr a tha seo ann am bàrdachd Ghàidhlig,
mar ann an Dàn do Eimhir XLVI: 'Tha sinn còmhla, a ghaoil, / leinn fhìn
ann an Dùn Èideann, / is t' aodann suaimhneach còir / a' falach leòn
do chreuchdan. / Tha agamsa mar chuibhreann dhìot / ceann grinn is
colainn reubte.'[3]

'S e dual eile a th' anns a' bhàrdachd aige am mothachadh dian a
th' aige air fulangas a' chinne-daonna. Tha seo ga phiobrachadh bhon
toiseach agus follaiseach sa bhàrdachd aige bho thùs gu èis. Tha 'càs an
t-saoghail' agus 'siùrsachd bhuadhan' (Dàn do Eimhir XIV)[4] ga bhuaireadh
mar a tha iad san dàn 'An Cuilithionn', far a bheil e a' dèanamh luaidh gu
mionaideach tro bhilean Clio air àmhgharan is 'breòiteachd is dallabhrat'
a' chinne-daonna.[5]

Dual cudromach eile, 's e eachdraidh. Tha e soilleir gu bheil e mion-
eòlach air eachdraidh na Gàidhealtachd, agus tha an t-eòlas sin follaiseach
ann an iomadh dàn. Seo eisimplir bho 'An Cuilithionn' far a bheil ainmean
dhaoine a bha an sàs anns na Fuadaichean agus ainmean-àite a' tighinn
còmhla, mar a tha tric a' tachairt:

An iar-dheas air ceann na Gàrsbheinn
chunnacas an Dotair Màrtainn
's bha MacAlasdair na h-Àirde
ag èaladh mu mhullach Blàbheinn;
bha Eòghann Mòr air Sgùrr an Sgùmain
's e 'g amharc sìos air Rubha 'n Dùnain …[6]

Tha eòlas mionaideach dhen t-seòrsa sin cumanta tron bhàrdachd aige agus tha sin a' cur blas Gàidhealach oirre. Ach chan e dìreach na h-ainmean. Tha an t-eòlas a th' aige air eachdraidh agus na dh'fhuiling na Gàidheil ga phianadh gu mòr. 'Air na leathadan uaine / ceò na h-eachdraidh ga shuaineadh, / cridhe, fuil is feòil mo dhaoine / an trom-laighe air na raointean …'[7] Tha àmhghar nan Gàidheal air sgàth Fhuadaichean, ana-ceartais agus chogaidhean nan uallach mòr air a spiorad, mar a chì sinn ann an dàin mar 'An t-Eilean', 'An Cuilithionn' fhèin agus 'Dà Dhòmhnallach'. Mar a thuirt Seamus Heaney mu dheidhinn, 's i a' Ghàidhealtachd 'the ancestral ground in which this poet's tap-root is profoundly lodged'.[8]

Tha an dual sin, dual na h-eachdraidh ionadail, ag èirigh gu nàdarra a-mach à dual cudromach eile: 's e sin an togail a fhuair e ann an Ratharsair. Mar a tha e fhèin a' sealltainn san ro-ràdh ann an *O Choille gu Bearradh*, thug an togail a fhuair e buaidh mhòr air. Fhuair e eòlas air na seann òrain bho a sheanmhair Màiri, a bhuineadh do Chlann MhicMhathain, agus bho Pheigi, piuthar a mhàthar. Bho sin a-mach bha gaol aige air na seann òrain. Bha an aon nì fìor a thaobh pìobaireachd. Bha athair na phìobaire agus chluinneadh e bràthair a mhàthar a' cluich ceòl clasaigeach na pìoba. Chuala e na h-òrain aig Uilleam Ros bho athair. Chuala e mu na Fuadaichean air Ratharsair agus mar a chaidh saighdearan bho na Camshronaich a chall anns a' Chiad Chogadh.[9] Bha sin uile na phàirt dhen dùthchas aige a bhiodh air a shnìomh dhan bhàrdachd a thigeadh bhuaithe nuair a thigeadh e gu aois.

Ach bha dualan cudromach eile a' nochdadh aig an àm seo cuideachd: 's iad sin creideamh agus poilitigs. Bhuineadh an teaghlach aige dhan Eaglais Shaoir Chlèirich, agus mar a sgrìobh Joy Hendry, 'Although MacLean relinquished Calvinism in favour of socialism at an early age, Calvinism continued to make a profound impact on him, influencing his thought as well as his language.'[10] Mar a tha MacGill-Eain fhèin ag ràdh san ro-ràdh a dh'ainmich mi shuas, 's e a bha a' cur dragh air gu h-àraidh mar a bha an Eaglais ag ràdh gun robh a h-uile duine, ach iarmad bheag a bha air an taghadh le Dia, a' dol a dh'Ifrinn chaillte gu sìorraidh. Tha iomradh air an Taghadh a tha seo gu math tric na chuid bàrdachd.

Tha co-fhaireachdainn agam ri MacGill-Eain. Chaidh mo thogail-sa mar bhalachan san Eaglais Shaoir agus bha na h-aon teagamhan agam 's a bh' aig MacGill-Eain. Bidh mi ag ràdh barrachd mun seo nas fhaide air adhart, ach 's fhiach rud no dhà a ràdh an-dràsta. Anns a' chiad dol-a-mach, feumaidh sinn sgaradh a dhèanamh eadar 'creideamh eaglaise' agus 'creideamh beò'. Tha 'creideamh eaglaise' glè thric air a sgrìobhadh sìos mar 'chreud' agus tha sin a' fàs gus a bhith nas cudromaiche na na tha am Bìoball fhèin ag ràdh ri duine fo stiùireadh an Spioraid Naoimh, rud ris an canainn-sa 'creideamh beò'. Bha e nàdarrach gun robh gille tuigseach òg a' cleachdadh a reusain gus sabaid an aghaidh creud a bha a' coimhead cho an-iochdmhor. Bha e nàdarrach cuideachd gun robh e nuair a bha e na bu shine air a tharraing gu creideamh nan Comannach, dòigh-smaoineachaidh a bha a' sàsachadh 'the passion of a moral activist', mar a th' aig Raymond Ross air.[11] Bha gràin aig MacGill-Eain air *elitism* sam bith. Ach, a rèir choltais, aig deireadh a latha cha robh earbsa na bu mhotha aige ann an Comannachd na bh' aige ann an creud no feallsanachd sam bith eile. Ann an 'Eadh is Fèin is Sàr-fhèin' tha e ag ràdh:

> Chan fhuirich an cridhe air a' mhachair;
> 's mòr as fheàrr leis a' chridhe
> ('s e cho càirdeach don spiorad)
> bhith 'n crochadh air piotan ris an stalla
> is fear mòr 'na cheannard ròpa,
> Calvin no Pàp no Lenin
> no eadhon bragairneach brèige,
> Nietzsche, Napoleon, Ceusair.[12]

Bheir sinn an aire gur e an cridhe 's nach e an eanchainn a tha a' cur earbsa anns na ceannardan mòra. Agus anns an dàn 'Palach' tha e ag ràdh: 'Chan eil ceann-teagaisg 'nam chainnt: / tha dusan Palach anns an Fhraing.'[13] Sheas an t-òganach Palach an aghaidh nan Comannach. Tha e mar gum biodh MacGill-Eain ag ràdh: tha gaisgich ann fhathast ach chan eil creud, no teacsa, ann as urrainn dhaibh a leantainn.

Thòisich mi le samhla – ròpa agus na dualan a tha a' cruthachadh ròpa mion-mhothachadh MhicGill-Eain. 'S iad na dualan a th' againn gu ruige seo gaol ann an iomadh cruth, aideachadh rudan a tha fìor phearsanta, eachdraidh ionadail, fulangas nan Gàidheal agus a' chinne-daonna, teaghlach, dùthchas agus togail, creideamh agus poilitigs. Tha dualan eile fìor chud-romach a dh'fheumte bruidhinn mun deidhinn airson ròpa iomlan MhicGill-Eain a thoirt còmhla, ach mus dèan mi sin 's fhiach stad airson mionaid airson ceist a chur: a bheil na dualan sin a dh'ainmich mi ga dhèanamh eadar-dhealaichte bho bhàird Ghàidhlig eile?

Dìreach a' gabhail riutha mar chuspairean air leth, chan eil mi a' smaoineachadh gu bheil. Gheibh sinn gaol a tha nas leithne na gaol na feòla ann an iomadh bàrd Gàidhealach – mar eisimplir, ann an 'Spiorad a' Charthannais' le Iain Mac a' Ghobhainn (c.1848–81).[14] Gheibh sinn fèin-aideachadh pearsanta ann an dàin Màiri Mhòr nan Òran, cho math ri dùthchas nan Gàidheal, ainmean-àite agus mar sin air adhart, agus co-fhaireachadh airson nam Fuadaichean agus fulangas nan daoine. Gheibh sinn an aon cho-fhaireachadh agus an aon fhaireachdainn mu dhùthchas ann am bàrdachd Mhurchadh MhicPhàrlain: 'Comann mo ghaoil, / O, 's sgaoilte comann mo ghràidh!'[15] Agus tha ceasnachadh aigesan cuideachd mu dheidhinn creideimh, gu h-àraidh san òran 'Am Fear Teiche', far a bheil an loidhne ''S m' eas-creidimh-sa ri 'g iarraidh cinnt.'[16] (Ach chan e idir an seòrsa mì-chinnt bhunaiteach a th' ann am bàrdachd MhicGill-Eain a tha seo.)

Ach gabhamaid aon eisimpleir eile: Dòmhnall Mac an t-Saoir, no Dòmhnall Ruadh Phàislig, aon de bhàird ainmeil dhualchasach na ficheadamh linn. Chì sinn, ged a tha na dualan a dh'ainmich mi mu thràth aigesan cuideachd, gu bheil an guth a tha na bhàrdachd gu tur eadar-dhealaichte bhon ghuth a tha ann am bàrdachd Shomhairle. Tha seo à 'Uibhist Uaine an Eòrna':

> An t-eilean tlachdmhor, 's mór mo bheachd
> Thug Rìgh nam Feartan fàbhor dhi
> Os cionn gach bad tha 'n Innse-Gall;
> Tha A Spiorad ann 's tha bhlàth orra,
> 'Gan treòrachadh g'A ionnsaigh fhèin.
> Tha 'm beath' a réir nam fàintean ann,
> Mar dhaoine diadhaidh, naomha, Crìosdail,
> Faoilidh, fialaidh, fàilteachail.[17]

Chan eil ceasnachadh sam bith anns a' ghuth seo. Tha e a' gabhail ris gu bheil Dia ann agus gu bheil a h-uile càil ag obrachadh gu ceart, òrdail fhad 's a chumas daoine ris na fàintean. 'S e seo an guth dualchasach, agus 's e guth a th' ann a gheibhear anns a' mhor-chuid dhe na bàird a bh' ann ro

MhacGill-Eain. Smaoinich a-nis air a' ghuth seo, a' chiad earrann anns an dàn 'Ùrnaigh' (Dàn do Eimhir XVIII):

A chionn nach eil Dia ann
agus a chionn nach eil Crìosda
ach 'na fhaileas faoin sgialachd,
chan eil ann ach: Dèanam làidir
m' aigne fhìn an aghaidh àmhghair.[18]

Thàinig an earrann sin às an dreachd de *Dàin do Eimhir* a dheasaich Christopher Whyte ann an 2002. Tha seo inntinneach, oir san dreachd a thàinig bho MhacGill-Eain fhèin ann an 1989 tha a' chiad trì loidhnichean a' leughadh 'A chionn nach eil dìon ann / agus a chionn nach eil m' iarrtas / ach 'na fhaileas faoin sgialachd ...'[19] Dh'atharraich an neach-deasachaidh am facal 'dìon' gu 'Dia' agus am facal 'iarrtas' gu 'Crìosda' seach gur e sin a bh' aig MacGill-Eain nuair a sgrìobh e an dàn an toiseach, mar a tha Whyte a' dearbhadh anns na notaichean aige aig deireadh *Dàin do Eimhir* (2002).[20]

Biodh an t-atharrachadh sin ceart no ceàrr, 's e a tha far comhair an-dràsta ach a bhith a' coimeas guth MhicGill-Eain agus guth Mhic an t-Saoir. Tha guth ùr ann am bàrdachd Ghàidhlig – guth an ana-creidis, guth an daonnaire: 'Dèanam làidir / m' aigne fhìn an aghaidh àmhghair.' 'S e saoghal feallsanachd a' bhitheileis a tha sin. Tha e a' cur nar cuimhne fheallsanachdan ain-diadhaidh mar a bh' aig Jean Paul Sartre agus Nietzsche. Dhaibhsan cha robh Dia ann a bheireadh cuideachadh seachad. Dh'fheumadh gach duine fa leth a roghainnean fhèin a dhèanamh agus a bheatha a dhealbh.

Saoil dè cho eòlach 's a bha MacGill-Eain air na feallsanaich Eòrpach? Tha e ag ainmeachadh grunn dhiubh anns an dàn 'An Cuilithionn' mar fheadhainn a bha 'Clio an t-saoghail' air a leughadh: 'Leugh mi Plato is Rousseau, / Voltaire, Condorcet is Cobbett, / Leonardo, Schopenhauer, Fichte, / Blok, Lenin, Marx, Nietzsche.'[21] Ach saoil an do leugh MacGill-Eain fhèin iad? A rèir Joy Hendry, ann an litir a chuir MacGill-Eain gu MacDhiarmid san dara leth dhe na Tritheadan thuirt e gun robh e 'reading nothing but Marxism in which I am considerably more proficient than I used to be.'[22] Agus ma bha e a' leughadh Mharx, tha e soilleir gun tàinig e fo bhuaidh feallsanachd Eòrpaich, oir bha buaidh mhòr aig feallsanaich Eòrpach mar Hegel, Rousseau agus Feuerbach air beachdan Mharx.

Air an làimh eile, thuirt Iain Mac a' Ghobhainn, 'Nor is it the case that MacLean has ever been ... an omnivorous autodidact, as Auden and MacDiarmid were ... The poetry is in the passion.'[23] Agus tha MacGill-Eain ag aontachadh ann an Dàn do Eimhir XV, 'Trì Slighean: Do Ùisdean MacDhiarmaid.' Chan eil e ag iarraidh 'slighe chumhang nan àrd-bheinn' a bh' aig MacDiarmid no 'an t-slighe chrìon ud ... / th' aig Eliot, Pound agus Auden'. Bha a dhùthaich fhèin na bu chudromaiche dha, agus am fiaradh a chuireadh na aigne le 'càs na Spàinnte, / cridhe feargach is nighinn àlainn.'[24] Dian-fhaireachdainn, mar a thuirt Mac a' Ghobhainn.

Ach, a dh'aindeoin sin, tha e soilleir gun robh dualan eile, dualan Eòrpach, ann am mion-mhothachadh MhicGill-Eain a bha ga dhèanamh tur eadar-dhealaichte bho bhàird Ghàidhlig a bh' ann roimhe. 'S iad na dualan sin 1) poilitigs shòisealach eadar-nàiseanta, 2) feallsanachd ana-creidmheach Eòrpach, mar a chunnaic sinn, agus 3) buaidh litreachais Eòrpaich agus Shasannaich. Tha na buaidhean Eòrpach sin taobh ri taobh ris na buaidhean Gàidhealach a dh'ainmich mi na bu tràithe. 'S e an t-strì a th' ann eadar na dualan ionadail agus na dualan Eòrpach, agus mar a tha iad air an snìomh còmhla, a tha a' dèanamh bàrdachd MhicGill-Eain cho cumhachdach, cho cudromach agus cho sònraichte. Mar a tha Iain Mac a' Ghobhainn ga chur anns an alt a dh'ainmich mi:

In the Thirties, MacLean set himself at the centre of his time in a way that Highland poets have not succeeded in doing. That is to say he was aware of a historical process which lay beyond Highland frontiers ...[25]

Sin iad na dualan a tha a' tighinn còmhla ann am bàrdachd MhicGill-Eain agus a tha a' cruthachadh a mhion-mhothachaidh. Ach dè, ma-thà, an sealladh slàn a bh' aige air an t-saoghal, dè a' *weltanschauung* a bh' aige? No an robh *weltanschauung* aige? Tha aon nì cinnteach: gun tàinig e fo bhuaidh dà *weltanschauung* chumhachdach, shlàn a bha gu tur an aghaidh a chèile. 'S iad sin creideamh na h-Eaglaise Saoire Clèirich, a bha a' creidsinn ann an Dia, ann an sìorraidheachd, ann an saoghal maireannach thar an t-saoghail seo, agus feallsanachd phoilitigeach Kharl Marx, a bha a' faicinn a leithid de chreideamh mar rud a bha ag èirigh à mac-meanmna, mar 'opium an t-sluaigh'. 'S e a bha Marx ag iarraidh ach an saoghal atharrachadh, far am biodh co-chomann far nach robh clas ann tuilleadh. Bha an gnìomh na bu chudromaiche na feallsanachd. Chuir e cùl ri saoghal spioradail Hegel agus bha e ag agairt gur anns an t-saoghal seo a bha slàinte.

Tha e soilleir bho a bhriathran fhèin gun do chuir MacGill-Eain cùl ri creideamh na h-eaglaise bhon a thòisich e a' sgrìobhadh bàrdachd an toiseach. 'S dòcha nach eil dàn ann an corpas na Gàidhlig a tha cho dubhach, eu-dòchasach ris 'A' Chorra-ghritheach' – a rèir choltais, a' chiad dàn a sgrìobh e leis an robh e fìor thoilichte.²⁶ Tha an treas earrann a' dol: 'Anfhannachd an strì, / aognaidheachd am brìgh, / gealtachd anns a' chrìdh, / gun chreid-eamh an aon nì.'²⁷ Ann an dàn a sgrìobh e fada às dèidh sin, 'A' Bheinn air Chall', tha e soilleir gu bheil e a cheart cho eu-dòchasach mu staid mhic an duine – 'a chionn 's nach tèid na sràidean ciùrrte / 's a' choille mhaoth an co-chur rèidh' – agus cuideachd eu-dòchasach mu chreideamh:

> Sìorraidheachd Dhante is Dhùghaill
> 'na seann solas ùr aig beagan
> agus neoni ghlas na h-ùrach
> 'na comhartachd chrìon phrann aig barrachd. ²⁸

Tuigidh sinn, saoilidh mi, gur e 'neoni ghlas na h-ùrach' a tha a' toirt cofhurtachd dha fhèin agus nach e 'an robair eile air a' chrann' (loidhne 31).

Chuir e cùl, ma-thà, ri creideamh agus *weltanschauung* na h-eaglaise. 'S dòcha airson greis bhig ron Dàrna Cogadh gun robh a dhòchas ann an Comannachd agus Arm Dearg na Ruis²⁹, ach cha do mhair sin fada. Ann an 1946 dh'aidicheadh e do MhacDhiarmaid gun robh e 'utterly at sea in politics these days, having … come to the conclusion that the Communist Party is no use for me'.³⁰ Agus, gu h-inntinneach, tha e ag ràdh anns an ro-ràdh airson an dàin 'An Cuilithionn', 'I never accepted the whole of Marxist philosophy, as I could never resolve the idealist-materialist argument'.³¹ Tha na facail sin a' sealltainn gun robh strì na inntinn fad a bheatha eadar sealladh Mharx, eadar feallsanachd nitheil (no *materialist*) agus feallsanachd an spioraid, mar a th' aig Fichte.³² Tha an t-strì a tha sin follaiseach ann an *Dàin do Eimhir*, far a bheil aodann Eimhir a' riochdachadh an iarrtais airson an t-saoghail shìorraidh. Cha cheadaich an tìde dhomh an t-strì sin a shealltainn gu mionaideach, ach tha daoine mar John Herdman air sin a dhèanamh mu thràth.³³

Mar a chunnaic sinn, tha mòran dhualan ann an mion-mhothachadh MhicGill-Eain, ach chan eil *weltanschauung* ann a tha a' tarraing a h-uile càil còmhla, an saoghal tìmeil agus an saoghal sìorraidh. Tha mi airson tionndadh a-nis gu aon dual no snàithlean a tha a dhìth ann am bàrdachd MhicGill-Eain. 'S e sin an saoghal os-nàdarra, no an saoghal ana-ghnàth-aichte, mar a tha Iain MacAonghuis ga ainmeachadh.[34] Faodaidh sin, bho aon shealladh co-dhiù, a bhith toirt leis nithean spioradail ann an saoghal a' Chrìosdaidh, gu h-àraidh obrachadh an Spioraid Naoimh. Bha an saoghal ana-ghnàthaichte riamh cudromach dha na Gàidheil an dà chuid air taobh a-muigh agus air taobh a-staigh na h-eaglaise. Saoilidh mise gum feum sinn mothachadh a bhith againn air rudan ana-ghnàthaichte a bhios a' tachairt agus mìneachadh a bhith againn dhaibh ma tha sealladh coileanta gu bhith againn air an t-saoghal. Tha rudan gu math iongantach a' tachairt ann am beatha dhaoine agus chan eil mìneachadh aig saidheans dhaibh.

Ged a tha MacGill-Eain ag ainmeachadh 'tannasg' anns an earrainn mu dheireadh dhen dàn 'An Cuilithionn', 's ann na mhac-meanmna a tha e. 'Chan eil ann ach an nì do-ruighinn, / an samhladh a chunnaic an t-anam, / Cuilithionn ag èirigh thar mara.'[35] Chan eil ann ach samhla coltach ris a' Chuilithionn fhèin.

Ach chan e samhla a bh' ann an saoghal an spioraid do Dherek Prince, a bha beò bho 1915 gu 2003, ach rud a bha a' riaghladh a bheatha bhon àm a chaidh iompachadh gu latha a bhàis. 'S e Crìosdaidh a bh' ann agus faodaidh sinn esan a ghabhail mar shamhla air an dual spioradail, creideamh ann an Dia agus ann an saoghal os-nàdarra.

Rugadh Prince anns na h-Innseachan. B' e Seanailear a bha na sheanair an Arm Bhreatainn agus b' e Caiptean a bha na athair. Bhuineadh iad do chlas a bha *pukkah* anns a h-uile dòigh – pàirt de dh'ìmpireachd Bhreatainn aig an àm. Chaidh Prince gu sgoiltean prìobhaideach agus an uair sin gu Eton agus Cambridge.[36]

B' e sàr sgoilear a bh' ann ann an Greugais, Laideann is Feallsanachd. Bha e ann an clasaichean an fheallsanaich ainmeil Ludwig Wittgenstein agus bha iad eòlach air a chèile. Fhuair e an Tripos clasaigeach le urram sa Chiad Chlas. Airson MA, sgrìobh e tràchdas air 'The Evolution of Plato's Theory of Definition'. Ann an alt san *Times* chaidh ainmeachadh mar 'an exceptional among exceptionals' air sgàth na h-obrach sgoilearachd aige.[37] Ach fhad 's a bha e ann an Cambridge bha e aonaranach, mì-thoilichte agus, coltach ri MacGill-Eain anns 'A' Chorra-ghritheach', 'gun chreideamh an aon nì'.

Dh'atharraich sin uile nuair a bha e san Arm aig àm a' Chogaidh. 'S ann sa Chorps Mheidigeach a bha e agus chaidh a chur gu Scarborough ann an Siorrachd York airson trèanadh. Dhrùidh e air cho còir, blàth-chridheach agus a bha muinntir Siorrachd York. Aon latha thug saighdear eile cuireadh dha a dhol gu eaglais, eaglais shoisgeulach no Chaingiseach. Cha robh an eaglais sin idir coltach ris an eaglais Anglican ris an robh e cleachdte, no, gu dearbha, ris an eaglais ris an robh MacGill-Eain cleachdte. Bha daoine a' togail an làmhan mar gum biodh ri Dia neo-fhaicsinneach, ag ùrnaigh gu pearsanta agus gu dùrachdach agus a' seinn laoidh barrachd air aon uair.[38]

Gun fhios dha, bha Prince air a dhol gu eaglais far an robh an coitheanal a' creidsinn gun robh an Spiorad Naomh ag obair fhathast ann am beatha dhaoine, mar a thachair aig Latha na Caingis mar a tha e air aithris sa Bhìoball ann an Gnìomharan nan Abstol. Thòisich an gluasad seo ann an Los Angeles aig toiseach na ficheadamh linn, agus a rèir eòlaichean tha a-nis suas ri 500,000 de 'Renewalists' air feadh an t-saoghail.[39] Agus mar a tha na h-ùghdaran sin, Micklethwait agus Woolridge, ag ràdh, 'Their beliefs are not for the fainthearted. Most adherents have witnessed divine healing, exorcisms or speaking in tongues'.[40]

Sin mar a thachair dha Derek Prince. Na dhuine òg ann an Scarborough, chaidh a bhaisteadh leis an Spiorad Naomh, chunnaic e mìorbhailean agus thachair rudan ana-ghnàthaichte na bheatha fhèin, rudan nach gabhadh a mhìneachadh tro a reusan. Bha e air Bìoball a cheannach agus a thoirt leis dhan Arm, a' sùileachadh a leughadh mar theacsa feallsanachd. Ach a-nis bha e a' sealltainn air mar Fhacal Dhè, agus bliadhnaichean às dèidh sin, às dèidh dha an t-Arm fhàgail, bha e na fhear-teagaisg ainmeil a' Bhìobaill tron bhuidhinn Derek Prince Ministries.

Gu h-inntinneach, bha e an làthair aig batal El Alamein, far an deach MacGill-Eain a leòn, ged nach robh esan aig uchd catha mar a bha Somhairle; ach 's e sgeulachd eile a tha sin.

'S e an leasan a tha mi ag iarraidh a thoirt à seo gun robh an seo duine, le inntinn gheur agus fhoghlamaichte, dhan do thachair nithean nach b' urrainn dha reusan a thuigsinn. Air sàillibh nan nithean sin, thòisich e a' creidsinn ann an Dia agus ann am mìneachadh spioradail air an t-saoghal.

Bha *weltanschauung* aige a bha a' dèanamh ciall dhe na chunnaic e agus dhe na thachair dha.

A-nis, 's e bàrd iongantach agus cudromach ann an iomadh dòigh a th' ann am MacGill-Eain, mar a tha mi air a shealltainn agus air a mhìneachadh. Bha mion-mhothachadh aige air iomadh nì, an dà chuid ionadail agus eadar-nàiseanta. Bha dìreach aon dual a dhìth air ròpa a' mhion-mhothachaidh aige airson *weltanschaunng* slàn a dhèanamh, agus 's e sin breithneachadh air na fèin-fhiosrachaidhean ana-ghnàthaichte – pearsanta (no *subjective*) agus neo-eisimeileach (no *objective*) – a tha air a bhith aig Prince agus milleanan dhaoine coltach ris.

'S dòcha gur e aon adhbhar airson sin an creideamh anns an deach a thogail, an Eaglais Shaor Chlèireach, nach eil a' gabhail ris gu furasta gum faod comharran poblach is pearsanta na Caingis a bhith fhathast gu follaiseach rim faicinn. Faodaidh gun tàinig MacGill-Eain fo bhuaidh creideamh eaglaise na òige agus gun do chuir sinn dallabhrat air an t-sealladh a bh' aige air creideamh.

Notaichean

1   MacGill-Eain, Somhairle, *Caoir Gheal Leumraich*, Christopher Whyte agus Emma Dymock, deas., Dùn Èideann: Polygon, 2011, t.d. 141
2   Ibid, t.d. 163
3   Ibid, t.d. 147
4   Ibid, t.d. 109
5   Ibid, t.d. 112
6   MacGill-Eain, Somhairle, *An Cuilithionn 1939 and Unpublished Poems*, Christopher Whyte, deas., Glaschu: Association for Scottish Literary Studies, 2011, t.d. 41
7   Ibid, t.d. 51
8   Ross, Raymond J. and Joy Hendry, eds, *Sorley MacLean: Critical Essays*, Edinburgh: Scottish Academic Press, 1986, t.d. 2
9   *O Choille gu Bearradh*, tdd. xi–xvi
10 *Sorley MacLean: Critical Essays*, t.d. 19
11 Ibid, t.d. 94
12 *Caoir Gheal Leumraich*, t.d. 251
13 Ibid, t.d. 261
14 MacLeòid, Iain N., deas., *Bàrdachd Leòdhais* (ath-fhoillseachadh), Steòrnabhagh: Acair, 1998, t.d. 92
15 MacPhàrlain, Murchadh, *An Toinneamh Dìomhair*, Steòrnabhagh: Stornoway Gazette, 1973, t.d. 13
16 Ibid, t.d. 41

17 *Sporan Dhòmhnaill: Gaelic Poems and Songs by the Late Donald MacIntyre, The Paisley Bard*, Somerled MacMillan, deas., Dùn Èideann: Oliver and Boyd for the Scottish Gaelic Texts Society, 1968, t.d.11

18 MacGill-Eain, *Dàin do Eimhir/Poems to Eimhir*, Christopher Whyte, deas., Glaschu: Association for Scottish Literary Studies, 2002, t.d. 65; *Caoir Gheal Leumraich*, t.d. 115

19 *O Choille gu Bearradh*, t.d. 16

20 *Dàin do Eimhir*, t.d. 205

21 *An Cuilithionn 1939*, t.d. 93

22 *Sorley MacLean: Critical Essays*, t.d. 19

23 Ibid, t.d. 46

24 *Caoir Gheal Leumraich*, t.d. 111

25 *Sorley MacLean: Critical Essays*, t.d. 49

26 Ibid, t.d. 16

27 *Caoir Gheal Leumraich*, t.d. 3

28 Ibid, t.d. 275

29 *O Choille gu Bearradh*, t.d. 63

30 *Sorley MacLean: Critical Essays*, t.d. 28

31 *O Choille gu Bearradh*, t.d. 63

32 *The Oxford Companion to Philosophy*, T. Honderich, ed., Oxford: Oxford University Press, 1995, tdd. 523–26

33 *Sorley MacLean: Critical Essays*, tdd. 165–75

34 *Dùthchas nan Gàidheal: Selected Essays of John MacInnes*, Michael Newton, ed., 'Looking at Legends of the Supernatural', Edinburgh: Birlinn, 2006, t.d. 459

35 *An Cuilithionn 1939*, t.d. 117

36 Mansfield, Stephen, *Derek Prince: A Biography*, Florida: Charisma House, 2005, tdd. 24–30

37 Ibid, tdd. 61–66

38 Ibid, tdd. 82–85

39 Micklethwait and Woolridge, *God is Back: How the Global Rise of Faith is Changing the World*, New York: Penguin Press, 2009, t.d. 17

40 Ibid, tdd. 17

10. Òrain Loch Aillse is Chinn Tàile

MÀIRI SÌNE CHAIMBEUL

Màiri Sìne Chaimbeul describes the singers and songs heard in Lochalsh and Kintail when Sorley MacLean was Headmaster of Plockton High School. Many of these had been recorded by Sorley's brother Calum MacLean. She also mentions the importance of 'The Dornie Manuscript' and the Ethnographic Wax Cylinders recorded by Lucy Broadwood between 1907 and 1909. She relates how Sorley's teaching made the old songs come alive for his pupils and how by showing respect for those who sang Gaelic songs and told Gaelic stories he raised their status and the status of Gaelic in the eyes of the wider community. He emphasised that 'without the songs and the stories we will be poor and dumb'.

Nuair a thàinig Somhairle MacGill-Eain dhan Phloc anns na Leth-cheudan, bha fhathast grunn dhaoine anns a' bhaile aig an robh Gàidhlig, agus bhiodh òrain Ghàidhlig aca nuair a bhiodh iad a' cruinneachadh ann an taighean air an oidhche, rud a bha tachairt gu math tric.

Seo feadhainn air a bheil cuimhne agam. Bhiodh m' athair, George MacKay, a' seinn 'Mo Nighean Donn an t-Sùgraidh'; Kenny John MacCoinnich, 'Fàilte Dhut 's Deoch-Slàinte Leat' – a chaidh a dhèanamh le fear às a' Phloc; bodaich à Port an Eòrna, Sammy Murchison agus a bhràthair – bhiodh òrain mar 'An Tìm a Bh' ann bho Shean' acasan. Bha a h-uile duine eòlach air an òran 'An t-Alltan Dubh' – Tommy Finlay às an Dòrnaidh mar bu thrice a bhiodh ga ghabhail – agus bha dhà no thrì aig Danny a' Phuist Oifis: 'Thig Trì Nithean gun Iarraidh', 'A Mhàiri Bhàn Òg' agus 'Bu Chaomh Leam Bhith Mire', a chaidh a dhèanamh, a rèir mo mhàthar, le a seann-seanair, Alasdair MacMhathain, am Fìdhlear Dall (Dòmhnall Fìdhlear a bh' air seanair mo mhàthar).[1]

Agus bhiodh Torcall MacNeacail le 'B' e Siud an Cùl, Seo an Cùl Bachlach' agus 'Ochòin, a Rìgh, Gura Mi Tha Muladach'. Bha rann a bharrachd aig Murchadh 'Ain Eachainn:

Ochòin, a Righ, nan robh pìob thombac' agam,
Mo spliùchan làn agus còrr is cairteal ann,
Bheirinn pìos do gach nàbaidh thachradh rium
'S chuirinn an còrr na mo phòcaid achlaise.

Bhiodh cuid dhe na boireannaich a' seinn cuideachd, mo mhàthair, Lexy MacKay, nam measg. Bhiodh i a' cluich na clàrsaich agus bha i air leasanan seinn fhaighinn, is mar sin bha an t-seinn aice, is dòcha, a' leantainn air stoidhle Marsaili Kennedy-Fraser – rud a bha gu math fasanta aig an àm, ged a tha sinne dualtach a bhith cur sìos air gu mòr an-diugh. Agus bhiodh i fhèin ag innse dhomh mu chailleach a bha a' fuireach an ath dhoras rinn, Ceit Dhonn NicRath, a bhiodh a' seinn rithe fhèin gun sgur nuair a bhiodh i a-muigh a' biathadh nan cearcan no a' crochadh aodaich.

Ri linn 's gun tàinig Somhairle MacGill-Eain a dh'fhuireach sa bhaile, thadhail Calum a bhràthair air a' chuid bu mhotha dhe na daoine sin, agus tha na clàraidhean sin nan adhbhar toileachais dhòmhsa. A bharrachd air na daoine seo, bhiodh feadhainn eile a' nochdadh sa bhaile, mar Seumas Caimbeul às an Dòrnaidh – a bha anns an sgoil sa Phloc agus a dh'ionnsaich seinn na h-eaglaise bho èildear sa bhaile. Bha tòrr òran aigesan bho cheann eile na sgìre – an Dòrnaidh agus Cinn Tàile – agus tha sinn gu math fortanach gun do chlàraich esan uimhir dhe na h-òrain aig Iain Mac Mhurchaidh, Bàrd Chinn Tàile, 's mar sin gun do chùm sin sàbhailte iad airson a' ghinealaich againn.

Bhiodh Alasdair Friseal à Achd Ille Bhuidhe a' tadhal air a' bhaile gach samhradh le a theaghlach. Bha e pòsta aig piuthar Thorcaill, agus bha guth binn socair aigesan agus stòras beartach de dh'òrain, cuid dhiubh a dh'ionnsaich e ann an Loch Aillse is Cinn Tàile agus cuid bhon sgìre aige fhèin.

Cuideachd, aig an àm ud, bhiodh Mòd anns a' Chaol gach bliadhna agus bha e mar chleachdadh gum biodh na daoine a bhuannaich am Bonn Òir aig a' Mhòd Nàiseanta a' nochdadh aig a' chonsart mu dheireadh, agus tha cuimhne mhath agam air Coinneach MacRath agus Seumas Mac-a-phì, Evelyn Chaimbeul agus Seonag NicCoinnich.

Bha buaidh aig Somhairle air a' bhaile ann an dòigh shònraichte, agus 's e sin gun robh e a' toirt urram dha na bodaich is na cailleachan sin aig an robh a' Ghàidhlig, òrain agus sgeulachdan, ged nach robh iad idir anns an fheadhainn a b' fheàrr dheth san sgìre. Agus leis a sin, thog e inbhe nan daoine sin agus inbhe na Gàidhlig suas ann an sùilean an t-sluaigh.

Bha aon bhodach gu h-àraid a bhiodh a' tadhal air Somhairle, glè thric air a shlighe dhachaigh às an taigh-òsta, agus chaidh mòran sgeulachdan a chlàradh bhuaithe le Calum MacGill-Eain: Iain Smoc, no Iain Fionnlasdan, às an Druim Bhuidhe. Agus leigidh mi leis fhèin facal no dhà a chantainn ribh:

> 'S minig a bha mi (bha mi) mun bhuideal
> Mar ri cuideachda shòlasach –
> Cha b' e 'n dram a bha mi 'g iarraidh
> Ach na b' fhiach an cuid stòiridhean.

> [Rann le Iain Mac Mhurchaidh]

> Agus oidhche mhath leat, a chàirdean mo ghaoil – tha mi toilichte a bhith nur measg air fad ann an cùil bheag anns a' Phloc![2]

Tha cuimhne agam, san dol seachad, air Somhairle a bhith ag innse dhomh gun robh ainm aig muinntir Loch Aillse a bhith socair sìtheil fo bhuaidh na dibhe, eucoltach ri cuid de dhaoine a bhios a' tòiseachadh a' sabaid nuair a bhios an deoch orra.

Bhiodh Somhairle ag innse, 's e a' gàireachdainn, gum biodh Iain Smoc ag ràdh ris nuair a bhiodh e a' toirt lioft dhachaigh dha – rud a dh'fheumadh e a dhèanamh aig deireadh gach oidhche – 'Na trì bàird a b' fheàrr a bha riamh ann an Alba: Iain Lom, Iain mac Mhurchaidh 's tu fhèin.' Mar gum biodh iad uile beò fhathast.

Nuair a bha mi fhìn san àrd-sgoil, bhiodh clasaichean againn le Somhairle air an leabhar *Bàrdachd Ghàidhlig* le W. J. Watson, agus bha dòigh aige air a' bhàrdachd sin a thoirt beò – gu h-àraid na h-òrain aig cùl an leabhair (ged nach eil càil san leabhar a dh'innseadh dhut gur e òrain a th' annta) – gus an tuigeadh sinne an saoghal anns an deach an dèanamh. Bha e mar gum biodh tu fhèin nad shuidhe nad 'ònar / air còmhnard an rathaid, / dh'fheuch am faiceadh tu 'fear-fuadain / tighinn o Chruachan a' cheathaich' ('Clann Ghriogair air Fògradh', t.d. 242). Mar a tha e fhèin ag ràdh san aiste 'Old Songs and New Poetry' (*Ris a' Bhruthaich*, t.d. 106), 'I am, for instance, quite sure that I thought "On the level of the road" one of the greatest of all Scottish poems long before I knew that there was an extant melody for it'.

Cha mhòr nach fhaiceadh tu 'long Dhòmhnaill', 'stiùir òir oirr', / trì chroinn sheilich' ('Tàladh Dhòmhnaill Ghuirm', *Bàrdachd Ghàidhlig*, t.d. 246). Agus beagan bhliadhnaichean an dèidh sin dh'ionnsaich Catrìona, nighean Shomhairle, fonn an òrain sin bho Cheit Phàdraig ann an Uibhist a Deas agus chuala mi i ga sheinn iomadh uair.

Tha am fiosrachadh sin airson dealbh a thoirt dhuibh air staid na Gàidhlig san sgìre nuair a bha mise òg. Ach, mar a chanas iad, dh'fhalbh siud is thàinig seo. Chan eil an saoghal mar a bha e. Nuair a bhios daoine òga a' cruinneachadh air an oidhche a-nise, bidh iad fhathast a' seinn, tha mi toilichte a ràdh, ach 's iad na h-òrain aca fhèin a bhios aca, òrain a chluinneadh tu ann am baile sam bith san dùthaich, agus tha sin air toirt orm smaoineachadh air cruinneachadh a dhèanamh dhe na h-òrain a bhuineas do Loch Aillse is Cinn Tàile, gus am bi e comasach dha daoine òga na h-òrain againn fhìn ionnsachadh agus an toirt beò a-rithist.

Agus, leis an amas sin, agus cuideachd seach gu bheil seo air tachairt ann an iomadh àite, an t-Eilean Sgitheanach, Leòdhas, Uibhist, shaoil leam gun robh a thìd' ann na h-òrain bhon sgìre seo a thoirt gu aire an t-sluaigh. Tha mi air tòiseachadh a' rùrach ann an iomadh àite gus òrain a lorg. Tha mi, mar a tha fhios aig gu leòr, air leabhar a chur ri chèile air beatha is bàrdachd Iain Mhic Mhurchaidh, agus bhiodh na h-òrain aigesan gu math cudromach ann an cruinneachadh sam bith a tha a' buntainn ri Cinn Tàile gu h-àraid. A bharrachd air a sin, tha mi air lethbhreacan fhaighinn dhe na clàraidhean a rinn Calum MacGill-Eain san sgìre sna Leth-cheudan. Agus chuala sibh eisimpleir mar-thà le Danny MacCoinnich. Mar a thuirt mi roimhe, tha a' chuid as motha dhe na daoine a dh'ainmich mi a' nochdadh air na clàran sin. Gu fortanach, rinn Seumas Caimbeul tòrr dhan BhBC agus do Sgoil Eòlais na h-Alba, agus tha Alasdair Friseal air mòran dhe na h-òrain aigesan a chur air clàr.

Bha inneal-clàraidh aig Torcall MacNeacail aig an aon àm agus tha teipichean agam a rinn esan, le measgachadh de dh'òrain agus còmhradh. Agus tha e gu math tlachdmhor dhòmhsa a bhith a' cluinntinn guthan nan daoine a bha timcheall nuair a bha mi a' fàs suas.

Tha goireas air leth eile againn, 's e sin 'Làmh-sgrìobhainn an Dòrnaidh'. Rinn an Dr Nancy McGuire obair mhòr air an làmh-sgrìobhainn seo mar phàirt dhen fhor-cheum aice, agus tha cuid dhe na h-òrain a tha anns an làmh-sgrìobhainn rim faighinn air na teipichean a rinn Calum MacGill-Eain san Dòrnaidh. Faodaidh sinn, mar sin, na fuinn 's na facail a chur ri chèile.

Agus mu dheireadh, tha stòras iongantach aig Leabharlann Bhreatainn ann an Lunnainn: 'Ethnographic Wax Cylinders' a chlàraich Lucy Broadwood eadar 1907 agus 1909. Am measg na th' ann tha suas ri ceud òran a chlàraich i fhèin agus fear an Dr Fearchar MacRath ann an Gàidhlig na h-Alba – ged nach aithnich thu sin ach air èiginn bho na h-ainmean a tha air an liosta. An rud a b' inntinniche dhòmhsa mun deidhinn, 's e gu bheil cuid dhe na fuinn beagan (agus uairean, mòran) eadar-dhealaichte bhon dòigh anns an cluinnear iad an-diugh, agus bhiodh e glè mhath coimeas a dhèanamh eadar na diofar dhreachan.

Nuair a thòisich mi a' smaoineachadh air seo a dhèanamh, mar as tric a bhios a' tachairt le rannsachadh, cha robh dùil agam gum biodh mòran ann, ach chì sibh fhèin gu bheil tòrr stuth a-muigh an siud, agus 's math a b' fhiach a tharraing ri chèile. Agus ma dh'ionnsaich mi aon rud bho Shomhairle, 's e gu bheil dualchas làidir agus prìseil aig na Gàidheil. Gun na h-òrain agus na sgeulachdan a thàinig thugainn bho na ginealaichean a bh' ann romhainn, bidh sinn bochd is balbh. Is ann leinne a tha na h-òrain sin agus cha bu chòir dhuinn an leigeil air dìochuimhne.

Notaichean

1 *Tobar an Dualchais*, 1952.10.16, Track ID: 23227 – Original Tape ID: SA1952.139
2 *Tobar an Dualchais*, Track ID: 1163 – Original Tape ID: SA1955.162

11. 'A mind restless seeking': Sorley MacLean's Historical Research and the Poet as Historian[1]

HUGH CHEAPE

The success and universal acclaim of Sorley MacLean's literary career and its continuing reverberations have tended to elide his output of historical research and contributions to wider fields of Celtic Studies and Scottish History. In Sorley's case as a natural tradition-bearer, the distinction between poet and historian must be an artificial one, and intellectual trends in historical studies serve to enhance the importance of his historical work. This essay looks at some of these trends and some topics which Sorley researched and published, at his intense interest in the literature, personalities and events of the more culturally secure seventeenth century, and the fruitful blend of archival research and oral tradition – for example, in his Raasay home.

History, like any academic discipline, is not necessarily a straightforward business. Of course, there are those who will argue that subjects and disciplines within the sciences are 'easier' or in some way more straightforward than those categorised within the humanities, and alternatively there are arguments for the greater difficulties of the sciences over the humanities. At the same time, all academic disciplines are subject to advance, decline, variation and change in their make-up and subject-matter and in their conceptual framework. The charting of change has become an academic discipline in itself and, in the sciences, has been closely studied. Changes in the sciences have been characterised as 'scientific revolutions' and as demonstrating convulsive change. The process is predicated on a tendency for outmoded paradigms for a discipline's theory or model to persist for some time after their obsolescence has set in. When the paradigm does eventually shift, this may occur rapidly, and the speed of change is then maintained by the subsequent concentration of resources on research into what are thought to be important questions.[2]

Historical paradigms, such as those confronting Sorley MacLean, seem to change in a more haphazard way; there are periodic shifts forward but more characteristically a sluggish revisionism in which pupils are mainly concerned to qualify the interpretations of the previous generation and, only rarely and at a risk to their own careers, challenging its assumptions. A more dubious influence may arise from the appropriation of a historical paradigm to a political agenda. History is coloured by the institutional configurations of higher education, academic labels and conventional terminology such as periodisation, and the national boundaries of academic disciplines. Bridging the divide between disciplines is a further challenge. Lip service at least is ritually paid to cross-disciplinary and multi-disciplinary studies, so that historians have recourse to economics, sociology, anthropology, archaeology and even literary theory, though less to physics, mathematics and, it must be said, to language, linguistics or socio-linguistics.

The centenary celebration of Sorley MacLean as 'renowned over hundreds' – *Ainmeil thar Cheudan* – prompts consideration of the poet as historian and assessment of his cultural and political legacy, particularly with regard to a 'national history'. The recognition and success of Sorley MacLean as poet has perhaps obscured his historical writing or distracted recent generations from it. Taken in isolation, this is still an important and lasting part of his output, with a lifetime of historical research and significant contributions to wider fields of Scottish History and Celtic Studies. In Sorley's case as a natural tradition-bearer, the distinction between poet and historian must be an artificial one, though recognisable in other contexts where misconceptions may arise from too ready assumptions that poetry depicts real-life people and events. Gaelic poetry still needs further scrutiny for its depictions of people and events, and to be accepted or discarded, as Sorley suggests in his published output. We can claim to be in a more liberal-minded academic atmosphere which will admit consideration of this genre of literary evidence. At the same time, intellectual trends in historical studies such as the shift in focus from parliamentary institutions and political elites to social structures and *mores* have opened the historian's mind to poetry and song, and these trends serve to highlight the importance of his historical work. This study argues for the emplacement of Sorley MacLean's research in the historical discourse in

Scottish Historical Studies and an *a priori* acceptance that Gaelic song and poetry may indeed supply a record, straightforward or otherwise, of something that actually happened.

The business of historians and their obligation to society is to remember what others forget. Sorley MacLean's self-conscious custodianship of family history and the memory of events, as well as his self-evident reflective powers, make him a historian to trade. In terms of his own family and its cultural context of the life of a Gaelic-speaking community through two World Wars within two generations, there is almost nothing too exceptional about this, and there are striking examples to corroborate it.[3] In the wider context of Britain and Europe today, where a generation seems to have grown up in a permanent present, we are served with stereotyping and banal definitions and lack an organic relation to the public past of the times we live in. Memory of event and cataclysm and the will to question and understand them is an understated though ever-present component of Sorley MacLean's poetry, but, however obliquely, he can be considered as much a remembrancer and chronicler as any twentieth-century historian. Contemplation of topics such as genocide, the rise of fascism, ecological dislocation and disruption, religious belief or death and renewal, to which Sorley's poetry holds a mirror, is outside the scope of this short paper. With this reflective and intellectual reach in his work, however, this study looks at some topics which Sorley researched and published, at his intense interest in the literature, personalities and events of the more culturally secure seventeenth century, and at his fruitful blend of archival research and oral tradition – for example, in his Raasay home.

Sorley MacLean's essays, lectures and learned papers which give voice to the strength of his ideas were scattered in a range of publications such as the *Transactions of the Gaelic Society of Inverness*, potentially reducing the impact of any thesis without the diligence of a dedicated researcher. Here, we are indebted to Professor William Gillies, to the MacLean family and to Acair Ltd, the Stornoway publisher, for gathering 'The Criticism and Prose Writings of Sorley MacLean' into the volume *Ris a' Bhruthaich*, first published in 1985.

The potential for a nudge to the paradigm of Scottish History grows from Sorley's fascination (as he describes it) with the vast body of 'folk' and 'sub-literary' song poetry of the sixteenth, seventeenth and eighteenth centuries. However, part of the power of Sorley MacLean's literary and critical output for us lies in its contemporaneity, or at least in its take on the recent past and the influence that the recent past had had on him. In this he writes about the twentieth century and his own lifetime. A public interest in him as commentator has grown with the intense scrutiny in Scotland given to topics such as 'clearance' and 'emigration' since the 1970s. In his introduction to *Sorley MacLean: Critical Essays*, published by Scottish Academic Press in 1986, Seamus Heaney wrote of the 'force of revelation' on hearing Sorley MacLean reading his poetry and characterised MacLean as 'a mind that is ravenous for conviction.'[4] The events which Sorley had experienced, such as the Spanish Civil War, or in which he had participated, such as the North Africa campaign, made him a twentieth-century writer in his search for answers or justifications. He was, as the social anthropologist would say, a 'participant observer', but also politically committed and, more significantly for considering the poet as historian, dissatisfied with the public record. A level of dissatisfaction and the intensity of questioning is part of the new historiography of the late twentieth century, growing more vigorously through the channels of the social sciences and spilling into historical studies through Marxist dialectic and the New Left politics of the 1970s.

Two early papers delivered to the Gaelic Society of Inverness in 1938 and 1939 demonstrate, as Seamus Heaney added to his characterisation of Sorley, that 'there's nothing antiquarian or archival in this drive' and that this research fired the engagement of a political mind. These papers respectively dealt with nineteenth-century subjects, 'Realism in Gaelic Poetry' and 'The Poetry of the Clearances', both remarkable treatments of their subjects for the time. In arguing for 'realism', the author achieves two main ends, with, in the first place, a vigorous counter-argument to the concept of the 'Celtic Twilight' and its votaries, and, secondly, the identification of an authentic voice. As he wrote, '... the Celtic Twilightists achieved the remarkable feat of attributing to Gaelic poetry the very opposite of every quality which it actually has.'[5] Sorley's later comment on this as 'an immature protest against the dominance even as late as 1938 of the "Celtic Twilight"' does not diminish its importance for us today as a considered statement on a topic which continues to reverberate.[6] The editor is to be congratulated for ensuring its reprinting in *Ris a' Bhruthaich*. Without acquaintance with the language, there is bound to be bland acceptance in the anglophone world of Marjory Kennedy-Fraser's *Songs of the Hebrides*, but there is a vital need for an alternative perspective on them rather than, as Sorley highlighted, 'the fashionable opinion that Mrs Kennedy-Fraser's work was the authentic culmination and treasury of Gaelic poetry and an invaluable presentation of it to the world, even in the English versions of the words of the songs'[7]. An authentic voice was identified in the oldest surviving popular poetry – that is, 'the largely anonymous, orally preserved and tradition-modified poetry which is contained in the simpler songs of the sixteenth, seventeenth and eighteenth centuries, and which survived, but at a much lower poetic level, well into the nineteenth century'.[8]

Sorley's survey and consideration of the poetry of the Clearances was the first of its kind in Scottish historical studies and lends weight to consideration of the role of the poet as historian. It is now almost forty years since the ground-breaking Highland historian, James Hunter, acknowledged Sorley MacLean's pre-eminent role as historian: '... there has been only one serious attempt to evaluate the impact of economic change on the Gaelic consciousness – and that by a Gaelic poet, Sorley MacLean – rather than by an historian.'[9] Speaking to the Gaelic Society of Inverness in February 1939, MacLean spared nothing in his recall of the plight of a people in the face of tyranny on a national scale. Historians or chroniclers of the Clearances such as Donald MacLeod (1857) and Alexander Mackenzie (1883) had opened up the subject and courted controversy. They made some distinctions between phases of clearance and emigration, between 1780 and 1820 and between 1820 and 1880, raising issues such as free-will or enforcement taken up by historians of our own time.[10] Economic determinism tended to shape views on the earlier period of emigration, but Sorley drew out an anomaly that, though there were clearances, they seemed to evoke little comment in verse. He recognised that one or two voices were raised in the eighteenth century – for example, John MacCodrum with his statement of an older view of the rights of the clan to the territory of their dwelling and Ailean Dall MacDougall in his 'Òran nan Cìobairean Gallda', with its invective and hatred focused on the Lowland shepherds who in every way were an offence to the senses, in how they looked, in how they sounded and in their offensive smell. MacLean also made a potent comment on this evidential imbalance: 'Of course, so much of the poetry of that period has been lost and much was undoubtedly kept out of the collections dedicated to aristocratic patrons that one cannot know the reaction of poets between 1750 and 1880.'[11] Social and economic dislocation and destruction filled the years from 1820 to 1860 but the poetry of the period was 'flabby and anaemic'.[12] Weakness might be defined in confusing the cause and effect of the Clearances – for example, in blaming Englishmen and Lowlanders for the crimes of the Highland chiefs, or in recognition of the clergy's acquiescence and occasional support for the landlords. Since, as Sorley emphasised, ministers of the Established Church were economically attached to the landlord, some actively supported the Clearances, or, in any process of censure, they would hide their criticism from their patrons. Highlanders' resistance, either physical or moral, was bound to be weak and the poetry of this period reflects this impotence. In Scottish historical studies in 1939, this was an extraordinary exploration of a topic in stasis, but Sorley's voice was a lone one.[13]

Sorley MacLean thus finds fault with nineteenth-century Gaelic poetry, describing the worthlessness of its matter and contrasting it to the oldest existing Gaelic poetry of the sixteenth, seventeenth and eighteenth centuries, which had survived into the nineteenth century. But for Sorley, there were lights in the gloom of the nineteenth century – for example, William Livingston's 'Fios chun a' Bhàird', with his strong message of Gaelic nationalism, and 'Éirinn ag Gul', with its sympathy for Ireland and the linking of the circumstances of the Gaels of Scotland and Ireland. Livingston, 'charged with the burden of history', uses long views to the past in 'Na Lochlannaich an Ìle' and 'Blàr Shunadail' to throw into relief the devastation of Islay in the nineteenth century. Sorley MacLean also invokes Dr John MacLachlan of Rahoy (1804–1874), who belonged in theory to a professional class or social stratum unaffected by the devastation and lived through the Clearances in Morven, Sunart and Mull, where they were particularly severe. Though MacLachlan is not considered a master-poet, Sorley draws on vital insights offered by MacLachlan's verse and 'a union of anger and piercing sorrow' evident in his songs.[14]

Sorley's presentation of the case against the Clearances is moderated by his views on the overall quality of the poetry of the nineteenth century, views that will be less deprecatory and more nuanced today, but nevertheless his search for the voice of the people was so successful as to persuade others to take up the cause – but not at the time.[15] His robust critique picked up contemporary voices seemingly unrecognised by historians and he described the importance of source material such as Archibald Sinclair's *An t-Òranaiche*, first published in parts between 1876 and 1879, with its records of personal experience. *Mutatis mutandis*, this is substantial historical evidence and Sorley has been an effective guide. He identified the poetry of Skye and Lewis which grew out of crofter resistance and which took courage and a lead from contemporaries such as Rev. Donald MacCallum, accused and imprisoned 'for inciting the lieges to class hatred', and Màiri Mhòr nan Òran. She was the poet of the Land League but with a respect for *uaisle* (nobility). Sorley identified the nostalgic retrospect as itself highly significant for popular views and attitudes. The 1939 paper was a tour-de-force on the poetry of social and political protest emerging from the Clearances and the Land Agitation. He considered the verse to be historical evidence on the perceptions and experiences of those caught up in the events, but in its totality and in spite of the clear incitement offered by Sorley, it has been little used by modern historians.

In the historiography of Scotland, there seems to be a less than strident side to this hunger for conviction revealed so compellingly in Sorley MacLean's late 1930s statements. With the wisdom of hindsight and the lessons offered by Sorley, any such shortcomings can be explained if not excused. In commemorating the birth of Sorley MacLean in 1911, it is worth reflecting on the state of Highland history at the time and in the years following. In short, there was little available to the ravenous mind in terms even of standard textbooks on Scottish history. The Cambridge 'history school' dominated British History, which, in effect, was English History with a nod towards Scotland and Ireland when they impinged on the onward and upward progress of English constitutional government. The writers of British History at the end of the nineteenth century included university teachers such as F. W. Maitland who belonged to a class of historians sometimes termed 'the constitutionalists' whose hold over Scottish academic historians was complete. A good example of those in thrall is Professor Peter Hume Brown (1849–1918), the first holder of the Sir William Fraser Chair of Scottish History and Paleography in the University of Edinburgh. His Cambridge University Press three-volume *History of Scotland*, published in 1902, was the standard text whose treatment of Scotland's past stopped with the Union and Rebellion of 1745, the inference being that Scotland had no history after 1707. Hume Brown's treatment of Highland history was almost as lurid and peremptory as that of James VI.

Can such sparse and dismissive handling be exonerated by pleas of ignorance of the sources? In fact, some remarkable advances were made in the immediately preceding generation or two, placing some intriguing documentation before Scottish historians. This was largely the work of one or two people. Donald Gregory (1804–1836) was from an academic family of great distinction which included professors of science, medicine and mathematics over many generations, and was descended, it was said, from the MacGregors of Roro in Glen Lyon. He was Secretary of the Society of Antiquaries in the 1830s and joined with another Edinburgh scholar, William Forbes Skene (1809–1892), in 1833 to found the Iona Club, named 'in commemoration of the Monastery of Iona, the ancient seat of Scottish learning', and its object being 'to investigate and illustrate the history, antiquities and early literature of the Highlands of Scotland'. The Iona Club had a Gaelic Committee as part of its Council whose members included Rev. Dr Norman MacLeod, *Caraid nan Gàidheal*, and Rev. Dr Macintosh Mackay, the scholarly minister of Laggan and editor of the Highland Society's Gaelic Dictionary. The Iona Club's main achievement was the publication in 1847 of a collection of papers edited by Gregory and Skene as *Collectanea de Rebus Albanicis*, including documents still under scrutiny such as the 'Genealogies of the Highland Clans extracted from ancient Gaelic MSS', now known as 'MS 1467'. In 1836 Donald Gregory published his *History of the Western Highlands and Isles of Scotland* from the reign of James IV until the death of James VI. When W. F. Skene published his *The Highlanders of Scotland* in 1837, he noted in the Preface 'the general neglect of Highland history', which he attributed to 'that extraordinary prejudice against the Celtic race, and against the Scottish and Irish branches of that race in particular which certainly biased the better judgement of our best historians'.

Skene himself was an assiduous collector and deposited a collection of Gaelic manuscripts in the Advocates' Library, where by 1862, largely through Skene's own efforts, there were sixty-five Gaelic manuscripts where formerly there had been only four. Spectacularly, he himself secured the 'The Black Book of Clanranald' from a street barrow in Dublin and the Fernaig Manuscript, which had been given to him by the trustees of Rev. Macintosh Mackay. It is notable that these two manuscripts alone make up most of the second volume of *Reliquiae Celticae*. Skene contributed an introduction to Thomas MacLauchlan's 1862 edition of the Book of the Dean of Lismore, and his majestic *Celtic Scotland: A History of Ancient Alban* (1876–1880) appeared in three bulky volumes, 'History and Ethnology', 'Church and Culture' and 'Land and People', and included many appendices of original documents.[16]

Sorley MacLean's fascination with the folk poetry of circa 1550–1800 was informed by his interest in the history of the period, and especially of the seventeenth century, a period which formerly had a grim reputation in British history in comparison to the sunburst of the eighteenth century and the 'Enlightenment'. If our studies (and sources) are over-compartmentalised, we may miss the bigger picture which may make more sense of Sorley's specialised insights. In the fifteenth and sixteenth centuries, for example, the Stewarts won and consolidated their power in Scotland. The emergence of the dynasty in the mid-fifteenth century was particularly owing to the shrewd judgement and ability of James II (1437–1460) and his dealings with over-mighty subjects. His marriage to Mary of Gueldres brought him guns and gunsmiths and technology from the Low Countries – and possibly Mons Meg. He overpowered the Douglases and broke the bond that they had made with the Earl of Ross and Lord of the Isles in 1455. There was a tale that the young king went for advice to Bishop Kennedy of Saint Andrews, who took up a sheaf of arrows and showed him that they could not be broken, that they were irresistible when united – but could be broken one by one. With his queen from Denmark, James III sustained the links with Europe and the Renaissance, as did his son, James IV (1488–1513), possibly the last King of Scots to be a Gaelic-speaker.

James IV saw to the fall of the Lordship of the Isles in 1493 and the promotion of the Campbells of Argyll, the Gordons of Huntly and the Mackenzies of Kintail as the Crown's lieutenants. Our obsession with the shifting ground of politics or the destructive power of weaponry tends to push into the shadows the fabric of everyday life which the songs portray. At this time Scotland shared in the Renaissance styles of Florence and Venice, and we can glimpse touches of the Florentine palace in Dùn Bheagain and Dùn Tuilm. The European Renaissance is evident in the lavish hospitality and display, and in the drift towards domestic comfort and the distinguishing between *sala* (or hall), *scrittorio* (or study) and *camera* (or bedroom). Furniture, though sparse in the Highlands and Hebrides by modern standards, yet followed a European formula of storage chests and fine beds, and the government passed sumptuary laws to try to limit the expenditure on finery originating in the eastern Mediterranean and the Middle East; and bedrooms were now not just for sleeping in but for receiving close friends and throwing intimate dinner parties. Life for men and women of the Renaissance followed a ritualistic pattern, and the Palazzo Medici was not so very far from Castle Tioram. Some of this Renaissance 'horizon' can be felt in the lament of Mary MacDonald for her MacDonald of Clanranald husband, who died in 1618:

> Is iomadh sgal pìobadh,
> Mar ri faram nan dìsnean air clar ...[17]

> *Many a blast of the pipe together with the noise*
> *of the dice on boards*
> *I listened to in your house, with the poetry*
> *and the bragging of the bards,*
> *To the books of history with red covers, and to poems,*
> *Together with pleasure without thirst – why for ever*
> *would I let you away from me?*

The richness of allusion and imagery is as Sorley taught us, though much of the surviving literature in Gaelic is an evocation of 'big house' culture, with its entertainment of music and song and the declamations and contentions of the poets. There are also subtle touches such as a tenderness in the moving from the *faram* of the great hall or *sala* to the *camera* or *seòmar* and intimate reflection in the subtle counterpointing of a female with a male domain and the emergence of differing social roles.

The material culture of Renaissance Europe was to be seen in the coinage, dress, weaponry, sculpture and buildings, no less than in attitudes and perspectives. MacLeod of Dùn Bheagain's household accounts tell us of silk, satin and velvet, gold and silver lace, gold and silver buttons, and 'doublets for his Honour's page'. A complaint by Inverness burgesses against a Glenelg man in 1618 for his theft of '4 dozen great blue bonnets, 20 dozen trumps, 3 dozen bow-strings, 4 dozen English garters and a barrel full of powder' seems to suggest that Gaelic culture was entirely European.[18] Chiming with the insights into material culture and human emotion, the literature reveals an easy cosmopolitanism which should reverse our perception of the Hebrides as hinterland. When John MacDonald of Aird, Benbecula, rehearsed the followers and admirers of his leader, MacDonald of Clanranald, he joined France, Italy and Uist together into one social theatre, and conspicuous consumption was not the preserve of a ruling class, if we can appreciate the lover's shopping list in 'Bothan Àirigh am Bràigh Raithneach'.[19]

For richness, variety and imagery without equal throughout Europe, Sorley laid before us the songs of Mary MacLeod, Iain Lom MacDonald of Keppoch, the 'Blind Harper' – An Clàrsair Dall – and Sìleas na Ceapaich, with their poetry of clan and chief, of politics and place, of conviction and belief. He drew out the poetry of hitherto less well-known poets, of Mairearad nighean Lachlainn, Alexander Mackenzie of Achilty or Alasdair Mac Mhurchaidh, and the cattle-lifter and ladies' man, Dòmhnall Donn Bhoth Fhionndainn. He drew attention to the prominence of the sea in poetry and the prestige of the ship both as symbol and as stage for life, and though this imagery supplied the desired metaphor for senses of value, it only made sense in the richness and accuracy of description. Sorley added the important observation that, against modern expectation, supernatural elements were not common in sea poetry. Reading the landscape as 'environment' may seem a recent fixation, but the great late sixteenth-century song of mountains and hunting, 'Òran na Comhachaig', could be the text for a modern 'conservation management plan' for the Highlands. To these riches he added the poetry from unnamed and unknown poets surviving *air bilean an t-sluaigh*, 'on the people's lips', to be committed to paper and print in the twentieth century. The period of the seventeenth century which drew the scrutiny and admiration of Sorley MacLean seems qualitatively different when viewed from the north and west of the British Isles. Using the enlightenment offered by him, we might risk a view that if the Gael was no better than his southern neighbours, he was certainly no worse.

In an interview with Sorley MacLean in September 1982, the late Donald Archie MacDonald of the School of Scottish Studies recorded a conversation with the poet on 'some aspects of family and local background'. In describing contemporary influences on a young poet, Sorley revealed how his views took cognisance of the environment and how part of his identity was deeply rooted in Skye and Raasay:

> I grew up at that time when symbolism was such a thing in European poetry … and my symbols almost automatically became the landscape of my physical environment. But, of course, that was always affected, blended with what I knew of the history of my people.[20]

With Sorley's robust delivery to hand in *Ris a' Bhruthaich*, we can more easily and confidently reconsider Highland and Hebridean history, not only in its own right but also towards a reconfiguration of Scottish historical studies. Our cultural baggage is indelibly marked with excuses about the lack of sources for Highland history, the mantra of 'no documents, no history', or 'tradition' as historically suspect. Sorley warns us that the documents and texts that we have grown used to are deferential to alien values and expectations. He encourages us to 'read the landscape' and take seriously the anonymous tradition of popular poetry and song. This is no isolated voice in a peripheral place but a civilisation at its most confident, successful and assertive, and this in the seventeenth century when all appears in confusion in British History and Scottish History. There would be nothing more liberating and empowering than to follow Sorley MacLean's lead and re-position Highland history on foundations so inspiringly laid by him. The wider meaning of this for Highland history is given a modern but no less potent voice by Aonghas MacNeacail. In his 1996 collection *Oideachadh Ceart agus dàin eile/A Proper Schooling and other poems*, he asserts the value of an oral culture as against one where written records are the sole proof of civilisation. He questions why 'tradition' should always be regarded as historically suspect and his poem 'Oideachadh Ceart' closes with the insistence that history should be redefined to accommodate memory:

> … agus a-muigh
> bha gaoth a' glaodhaich
>
> *eachdraidh nam chuimhne*
> *eachdraidh nam chuimhne*[21]

Notes

1 The title of this essay adopts the line 'Inntinn luasganach a' sireadh' from 'A' Chorra-Ghridheach' in *17 Poems for 6d* (1940) to symbolise the poet's stance; also in *Caoir Gheal Leumraich*, Christopher Whyte and Emma Dymock, eds, Edinburgh: Birlinn 2011, pp. 2–3

2 See Thomas S. Kuhn, *The Structure of Scientific Revolutions*, Chicago: University of Chicago Press, 1962 (and subsequent editions).

3 See, for example, Calum Ferguson, *Children of the Black House*, Edinburgh: Birlinn, 2003, which draws on the memories of the author's mother and faces issues such as the psychological trauma of the First World War in an island community.

4 *Sorley MacLean: Critical Essays*, Raymond J. Ross and Joy Hendry, eds, Edinburgh: Scottish Academic Press, 1986, p. 2

5 *Ris a' Bhruthaich: The Criticism and Prose Writings of Sorley MacLean*, William Gillies, ed., Stornoway: Acair, 1985, p. 20

6 Ibid, p. 3

7 Ibid, p. 3

8 Ibid, p. 20

9 James Hunter, *The Making of the Crofting Community*, Edinburgh: John Donald, 1976, p. 4. I am extremely grateful to Professor Norman Macdonald, Portree, for this reference and for the reminder of its significance.

10 See for example Eric Richards, *A History of the Highland Clearances: Agrarian Transformation and the Evictions 1746–1886*, London: Croom Helm, 1982; and J. M. Bumstead, *The People's Clearance: Highland Emigration to British North America 1770–1815*, Edinburgh: Edinburgh University Press & The University of Manitoba Press, 1982.

11 *Ris a' Bhruthaich*, p. 51, questioning also the 'silence' about the scandalous experiment in slave-trafficking from Skye in 1739, 'that grim foretaste of the Clearances, *Saoitheach nan Daoine*'

12 Ibid, p. 57

13 Following James Hunter's singling out of the work of Sorley MacLean, another twenty years passed before this subject was revisited – for example, *Tuath is Tighearna*, ed. Donald E. Meek, Edinburgh: SAP for the Scottish Gaelic Texts Society, 1995; and Hugh Cheape, 'Song on the Lowland Shepherds: popular reactions to the Highland Clearances', in *Scottish Economic and Social History* 15 (1995), pp. 85–100.

14 *Ris a' Bhruthaich*, p. 58

15 See *Caran an t-Saoghail*, Donald E. Meek, ed., Edinburgh: Birlinn, 2003

16 Further and more searching exploration of Highland history was not to appear until the 1920s and '30s, with I. F. Grant, *Every-day Life on an Old Highland Farm* (1924), Audrey Cunningham, *The Loyal Clans* (1932) and W. C. Mackenzie, *The Highlands and Isles of Scotland: A Historical Survey* (1937), which was strong for the sixteenth century.

17 Rev. A. Macdonald and Rev. A. Macdonald, *The Macdonald Collection of Gaelic Poetry*, Inverness: The Northern Counties Newspaper and Printing and Publishing Company, 1911, p. 28

18 F. T. MacLeod, 'Notes on the Dunvegan Charter Chest', in *Transactions of the Gaelic Society of Inverness*, Vol. XXVIII (1912–1914), pp. 204–205 & 207

19 *Bàrdachd Ghàidhlig* (second edition), William J. Watson, ed., Glasgow and Stirling: An Comunn Gàidhealach, 1932, p. 140 & pp. 192–94
20 *Sorley MacLean: Critical Essays*, p. 220
21 '… and outside / a wind was crying / *history in my memories* / *history in my memories*': Edinburgh: Birlinn, 1996, pp. 12–17

12. Nature, Socialist Politics and Love in Sorley MacLean's Poetry[1]

NORMAN BISSELL

I met Sorley MacLean just once, twenty-one years ago at Waterstone's bookshop in Glasgow at the launch of his collected poems *O Choille gu Bearradh/From Wood to Ridge*, and he kindly wrote on my copy 'Do Thormod le dùrachd, Somhairle MacGill-Eain 7.4.90'. Like everyone else who has heard him, I was spellbound by the music of his voice and the measured dignity of his reading of his poems.

Since I don't have Gaelic, I'm sorry I can't really do justice to his work or appreciate fully the contribution he made to Gaelic poetry, but I hope that enough will come through in this reading of his work in translation to be of some value.

I went into Waterstone's again recently and asked the young man at the main desk of the biggest bookshop in Glasgow what they had of Sorley MacLean. He asked me 'How do you spell Sorley?' And when I did, he told me they had nothing. When I mentioned this to another member of staff I recognised who used to work in John Smith's, then Ottakars before it was taken over, he smiled and shook his head. I'm sure you'll agree that this tells us more about the sad decline in the book trade than it does about the significance of Sorley MacLean, but it does point up the importance of events like this conference.

In his ground-breaking book *On The Other Side of Sorrow: Nature and People in the Scottish Highlands*, James Hunter showed that the poetry of Sorley MacLean stands proud within the long tradition of literary expression of the natural world which goes back to the Celtic monks, Alasdair Mac Mhaighstir Alasdair and Duncan Bàn MacIntyre. His title is taken from the closing lines of 'An Cuilithionn':

> Beyond the lochs of the blood of the children of men,
> beyond the frailty of plain and the labour of the mountain,
> beyond poverty, consumption, fever, agony,
> beyond hardship, wrong, tyranny, distress,

> beyond misery, despair, hatred, treachery,
> beyond guilt and defilement: watchful,
> heroic, the Cuillin is seen
> rising on the other side of sorrow. (p. 414)

Even in this most political of epic poems he comes back to the mountain and his cherished belief that it symbolises a way of going beyond humanity's self-created problems, if we can but realise this.

Sorley was very aware of this rich literary tradition from his reading of earlier Gaelic poets and from the oral tradition he was brought up in within his family, and his deep feeling for nature comes through in all of his work, but particularly in poems like 'The Heron' and 'The Woods of Raasay'.

In 'The Heron' he observes it closely and precisely:

> A demure heron came
>   and stood on top of sea-wrack.
>   She folded her wings close in to her sides
>   and took stock of all around her.
>
> Alone beside the sea
>   like a mind alone in the universe,
>   her reason like a man's –
>   the sum of it how to get a meal. (p. 2)

He contrasts the single-mindedness of the heron with his own troubled mind:

> I am with you, alone,
>   gazing at the coldness of the level kyle,
>   listening to the surge on a stony shore
>   breaking on the bare flagstones of the world.
> [...]
> My dream exercised with sorrow,
>   broken, awry, with the glitter of temptation,
>   wounded, morose, with but one sparkle;
>   brain, heart and love troubled. (p. 4)

'The Woods of Raasay' has many beautiful passages which describe the woods with great flair and passion:

> The great wood in motion,
>   fresh in its spirit;
>   the high green wood
>   in a many-coloured waulking;
>   the wood and my senses
>   in a white-footed rapture;
>   the wood in blossom
>   with a fleeting renewal.
>
> The sunlit wood
>   joyful and sportive,
>   the many-winded wood,
>   the glittering jewel found by chance;
>   the shady wood,
>   peaceful and unflurried,
>   the humming wood
>   of songs and ditties. (pp. 56–58)

Yet he also speaks of his people and of the love for a woman:

> Graveyard on each south slope of the hillside,
>   the two rich graveyards of half my people,
>   two still graveyards by the sea sound,
>   the two graveyards of the men of Raasay returned,
>
> returned to the repose of the earth
>   from the sun's day of the round sky;
>   a graveyard shaded from the breath of the sea,
>   the two graveyards of the loins of the land. (p. 62)
> [...]
> What is the meaning of giving a woman
>   love like the growing blue of the skies

rising from the morning twilight
naked in the sun? (p. 64)

For Sorley, he and his people were inextricably part of the land and insepa-
rable from nature, and this is to be found throughout his work.

As a young man he was radicalised like so many of his generation by the
spread of fascism in Europe in the 1920s and 1930s and above all by the
bitter struggle in Spain in which Franco's army, with military assistance from
Hitler and Mussolini, triumphed over the Republican forces who had only
ill-equipped international volunteers to aid them. This and his friendship
with Hugh MacDiarmid led him to study Marx and Marxism and to become
a socialist, and one, incidentally, whose political views, particularly his
position on fascism, were more grounded and reliable than MacDiarmid's.

He has many powerful political poems from this period like 'Calvary'
(p. 20), 'Cornford' (p. 26), 'The Clan MacLean' (p. 30), 'A Bolshevik' (p. 134)
and 'Let me lop ...' (p. 134) which reflect with sadness and admiration on
those who have given their lives for the cause like Karl Liebknecht in
Germany, John Cornford, Julian Bell and Garcia Lorca in Spain, and John
Maclean in Scotland, who combined a belief in communism with the need
for Scotland's independence and advocated a Scottish Workers' Republic.

These views would still be considered very challenging in the Highlands
and Islands today, but they must have been incendiary in the 1940s. One of
the most effective of these poems is 'A Highland Woman' (p. 16), which
denounces her back-breaking work and premature death, and the failure
of the Christian religion to offer her any hope in this life. It reminds me of
some of Bertholt Brecht's poems about those nameless people who spend
their lives working without reward or recognition other than by the poet.

Later poems like 'Palach' (p. 260) about the young Czech student Jan
Palach who set fire to himself in Wenceslas Square in January 1969 in protest
at the Russian invasion of Czechoslovakia, and 'The National Museum of
Ireland' (p. 270) about the execution of the Edinburgh socialist James
Connolly in Dublin in 1916, show that he had lost none of his radical politics.

His studies and socialist beliefs equipped him to understand more fully
the historical context of the Clearances and the decline of his language and
culture. That understanding was particularly crucial in the writing of 'An
Cuilithionn'/'The Cuillin'.

A lot has already been said about this poem and time is short, so I will just add that I see it as a mighty struggle in the poet's mind between the forces of darkness, the morass of fascism which is spreading across the world, and the forces of light, led by the Russian Red Army, which are resisting them. These are symbolised by the Skye stallion, first gelded, then rejuvenated, Clio the muse of history, the different coloured roses, the rise of the waves, and by the mountain itself. From the depths of despair in Parts III and IV (pp. 367ff) he sees hope by the end in the strength of the people and the landscape.

This kind of politics marked a real departure in the world of Gaelic poetry and establishes him as a twentieth-century modernist and radical innovator in ways akin to MacDiarmid and his work in Scots.

His *Dàin do Eimhir/Poems to Eimhir* present a sequence of love poems which are also part of a struggle between love and reason, between the heart and the brain, and between his desires and the call of Spain. As Donald MacAulay has famously said, 'After the publication of this book Gaelic poetry could never be the same again.'[2]

It was published in 1943 by William MacLellan, who also published MacDiarmid, and I think it is important today to recognise and appreciate the significant pioneering service that MacLellan gave to poetry in Scotland.

But for me Sorley's most successful love poem is for his brother: 'Elegy for Calum I. MacLean'. Its beginning is stunning:

> The world is still beautiful
> though you are not in it,
> Gaelic is eloquent in Uist
> though you are in Hallin Hill
> and your mouth without speech.
>
> I can hardly think
> that a Gael lives
> and that you are not somewhere to be found
> between Grimsay and the Sound (of Barra),
> kindling ancient memory
> with kindness and fun … (p. 276)

And it traces all the places that Calum touched in his life and what he meant to them and their people, how he hid from his kind the 'four years of agony' before his death, and recounts the other places in which he could have been buried before concluding:

> And though he is not in Clachan
> in Raasay of the MacLeods,
> he is quite as well in Uist.
> His debt was great to Clan Donald. (p. 288)

For Sorley there is no separation between his people and the places where they lived and died, and I believe it is this sense of belonging to a place and love of that place embodied in the Gaelic word *dùthchas* which provides the key to an appreciation of his work as a whole.

In his recent book about Norman MacCaig, *At the Loch of the Green Corrie*, Andrew Greig has some interesting Sorley anecdotes to tell, and one of the most revealing is this:

> When Norman introduced me to Sorley MacLean, last of the high Gaelic bards, a singer of his people's songs who would have been proscribed by the Statutes of Iona, the one who hauled Gaelic poetry into political modernity, the very first thing Sorley said to me was 'And who are your people?'
>
> Not 'How are you?' or 'What do you do?' While Norman looked on amused, I explained my father's family were from Arbroath on the east coast, not part of the clan system, and my mother was from Northumberland.
>
> 'Yes, but who are your people?'
>
> [...]
>
> I later saw him several times, on first meeting a fellow Gael, exchange names, places, occupations, physiognomies, dates until he finally established to his own satisfaction who that person's people were. Then he could relax. Then he knew who that person was. Sorley had that memory and cast of mind to an extraordinary degree, but it was highly typical of his culture.[3]

This is much more than an interest in genealogy. It is the *dùthchas* of his Gaelic heritage. This is what he brings to bear most marvellously in 'Hallaig' and 'Screapadal'.

In 'Hallaig' (p. 230) his love becomes 'a birch, a hazel, a straight, slender young rowan … the girls a wood of birches … their laughter a mist in my ears' and it will slay 'Time, the deer, [which] is in the wood of Hallaig'. His love of the people who were once in that place is so strong that it transcends reality and brings Hallaig back to life.

'Screapadal', one of the last of his *Collected Poems*, also evokes that sense of place and people in detailed descriptions of

> the pine wood dark and green … limestone whiteness in the sun …
> A steep brae with scree-cairns … the dead written names/ of the
> children, men and women / whom Rainy put off the land … [and]
> the periscopes and sleek black sides / of the ships of the death / that
> killed the thousands of Nagasaki, / the death of the great heat and
> the smoke. (pp. 320–28)

The beauty of Screapadal could not be destroyed by those who cleared the people from the land but it is now threatened by the hydrogen and neutron bomb.

'Screapadal' is a warning to us about what is happening to our seas and land as a result of political decisions, and it brings together most tellingly the trinity of Sorley MacLean's passions: his love of nature; his love of the people who once lived there; and his politics, which present such a clear-eyed view of the reality in which we live.

Notes

1 All page references to the poems of Sorley MacLean are to Sorley MacLean, *Caoir Gheal Leumraich/White Leaping Flame*, Christopher Whyte and Emma Dymock, eds, Edinburgh: Polygon, 2011.

2 *Nua-bhàrdachd Ghàidhlig/Modern Scottish Gaelic Poems*, Donald MacAulay, ed., Edinburgh: Southside, 1976, p. 54

3 Andrew Greig, *At the Loch of the Green Corrie*, London: Quercus, 2010, pp. 185–86

13. Visions and Quests in the Poetry of Somhairle MacGill-Eain[1]

MÁIRE NÍ ANNRACHÁIN

Two pervasive concepts underpinning Somhairle MacGill-Eain's poetry are visions and quests. They structure significant portions of it, including the pieces that have acquired the highest status over the decades, such as 'Coilltean Ratharsair', 'Hallaig' and 'Coin is Madaidhean-allaidh'. Images and intimations of visions and quests, and explorations of their effect on each other, are almost ubiquitous, to the point of obsessiveness, as structuring concepts for MacGill-Eain.

'Coilltean Ratharsair'

Consider first 'Coilltean Ratharsair' ('The Woods of Raasay'). After an initial rhapsodic hymn to the woods of Raasay, the main event, so to speak, is the interplay between a mysterious, almost mystical face that appears like a vision to the speaker of the poem and the impulse the face generates in him to leave the island and travel across the sea to Skye. Everything starts out peacefully, with a suggestion of the paradisiacal in the image of beautiful woods, protecting and refreshing the speaker of the poem. Soon, however, a strange vision appears: 'Bhuair aodann sàmhchair choilltean' ('A face troubled the peace of the woodlands')[2]. The speaker rows out to sea towards the golden crown pieces cast by the moon on the water. I have argued elsewhere that the poem is an ironic reversal of Gaelic and international folktales that tell of a young man's journey on a quest, inspired by his love of a young woman.[3] In conventional folktales, a young man often sets out on an arduous quest that requires him to best some form of frightening monster or the like. After successfully completing the quest, the man returns and marries his love. The quest is central to 'Coilltean Ratharsair', where the speaker, presumably a young man, rows out to sea towards the golden coins the moon scattered on its surface, in themselves an unambiguous echo of the treasure that motivated many a quest. He subsequently struggles with the monster he encounters on the Cuillin mountain range: "S e Sgùrr nan Gillean a' bheithir / cholgarra gharbh le cheithir / binneanan carrach ceann-chaol sreathach' ('Sgurr nan Gillean is the fire-dragon, / warlike, terrible with its four / rugged headlong pinnacles in a row').[4] The fight is daunting and heroic against a formidable opponent: 'Thàinig an sitheadh bhon Chuilithionn / … lotadh a' mhaothanachd le uilebheist' ('The thrust came from the Cuilinn / … the tender softness was stung by a monster').[5] The return home is, ironically, not to new life but to death, and his incorporation into his community is not as a fully functioning adult man who has proven himself but as a person who has an affinity with, or at least a consciousness of, a group who have died, the men of Raasay:

> Cladh air dà shlios dheas an fhirich,
>   dà chladh saidhbhir leth mo chinnidh,
>   dà chladh sàmhach air bruaich na linne,
>   dà chladh fir Ratharsair air tilleadh.

> *Graveyard on each south slope of the hillside,*
>   *the two rich graveyards of half my people,*
>   *two still graveyards by the sea sound,*
>   *the two graveyards of the men of Raasay returned.*[6]

Far from winning the woman with the troubling face, the poem ends in disarray, with the wood described as a jewel in *blindness,* and the traditional ending of quests is found to be unreliable: 'chan eil eòlas / air crìoch dheireannaich gach tòrachd' ('there is no knowledge / of the final end of each pursuit'). This represents Gaelic's most recent major statement about the pain and destruction expressed through images of questing, a tradition that extends at least as far back as the Greek myth of Actaeon, who, while out hunting, spied on Diana / Artemis as she bathed and was torn apart by his own hunting dogs, which she turned on him. It is not entirely surprising that Actaeon should be explicitly acknowledged in 'Coilltean Ratharsair', when the speaker says he recognised him: 'b' aithne dhomh Actaeon brùite' ('I recognised the bruised Actaeon').[7]

'Hallaig'

Nowhere is the dynamic of vision and quest more clearly played out than in 'Hallaig'.[8] The subtitle 'Tha tìm, am fiadh, an coille Hallaig' ('Time, the deer, is in the wood of Hallaig') leads us at once into hunting territory, arguably the most iconic form of quest in Scottish Gaelic literature. The deer of the subtitle is introduced into the poem proper towards its end, where the hunting theme is made even more explicit: 'thig peilear dian à gunna Ghaoil; / 's buailear am fiadh a tha ... / a' snòtach nan làraichean feòir' ('a vehement bullet will come from the gun of Love; / and will strike the deer ... / sniffing at the grass-grown ruined homes').[9] Haunting this hunting image is the repeated clearance of the townships of Raasay, and of the township of Hallaig in particular. Sorley MacLean explained in a film directed by Timothy Neat that he succeeded in tracing his family as they were moved – almost hunted – from one townland to another.[10]

The poem's preoccupation is not only with the catastrophic clearance of the people of Raasay and the more general sorrow of inevitable death; it also attempts to generate a redemptive vision. This takes the form of an otherworldly encounter with the dead, who had been cleared and are now deceased, but are resurrected in the trees, which spread unfettered when the people left. The poem is an extraordinary reversal of one of the fundamental tenets of Gaelic poetry, which traditionally maintained that land prospers when its rightful sovereign is in place and ruling wisely, and withers when he dies.[11] This belief was used throughout the classical Gaelic tradition as a means of affirming sovereignty. But in 'Hallaig', in a manner it would be difficult to imagine earlier Gaelic poets endorsing, the land blooms not only despite the catastrophic loss of the people, but indeed directly because of it. The trees have literally taken the place of the cleared people, but in doing so they transcend the obvious, mundane and metonymic type of representation that would derive from their having simply replaced the people within the passage of time. On the contrary, they are metaphori-cally similar to the people to the point where they are in fact a magical, otherworldly representation of them:

> Tha iad fhathast ann a Hallaig,
> Clann Ghill-Eain 's Clann MhicLeòid,

na bh' ann ri linn Mhic Ghille Chaluim:
chunnacas na mairbh beò.

Na fir 'nan laighe air an lèanaig
aig ceann gach taighe a bh' ann,
na h-igheanan 'nan coille bheithe,
dìreach an druim, crom an ceann.

They are still in Hallaig,
MacLeans and MacLeods,
all who were there in the time of Mac Gille Chaluim:
the dead have been seen alive.

The men lying on the green
at the end of every house that was,
the girls a wood of birches,
straight their backs, bent their heads.[12]

Meg Bateman refers to a 'peculiarly reciprocal relationship between man and trees'.[13] She recalls that the medieval text *Auraicept na n-Éces* draws on human rankings to distinguish between 'chieftain, peasant, shrub and herb trees'; and she notes that 'words such as *fiùran, bile, geug, gallan* and *slat* ("sapling", "sacred tree", "branch", "scion" and "shoot") are used interchangeably of both people and trees' in more recent texts. These tropes have such a common currency that they may be considered virtually dead metaphors, though their beauty, particularly in the song tradition in both Scottish Gaelic and Irish, makes such a judgement seem harsh. 'Hallaig' is startlingly radical in its allowing nature to flourish in the exceptionally wrenching absence of the people through clearance as well as death, and simultaneously quite traditional in its representation of people by trees. The metaphoric basis of the older poetry, in which the trees were the vehicle and the people the tenor, as when a young man might be described as a sapling, falls back in 'Hallaig' into a form of otherworldly vision that retains the concept of the trees representing the people.

The Otherworld appears in many facets of the poem, most obviously in the vision of the living dead. It can also be detected in the ghostly connotations of 'tathaich', meaning both 'to haunt' and 'to frequent', the reference being 'far a bheil an sluagh a' tathaich' ('where the people are frequenting / haunting'), as well as other non-realistic details such as 'coiseachd gun cheann' ('endless walk' but also 'headless walk') and the assertion that the girls in their walking return from the land of the living: 'a' tilleadh às a' Chlachan, / à Suidhisnis 's à tìr nam beò' ('returning from Clachan, / from Suidhisnis and from the land of the living').[14] 'Ceò' ('mist'),[15] too, has definite otherworldly connotations, and is very often the site of otherworldly encounters with fairy women, or, in the case of Ireland, with the goddess who personified the land of Ireland. Directly after the subtitle, moreover, the poem starts with an explicit if metaphoric statement that an early way of seeing is suspended, namely his former way of seeing the world from his home, leaving the way open for a new and potentially otherworldly perspective: 'Tha bùird is tàirnean air an uinneig / trom faca mi an Àird an Iar' ('The window is nailed and boarded / through which I saw the west'). In Scottish Gaelic poetry 'Chì mi' ('I see') commonly expresses imagining, remembering, or seeing through second sight. Màiri Bhàn, for instance, in the song 'A Mhàiri Bhàn as Àille Sealladh', when told that her lover and the rest of the crew had drowned, says she can see him in his boat, following the white birds, presumably the day before, as he set out on his last trip: "S chì mi long a' falbh gu siùbhlach ... / 'S mo leannan fhéin làmh 'ga stiùireadh ... / Chì mi, chì mi, chì mi, thall ud, / Chì mi na h-eòin chruinne gheala ... / Mo ghiamanaiche féin 'gan leantail. ('I see a ship travelling swiftly ... / My own lover's hand is steering her ... / I see, I see, I see yonder, / I see the round white birds ... / the hunter himself following.')[16]

There is a dark irony in 'Coilltean Ratharsair', where the normal pattern of the folktale quest comes to nought. A similar dark irony suffuses 'Hallaig', as the encounter with an otherworldly woman, and even an entire population, inverts the normal relations of Gaelic sovereignty, inviting us both to see the cleared people alive in the trees that literally replaced them, and also to accept that nature can flourish despite the destruction of human society. A further irony arises from the sense of inevitable failure, despite what seems at first glance to be a hopeful revision of the traditional Gaelic concept of the sympathetic response by nature to the affairs of humans. Even were the poem's vision of the living dead to offer some relief from the extreme suffering brought about by the facts of history, it would not be enough, for two reasons. First, it has been recognised that the poem acknowledges that its own vision is temporary.[17] The deer of time, introduced in the subtitle, may well be shot, but it is only as long as the 'I', the speaker of the poem, lives that it will be immobilised: 'chan fhaighear lorg air fhuil rim bheò' ('his blood will not be traced while I live').[18] Second, the originary violence of the clearance from the land is neither overcome nor repudiated nor healed; it is rather to be met with an equivalent violence: 'thig peilear dian à gunna Ghaoil' ('a vehement bullet will come from the gun of love').[19] The bullet may be fired from love, but that simply serves to underline the fact that the selfsame act of violence can be claimed by the forces of oppression and of love without distinction, although it is safe to say that most would accept that killing a deer and clearing human communities off their land are of very different orders of magnitude.

'Uamha 'n Òir'

The long and fragmentary poem 'Uamha 'n Òir' ('The Cave of Gold')[20] is an evocative new version of the story of the Lughnasa Musician who entered a cave in search of treasure and was more or less taken prisoner. He is obliged to play music indefinitely in order to ward off the cave's terrifying monster. In Scotland, the tune and accompanying story have become amalgamated with a story about the MacCrimmon pipers. It is a well known vernacular song. Virginia Blankenhorn[21] and Daniel Melia[22] have clarified the various strands of the song in an exemplary fashion, while Máire MacNeill[23] has an excellent account of the original story.

MacGill-Eain's poem is long, difficult and complex. It starts with:

> Chaidh fear a-staigh a dh'Uamha 'n Òir
> is chaoidh e dhìth gun trì làmhan,
> nach robh a dhà dhiubh anns a' phìob
> agus an tèile sa chlaidheamh.

> *A man went into the Cave of Gold*
> *and bewailed his lack of three hands,*
> *that two of them were not on the pipes*
> *and the other on the sword.*[24]

The poem contains a good deal of agonised questioning, not unlike 'Coilltean Ratharsair' and 'An Cuilithionn'. This is overlaid on a narrative that tells of at least two musicians entering the cave, following each other down, and each encountering 'gall' uaine bhàis' ('the green bitch of death').[25] Significantly, the journey, or quest, follows the pattern of 'Coilltean Ratharsair', and clearly represents one of MacGill-Eain's deepest and most obsessive concerns, namely, the abandonment of paradise. The paradisiacal aspects of 'Dùis MhicLeòid' ('the Land of MacLeod') are crystal clear, a place construed as a combination of Gaelic and biblical abundance, with honey and spices, bread and wine, and Gaelic entertainment, the hallmark of a glorious chief in rightful leadership:

> na bruthaichean gorma 's na lochan,
> na rubhannan, na h-eileanan 's na tràighean,
> an t-aran, an fheòil 's am fìon ...

> 's a' mhil 's an spìosraidh air a bhilean
> agus na seilleanan 'na chluasan,
> an sùgradh 's am moladh 's an ceòl,
> na geallaidhean binne 's na duaisean
> is brìodal labhar an òil ...

> *the green braes and the lochs,*
> *the headlands, the islands and the shores,*
> *the bread, the flesh and the wine ...*

> *when the honey and spices were on his lips*
> *and the bees in his ears,*
> *the love-making, the praise and the music,*
> *the sweet promises and the rewards,*
> *and the soft eloquent words of the drink ...*[26]

Paradise was not enough. The poem's first piper embarks on a futile quest into the cave, just as the character in 'Coilltean Ratharsair' left his paradisiacal island to row out to sea. The piper of 'Uamha 'n Òir' is overcome by the experience of death and destruction, not through the frightening monsters of the Cuilithionn but through a green monster in the cave. The poem launches into questions, many of which have to do with trying to understand why he left, when all had been perfect. It focuses on trying to understand the motivation that lay behind precisely the same type of abandonment of paradise that 'Coilltean Ratharsair' narrated. The poem finds no explanation for his leaving, not even the suggestion of clearance, which seems to me to raise interesting questions in a Scottish context, for another day. He was free:

> 's gun e ri cosnadh an dìol-dèirce
> 's gun e ga bhioradh leis an àrdan
> ach rathail làidir sona òg ...

> Cha robh bàirligeadh ann,
> cha robh sgiùrsadh fon ghrèin
> ach am facal diùid fann
> eadar an eanchainn 's an cridhe ...

> *free from the poor wretch's labour,*
> *not pierced by a wounded pride,*
> *strong, fortunate, happy, young ...*

> *There was no summons to quit,*
> *there was no scourge on earth*
> *but the shy faint word*
> *between the brain and the heart ...*[27]

It also seems that the character simply forgot how lucky he was. He even forgot how the day touches the 'grey glue' with gold.[28] This is a far cry from the allure of the mysterious face and the exigencies of history which we saw precipitating the quest in 'Coilltean Ratharsair' and 'Hallaig' respectively. The poem foregrounds the question of motivation but finds no convincing explanation. It shies away from any moral judgement.

At this point a second man leaves a post-lapsarian, desolate, contaminated world, in an attempt to rediscover a lost paradise. He was motivated by a heroic though fruitless combination of despair and courage. His sword was 'heavy and blunt with despair' ('trom is maol leis an eu-dòchas')[29] and he had 'a courage that would not willingly surrender' ('treunt[as] / nach dèanadh strìochdadh ga dheòin').[30] He was also motivated by an inexplicable force that may or may not have been different from despair and courage, and that is characterised as 'sireadh nach do thuig e' ('the quest he did not understand').[31] Here, too, he knew – from the music – that it was highly unlikely that he would ever return, with the result that he too seems to have undertaken a doomed quest, although he also recognised that his art would have strength.

The two men in the cave appear to be two sides of the one person, the first leaving paradise to enter the cave, and the second wandering with eyes wide open from a bad situation into an even worse one in the cave. Both quests are equally inexplicable and doomed. The vision/visual is less important in this poem, because the overriding image is that of music, of its fascination and power. Towards the end of the poem the visual memory of the paradisiacal land of MacLeod has dimmed as the land becomes inaccessible:

> Mo dhìth, mo dhìth
> le ceann is cridhe,
> sùil chiar sa cheann
> 's gun sùil sa chridhe.

> *My lack, my lack*
> *with head and heart,*
> *dim eye in the head*
> *and no eye in the heart.*[32]

This clearly represents a return to the blindness with which 'Coilltean Ratharsair' ended, as well as the frozen eye at the start of 'Hallaig' that is followed by a sadly only temporary vision that suggests a redemptive alternative.

'Coin is Madaidhean-allaidh'

'Coin is Madaidhean-allaidh' ('Dogs and Wolves')[33] is another important poem that produces and reproduces a pattern of vision and quest. A wild careening hunt is described, where the speaker's unwritten poems are described as menacing dogs and wolves 'luath air tòrachd an fhiadhaich' ('swift in pursuit of the quarry'). The quarry is beauty itself, specifically 'fiadh do bhòidhche ciùine gaolaich' ('the deer of your gentle beloved beauty').[34] This reference to 'your beauty', in the penultimate line of a poem of twenty-four lines, announces at almost the last minute that the entire poem was an apostrophic address to the absent beloved, whose absence in life is mirrored by her almost total absence from the poem. It seems that a wish is expressed by the introduction of the beloved after a lengthy and agonised absence, in the body of the poem, that she might make an equivalent appearance late in the day in life. It is a feature of Gaelic songs that they frequently shift between first, second and third person address; in this poem that particular feature is put to good use as a formal expression of the almost complete absence of the beloved.

There is evidence of a type of vision, too, expressed by 'chì mi' ('I see'), the verb referred to above in relation to 'Hallaig' and the only verb in 'Coin is Madaidhean-allaidh' that does not appear as a verbal noun. This absence of active verbs might be considered strange in a poem of such hurtling movement, although admittedly not every verbal noun refers to movement: *a' breacadh, a' leum, a' ruith, a' gabhail, a' sireadh, a' sianail* ('dappling, leaping, running, taking, making for, shrieking'). Together they ensure that the one active verb, 'chì mi' ('I see'), stands alone. Here the specificity of the Gaelic tradition comes into its own and allows this exceptional verbal form to become a clear expression of a world in which normal patterns are inverted. 'Chì mi', in Gaelic, is an obvious invitation to read the whole impossible scenario as an otherworldly vision of wild charging animals. In this context, although the identification of 'mo dhàin neo-dheachdte' ('my unwritten poems') as dogs and wolves is a clear metaphor, more is at stake than a mere metaphor. Modern literary theory may see little distinction between 'my unwritten poems *are* wild dogs' and 'my unwritten poems *are as* wild dogs'. In a specifically Gaelic context, however, where the otherworldly vision is still so recent, so alive, it is more difficult to reduce 'chì mi mo dhàin neo-dheachdte … gadhair chaola 's madaidhean-allaidh' ('I see my unwritten poems … lean greyhounds and wolves') to the metaphor, or more strictly the simile, that would be created by, say, a hypothetical 'chì mi mo dhàin neo-dheachdte mar gum biodh iad nan gadhair chaola is nam madaidh-ean-allaidh' ('I see my unwritten poems as though greyhounds and wolves'). 'I see' still signals strongly the idea of an otherworldly vision. I have argued elsewhere that the relative scarcity of metaphor in most Gaelic poetry is explained by the alternative facility provided by the Otherworld for the expression or construction of an identity that violates truth conditions.[35] This contention is borne out by the otherworldly status of the vision that would be amenable to a metaphoric reading in other cultural contexts.

'Fuaran'

This paper has so far examined a number of MacGill-Eain's best known poems. The pattern of vision and quest is not confined to the iconic pieces but can be found throughout his work, sometimes in ways that are subtle to the point of risking over-interpretation or forcing the text. Mindful of the risk, I offer the following reading of the short and intriguing poem 'Fuaran' ('A Spring').[36] It seems to be that that vision and quest can be seen to structure this poem, albeit obliquely. It is short enough to reproduce the entire text here:

Tha cluaineag ann an iomall slèibh
far an ith na fèidh lus biolaire;
'na taobh sùil uisge mhòr rèidh,
fuaran leugach cuimir ann.

Air latha thàinig mi lem ghaol
gu taobh a' chaochain iomallaich,
chrom i h-aodann sìos ri bhruaich
's cha robh a thuar fhèin tuilleadh air.

Ràinig mi a' chluaineag chèin
a-rithist leam fhèin iomadh uair,
agus nuair choimhead mi san t-srùthlaich
cha robh ach gnùis tè m' ulaidh innt'.

Ach bha na glinn is iad a' falbh
is calbh nam beann gun fhuireach rium,
cha robh a choltas air na slèibhtean
gum facas m' eudail ulaidhe.

At the far edge of a mountain there is a green nook
where the deer eat watercress,
in its side a great unruffled eye of water,
a shapely jewel-like spring.

One day I came with my love
to the side of the remote brook.
She bent her head down to its brink
and it did not look the same again.

I reached the distant little green
many a time again, alone,
and when I looked into the swirling water
there was in it only the face of my treasure-trove.

But the glens were going away
and the pillared mountains were not waiting for me:
the hills did not look
as if my chanced-on treasure had been seen.

There are several references to sight, some of them figurative: 'sùil uisge mhòr rèidh', 'caochan', 'choimhead', 'facas' (respectively 'great unruffled eye of water', 'a brook' but with a suggestion of 'caoch' meaning 'blind', 'when I looked', and 'had been seen'). There are clear indications of strange, magical transformations, as in a vision. 'Cha robh a thuar fhèin tuilleadh' on the water; it did not 'look the same'. The initially reflected face of the beloved remained on the water over time and over the course of many visits. Yet, while this strange fleeting reflection became permanent, the massive landscape, as the mountains, arguably the phenomena least likely to succumb to sudden change, started to move away. The issue is expressed in terms of what was or was not *seen*: 'cha robh a choltas air na slèibhtean / gum facas m' eudail ulaidhe' ('the hills did not look / as if my chanced-on treasure had been seen'). The normal pattern of the world was reversed, became topsy-turvy, non-realist, otherworldly, in a manner reminiscent of the impeded sightline at the start of 'Hallaig' where the window was nailed and boarded, which was followed by a new, otherworldly vision: 'chunnacas na mairbh beò' ('the dead have been seen alive').[37]

Just as the visionary dimension of this poem is clear, the same can be said of a form of quest or hunt. I read this poem as a transformation of what is inarguably one of the most beautiful songs in Scottish Gaelic, 'Òran an Amadain Bhòidhich', often known as 'Mairead Òg',[38] a song on which MacGill-Eain commented,[39] and by which he was influenced. He identified with the plight of its speaker or composer, An t-Amadan Bòidheach ('The Handsome Fool'), most notably in Dàin do Eimhir XIII, where he identifies his beloved with a veritable list of renowned literary or quasi-literary heroines, including Deirdre, Maeve of Connacht, Maud Gonne and 'Mairearad an Amadain Bhòidhich' ('the Handsome Fool's Margaret'). An unwarranted sense of modesty made him reject the suggestion that he was on a par, as an artist, with An t-Amadan Bòidheach, asserting rather that they were not compa-rable: 'Agus a chionn nach mise … 'n t-Amadan Bòidheach' ('And since I am not … the Handsome Fool').[40] 'Mairead Òg' tells of the accidental shooting of his young wife by a young man, who is then driven mad with grief. His mother, hostile to his wife, sent her out to wash the clothes in a nearby loch and sent her son out to shoot ducks, with evil intent. It is, therefore, a song which has an episode of hunting or fowling (a typical quest) at its heart, but in 'Fuaran' this is transformed into the type of vision I described above. The evidence for seeing 'Mairead Òg' as an intertext is subtle but persuasive. Consider the pool of water, for instance, the loss of one's love, and in particular the linguistic echoes. Compare, for instance,

> Ràinig mi a' chluaineag chèin
> a-rithist leam fhèin iomadh uair,
> agus nuair choimhead mi san t-srùthlaich
> cha robh ach gnùis tè m' ulaidh innt'.

with 'Mairead Òg': 'Nuair ràinig mi an linne chaol / 'S ann bha mo ghaol a' sruladh innt'.'

This is sufficient for me at any rate to hear 'Mairead Òg', a song of tragic hunting and the loss of love, as a deep intertext in 'Fuaran'. A separate question relates to the interpretation of the content of MacGill-Eain's poems

– the absence of the beloved – with that of the earlier song, where the young man unwittingly killed his love as he carried out his family's instructions, but that is beyond the scope of this paper.

'Traighean'

Finally, I refer briefly to 'Tràighean' ('Shores'),[41] a poem in which a number of sea shores, those of Talisker on Skye, Calgary on Mull, Hòmhsta on Uist, Moidart on the mainland, and finally Mol Stenscholl in Staffin on Skye, are imagined in sequence, like a journey around Skye, out to its neighbours, finally returning to Skye. This journey is pitted against the Otherworld in various guises, as though the geographical journey were to be interrupted by impossible events, such as the horse-shaped mountain ridge Priseal bowing his head, the arrival of the day of doom ('luan'), and an eternal wait: 'dh'fheithinn-sa … gu sìorraidh' ('I would wait … forever'). It may stretch the text to interpret these otherworldly events as forms of vision, but if so, the stretch is small, and in the context of MacGill-Eain's complete work has, I believe, some authenticity. This preoccupation with the vision and quest in his work is closely linked in this poem with two notable features of traditional Gaelic love songs. They frequently express the desire to be in a far-away place with the beloved, often a remote wilderness, and they frequently say that they will love the beloved until some impossible or miraculous event might occur. To take just one example of each, see first 'Gur Tu Mo Chruinneag Bhòidheach': 'Dheighinn leat an ear 's an iar … Dheighinn a Dhùn Èideann leat, / gu sràid nan ceuman còmhnard … Dheighinn leat a dh'Èirinn, / gu fèill nam mnathan òga … Dheighinn leat a dh'Uibhist … Dheighinn leat a Shlèibhte/ is nam b' fheudar dhan an Òlaind' ('I would travel east and west [with you] … I would travel to Edinburgh with you, to the street of the level pathways … I would go with you to Ireland, to the feast of the young women … I would with you to Uist … I would go with you to Sleat and if necessary to Holland').[42] Second, 'A Dhòmhnaill nan Dòmhnall' expresses a desire for the impossible : 'nam biodh tu mar shionnach / air an tulaich ud thall,/ agus mise mar eala / air bharraibh nan tonn, / Nàile! Rachainn ad choinneamh …' ('… if you had been a fox / on that hill over there, / and I had been a swan / on the tops of the waves / och! I'd have gone to meet you').[43]

Conclusion

In this paper I have looked at a small number of examples of the ways in which visions and quests together underpin MacGill-Eain's poetry. I have suggested that 'Coilltean Ratharsair' offers a dark and ironic retelling of what seems to be a fundamental concern in traditional folktales, namely the pursuit of love, via a right-of-passage quest that acts as a test; that 'Hallaig' attempts to come to terms with a darker original form of hunt or quest, namely that of the Clearances, and in doing so shifts gear from displacement from the land into the final displacement through death, but in doing so fails to find any lasting redemption; and 'Uamha 'n Òir' completes a trinity of poems in its exploration of a third type of quest, one that appears to have no meaning, is quite mysterious, and yet compelling. 'Coin is Madaidhean-allaidh', 'Fuaran' and 'Tràighean' offer further examples of the repetition of the pattern. The latter two show only faint evidence of a vision and a quest, but the trace can be seen within the context of MacGill-Eain's overall work. 'Fuaran' resonates with the vision and the quest primarily by aligning itself with 'Mairead Òg'; 'Tràighean' does so by echoing the encounter between named places and otherworldly experiences we saw earlier in 'Coilltean Ratharsair' and 'Hallaig'.

The list is far from exhaustive. Many further questions remain unexamined, primary among which is the effectiveness of the vision and the quest, either singly or together, as strategies for overcoming various challenges, in particular that of death, a question to which I hope to return.

Notes

1   A portion of this paper appeared initially in Irish in my *Aisling agus Tóir: An Slánú i bhFilíocht Shomhairle MhicGill-Eain*, Maigh Nuad: An Sagart, 1992. This paper expands on that analysis and offers a flavour of the original publication to a readership unfamiliar with Irish.

2   MacLean, *Caoir Gheal Leumraich*, pp. 60–61

3   Ní Annracháin, Máire, 'Sorley MacLean's "The Woods of Raasay"' in *Lainnir a' Bhùirn/ The Gleaming Water: Essays on Modern Gaelic Literature,* Emma Dymock and Wilson McLeod, eds, Edinburgh: Dunedin Academic Press, pp. 71–86

4   *Caoir,* pp. 60–61

5   Ibid, pp. 62–63

6   Ibid, pp. 62–63

7   Ibid, pp. 62–63

8   Ibid, pp. 230–31

9   Ibid, pp. 234–35

10   Neat, Timothy (film), *Hallaig: the Poetry and Landscape of Sorley MacLean*: The Island House Film Workshop, 1984

11   Ní Annracháin, Máire, 'Where Shall Wisdom be Found? Somhairle MacGill-Eain's Answer to Job' in *Cànan & Cultar/Language & Culture: Rannsachadh na Gàidhlig 4*, Gillian Munro and Richard A.V. Cox, eds, Edinburgh: Dunedin Academic Press, 2006, pp. 127–49

12   *Caoir*, pp. 232–233

13   Bateman, Meg, 'The image of the tree in Gaelic culture' in *Rannsachadh na Gàidhlig 6*, Nancy R. McGuire & Colm Ó Baoill, eds, Aberdeen: An Clò Gàidhealach, 2013, p. 35

14   *Caoir*, pp. 232–33

15   Ibid, pp. 234–35

16   Campbell, John Lorne, ed., *Songs Remembered in Exile*, Aberdeen: AUP, 1990, p. 187

17   MacInnes, John, *Dùthchas nan Gàidheal*, ed. Michael Newton, Edinburgh: Birlinn, 2006, p. 419

18   *Caoir*, pp. 234–35

19   Ibid, pp. 234–25

20   Ibid, pp. 294–15

21   Blankenhorn, V. S., 'Traditional and Bogus Elements in MacCrimmon's Lament, *Scottish Studies* 22, 1978, pp. 45–67

22   Melia, D. F., 'The Lughnasa Musician in Ireland and Scotland', *Journal of American Folklore*, 1967, pp. 365–73

23   MacNeill, Máire, 'The Musician in the Cave', *Béaloideas* 57, 1989, pp. 109–32

24   *Caoir*, p. 294

25   Ibid, pp. 310–11

26   Ibid, pp. 296–97

27   Ibid, pp. 296–97

28   Ibid, p. 298

29   Ibid, pp. 298–99

30   Ibid, pp. 300–01

31   Ibid, pp. 302–03

32   Ibid, pp. 312–13

33   Ibid, pp. 132–35

34   Ibid, pp. 134–35

35   Ní Annracháin, Máire, 'An Teanga Fhíortha' in *Téacs agus Comhthéacs: Gnéithe de Chritic na Gaeilge*, M. Ní Annracháin and B. Nic Dhiarmada, eds, Cork: CUP, 1998, pp. 348–49

36   *Caoir*, pp. 6–7

37   Ibid, pp. 232–33

38   Gillies, Anne Lorne, *Songs of Gaelic Scotland*, Edinburgh: Birlinn, 2010, pp. 348–49

39   MacGill-eain (sic), Somhairle, *Ris a' Bhruthaich: Criticism and Prose Writings*, ed. William Gillies, Stornoway: Acair, 1985, p.24

40   *Caoir*, pp. 108–09

41   Ibid, pp. 140–41

42   *Songs of Gaelic Scotland*, pp. 423–24

43   Ibid, pp. 339–40

14. Editing MacLean: an Interview with Christopher Whyte

Christopher Whyte's contribution to the 2011 conference corresponded very closely with his introductory essay in the book An Cuilithionn 1939 and Unpublished Poems, *which he edited and which was launched as part of the conference. He preferred to make his contribution to this book via an interview, and an edited transcript of a conversation with Ian MacDonald follows.*

IMD: Christopher, when did you first come across the poetry of Sorley MacLean?

CW: While I was still studying at Cambridge, very, very late one night in somebody's flat close to Glasgow University, I spoke to a man called John Manson, from Coatbridge (not, I think, the John Manson who subsequently became known as working on MacDiarmid). He had retained his class and his nationalist affiliations despite three years at Cambridge. He told me that MacDiarmid had read more than either Pound or Eliot and that I had to read MacDiarmid's *Lucky Poet*. That was the book that unlocked the whole treasure-chest of modern Scottish literature for me. I wasn't particularly aware of it, but I'm sure that's where the first mention of Sorley MacLean came to me. I actually read some of the poems, in Iain Crichton Smith's translations, in a bookshop in Gower Street in London in 1974 or 1975, and decided I really had to learn Gaelic, in order to have direct access to MacLean. In the spring of 1975 I went regularly to the Mitchell Library with a notebook and copied out large swathes of the 1943 book, *Dàin do Eimhir agus Dàin Eile*, not really understanding very much – it was a kind of hieroglyphics to me at the time. That's when I noticed that, infuriatingly, there were gaps in the numbering of the poems and that the original text as published was incomplete. It sowed the seeds of a curiosity which led me to produce, nearly thirty years later, the edition that was published by the ASLS in 2002.

IMD: Well, you've done more than anyone to fill the gaps. When did you actually first meet Sorley MacLean himself?

CW: It was in August 1984, in the staff club in Edinburgh University. I had been in Italy for some ten years at that point. I knew very few people in Scotland, and was trying to translate the fullest possible text of the *Dàin do Eimhir* into Italian. About twelve of these poems were published in a literary review called *Linea d'Ombra*, based in Milan. The problem was that I was working with Dwelly, Roderick Mackinnon's *Teach Yourself Gaelic* and MacLaren's book on Gaelic. There were passages I just could not understand. I wrote to Sorley MacLean and Derick Thomson, asking to see them, so that I could get more information. Sorley arranged for us to meet late one afternoon – for some reason I think it was a Thursday – in the Edinburgh University Staff Club, Adam House, which at that time was the Festival Club.

It was a very strange occasion, because we were completely at cross-purposes. All I wanted was to show him the problematic passages, so that he could explain the idioms and give me a literal English translation. But it became clear that Sorley's intention was very different: he wanted to tell me the story behind the poems. I was distinctly embarrassed and felt it was slightly inappropriate, because I thought: 'Who am I for him to be sharing this apparently very intimate material with?' And a part of me couldn't help thinking: 'Well, clearly I'm not the first neophyte to present himself and to be initiated into the mysteries of the love story.' I went away from that meeting quite frustrated, because I hadn't got what I wanted. A few days later I went to see Derick Thomson in his office at Glasgow University. Derick explained the passages to me perfectly well, which was what I was looking for, and sent me away.

That meeting with MacLean was an odd one. I didn't get what I was looking for, I got something I wasn't looking for and, at the time, wasn't particularly interested in. I don't know what account Sorley would have given of the meeting – probably it didn't register very strongly in his memory. But for me it has a haunting quality, even over thirty years later. That was my first encounter with MacLean.

In the course of it he actually told me that one of the two men associated with the Scottish Eimhir had been 'a notorious homosexual' – his very words. It didn't occur to him that the person he was speaking to might be homosexual too! For me, it was very peculiar, coming on another gay man at the heart of the tangled web which had given rise to the greatest Gaelic love poetry of the twentieth century.

In 1990 I published an essay called 'The Cohesion of *Dàin do Eimhir*' (of course, Sorley was still alive at the time) which very much went in the face of his own presentation of the cycle after 1977, because the essay said that this was really a complete work with its own organic structure and meaning, and that the poems needed to be put back together as a sequence. I never heard anything about his own reaction. By that stage, I was somebody who had a strong association with Derick Thomson. This may have coloured his attitude to me on the few other occasions when we did meet.

IMD: Well, even in those days when you first encountered MacLean, there were still gaps in the published material. We now have *An Cuilithionn 1939*, which is the original version and which is fairly different from the version which was published much later, first of all partly in *Gairm*, then in *Chapman*, and then as part of the collected poems, *O Choille gu Bearradh*, shorn of about a quarter of its length. Why do you think it's important to have that first version of 'An Cuilithionn'?

CW: My own feeling is that MacLean was undisputedly a genius. He was a poet of such stature that everything he wrote needs to come into the public domain. And as an editor, for example of the unpublished poems, I don't feel like saying I saw forty-five poems and, in my opinion, these are the ones that deserve to get into print. I think it is standard practice for writers of this stature (it is happening quite early with MacLean) for everything to come into the public domain, with the idea that within twenty or thirty years some sort of a consensus will be reached about the quality and the importance of this material. The later 'An Cuilithionn' is an abridgement. That is an absolutely accurate statement. MacLean went in for cutting and pasting. The additional material doesn't go much over twenty lines, mostly in dribs and drabs here and there. So it's fair to say that everything that's there in 1989 was already there in 1939.

IMD: You're saying there's been almost no rewriting?

CW: A very little rewriting, but it's basically an abridgement. The person who reviewed *Caoir Gheal Leumraich* for the *Edinburgh Review* got the wrong end of the stick. The original version was never published. The reviewer speaks of the newly published materials as if it were a question of prologues, which it's not. It was a matter of putting back the bits that had been cut out. Almost everyone who has read one of these sections, which Emma Dymock, my co-editor on the collected poems, speaks of as 'the Cuillin praise song' (it's part of Section VII), seems to agree it is one of the pinnacles of MacLean's achievement. Until June 2011 this was unpublished; it simply had not got into print. There is little room for argument about the importance of bringing the original version into the public domain so that discussion can start. It's a very different poem architecturally.

One issue is MacLean's subsequent claims that 'An Cuilithionn' was unfinished. It's hard to find evidence from around the time of writing that this was the case. When I originally asked MacLean, at that first meeting, about the missing *Dàin do Eimhir,* he spoke of a lost notebook. But the material was available in the special collections at Aberdeen University Library. There were also various copies among MacLean's papers, and so it's almost like – how can I say this? – coming across someone who wants to give a different version of himself four decades later. The two versions of 'An Cuilithionn', if you like, reflect two very different MacLeans, with the added fact of the second version being an abridgement. The architecture of the 1939 poem suggests to me a completed whole with its own echoes and anticipations, its own verbal echoes and key words.

IMD: And I think at one point, decades ago, when he was writing to Douglas Young, he did use the words 'when I finished "The Cuillin" about New Year 1940'.

CW: Yes. Yes.

IMD: And at the same time, in the newest collected poems (*Caoir Gheal Leumraich*) you've published what you might call the 1989 version of 'An Cuilithionn', and you're giving that, as it were, its own status as almost a different kind of artefact, although they are clearly closely related.

CW: I think that's a diplomatic position, correct and appropriate at the present moment. My own gut feeling is that the 1939 poem should take precedence. I wouldn't be surprised if, in forty or fifty years' time, that will be the text that is given central place, rather than the 1989 abridgement. But the 1939 poem entered the public domain in June 2011. The new *Collected* was published in November 2011. It's far too early to make that substitution. There needs to be an ongoing critical debate and then, within twenty or thirty years, some sort of a consensus may emerge – as I think a consensus has emerged to the effect that *Dàin do Eimhir* should be read as a sequence, rather than as scattered, unconnected individual poems.

IMD: Just for clarity: you said there was very little rewriting or new material in the 1989 'An Cuilithionn'. Is there much in the way of rearrangement?

CW: No. There have been no significant changes to the order of the passages, just some minor adjustments. Passages have been cut – that's all. Some of the most topical passages which were cut are at this distance of time absolutely fascinating – for example, attacks on individual figures. It would appear that one of these was the headmaster of Portree High School – the new headmaster who was one of the reasons why MacLean went to Mull. Then there's Flora MacLeod of Dunvegan. It's understandable that, in 1989, MacLean should have felt a degree of embarrassment, but nowadays I think this adds to our fascination, because it's very much a poem of its time, of those months preceding the outbreak of war and immediately following it, which in terms of European history constitute a crucial moment.

IMD: I suppose he was under pressure from other individuals too, as well as from his own feelings to do with the politics of the poem. For example, I think that at one point Robin Lorimer said to Sorley in writing: 'Do you *believe* this now? If not, should you excise these lines? The test is do you *want* to say this now?' So there were pressures.

CW: For me you are connecting to another very important aspect of 'An Cuilithionn', namely, that the poem was disowned by MacLean as early, probably, as 1944–45, partly under the influence of Sydney Goodsir Smith, with whom MacLean and his wife shared a flat in Edinburgh. Goodsir Smith had taught English to members of the Polish army in exile, and so had direct information about the behaviour of the Soviet troops when they approached Warsaw. This would appear to have had a ricochet effect on MacLean, who felt the need to distance himself from what he himself had written about Stalin and the Red Army.

But the poem brings us face to face with the whole issue, during the preceding two decades, of the collusion of Western intellectuals and writers in the Bolshevik and, more particularly, the Stalinist experiment in Soviet Russia. That's a hugely important issue, particularly now that Soviet Russia no longer exists. How could so many brilliant men – principally males, because there's a gender aspect to this too, of 'macho' toughness – knowingly, or unknowingly, lend their support to an absolutely criminal regime which was one of the victors in the war (one more reason why it was so difficult to say the truth about them). Now, I think this is a source of profound embarrassment when one reads 'An Cuilithionn'. It's certainly a source of embarrassment for me. I believe that embarrassment to be, potentially, very fruitful. It connects us to something that goes way beyond the field of Gaelic writing, or even Scottish writing, to what I would call 'leftism', namely the enthusiastic support offered by people, by intellectuals, living in western parliamentary democracies, for a totalitarian regime operating on the far side of Europe. Almost nobody put their ideas into practice and went to live under that regime. The turn-of-the-century German painter Heinrich Vogeler was one. But there were remarkably few.

IMD: Ironically, I suppose the point might be made, though I'm not sure that any of those people you mention made it, that the Russian contribution to the victory over Germany in the Second World War was a crucial one. But I don't recall hearing that that was said, even though, as I understand it, a lot of barbarity was involved as well as a kind of by-product of that.

CW: I think that these are very interesting questions. Ian, you'll know that for the last seven years I've lived in Hungary, in Budapest, and let's say that in that context the heroic discourse about the Red Army's liberation of Eastern Europe doesn't really hold, it doesn't ring true – because this was perceived as one more catastrophe (though at the same time, it has to be said that it ensured the survival of a significant proportion of Budapest's Jewish population). There's a joke that, in Vienna, people are supposed to have said they could survive a Third

World War but they could never survive a third liberation! There are whole areas here that have been comparatively unexplored – for example, in Germany in the last five years people have begun to talk about the systematic raping of German women that took place at the hands of Russian soldiers. There are associated questions, such as 'Can a German civilian be a victim?' and 'Can a German soldier be a victim?' Then there is the vexed question of which was worse: Bolshevism or Nazism? I don't think it's useful to try and answer it. I do think the fact that the Red Army defeated the Nazi army in Eastern Europe doesn't justify any of the things that went on. MacLean's later attitude to 'An Cuilithionn' suggests that he was for a while of the same opinion.

While I was working on the edition of *An Cuilithionn 1939*, I was also translating the poetry of Marina Tsvetaeva (1892–1941) from Russian into English. This was very reassuring for me. Although I was very keen to do the edition, to some extent it meant looking backwards to something I had left behind – Scotland and academic life. I needed to have a foot in both camps, if you like: a foot in Gaelic Scotland and a foot in something much broader. I could say translating Marina Tsvetaeva offered me a balance. It even kept me sane, given that returning to work on MacLean's poetry, five years after abandoning Scotland, felt like being dragged back into the past – not quite kicking and screaming, but nearly!

After seventeen years in emigration, Tsvetaeva returned to the Soviet Union in June 1939, very much against her better judgement. Within four months, both her husband and her daughter, enthusiastic supporters of Stalin, had been arrested. Her daughter was pregnant, by a man who turned out to have been an informer for the regime. She was so badly beaten with rubber truncheons during interrogation that she lost her child. This happened precisely while MacLean was working on 'An Cuilithionn'. It was standard practice at the time. The daughter was rehabilitated in 1956 – in other words, she got a certificate saying the charges against her were totally unfounded, even though she had signed a full confession.

It's a small detail, concerning one woman out of thousands, but it should be sufficient to make any of us read 'An Cuilithionn' with profound discomfort. The discomfort provoked is what makes this poem so important. Placing that event beside the idealisation of Stalin in MacLean's poem sets all sorts of crucial questions resonating. It raises the hugely disturbing question of the prolonged support offered by writers and intellectuals in the West for a regime characterised by an appalling degree of criminality systematically applied. The fact that Stalin's armies defeated Hitler's does nothing to change the nature of the regime he headed. Within five years of writing 'An Cuilithionn', MacLean became totally alienated from his poem for these very reasons. It would be wonderful if they made it a bad poem, but they don't. You can write splendid poetry in support of a mistaken political cause. MacLean was not the only one to get it wrong – far from it.

I don't think we should try to avoid this paradox, that it was Stalin's Russia that defeated Hitler. We need to look it in the face.

The most surprising thing about the 2011 conference for me was the violent reaction provoked by anyone daring to criticise MacLean's leftist affiliations – as if that were still unacceptable in Scotland today, for men of my own age or slightly older. I'm not sure, but I suspect this may be what led Aonghas MacNeacail to speak of my introduction as 'tendentious' when he reviewed the edition. I say 'men' deliberately, because MacLean's sympathies for Soviet Russia have a decidedly 'macho' tinge. Showing how tough you are by backing, even in retrospect, a supposedly tough regime ('inhuman', 'criminal' or 'amoral' might be more appropriate words) still holds its charms for some people today. 'An Cuilithionn' is an aggressively masculine poem. Apart from a reference to the Eimhir figure and Màiri Mhòr, given third place among its patrons, the only other female presence, Lenin's widow Krupskaya, was rapidly excised.

IMD: The book *An Cuilithionn 1939 and Unpublished Poems* was launched at the conference and you spoke very eloquently about it in a way reminiscent of the way you're speaking now. *Caoir Gheal Leumraich*, the latest and largest collected edition, which is fairly close to being complete, came out in November 2011, some five months after the conference on MacLean, and it's interesting that the photographs of MacLean which we see on the front and on the back cover show him as a fairly young man. Now, we've become used to those superb photographs by Jessie Ann Mathew and Sam Maynard and Timothy Neat and various other people – memorable photographs of him in his late middle age or old age – but I take it that here the policy is to remind us that most of the great poetry was composed by a much younger MacLean. Where did the idea of using the youthful photographs come from?

CW: It came from the poet's daughter, Ishbel Maclean, and it seems to me a splendid idea because it underlines the fact that, when you approach MacLean's poetry now, you are confronted by two different people. The young man who wrote the poetry, he says in a letter to Douglas Young, was near suicidal much of the time because of his emotional involvement with the Scottish Eimhir. He had a strong sympathy for Bolshevism, and saw it, if you like, as the only hope of defeating fascism, as did many intellectuals of the time. I'm also pretty sure that when he went to fight in the war he believed he wouldn't come back. And if that creates desperation, it also certainly loosens your tongue because, if death is round the corner, there's no reason why you shouldn't go to the heart of the matter and say everything that needs to be said.

The older MacLean was, I think, embarrassed to a certain extent by the younger figure, and embarrassed by some of the things that he had said. He was a very respected member of a Highland community, a headmaster with a crucial role there – a totally different set of circumstances. He had been unjustly denied recognition and celebration for three or four decades and finally he was getting something of what he deserved. So his attitude to the material and to that younger man was very ambivalent. My own experience as editor involved having to confront these two figures. Because the older MacLean, if you like, had had his say, for me as editor it was important to bring the younger MacLean out in all his uncomfortable, sometimes scandalous sincerity. That's why the photographs on the cover of the book are so splendid and convey something of the same message – that sense of an edge of danger.

IMD: I think that one thing no-one would dispute is MacLean's courage and the depth of his feelings for people's suffering, and I must say that I found it moving when in the National Library to be able to handle some of the material that he actually had with him in the desert and wrote on – some of the notebooks.

CW: Something that's worth broaching is the knotty question of a biography of MacLean, and certainly, as far as I can see, MacLean's conduct regarding each of the two women he bracketed underneath the name of Eimhir was impeccable. What brings this to mind when you talk about the war is that it's clear MacLean would have loved to go to fight in Spain but for family reasons was unable to go. I hope I'm getting my facts right here. He asked to be released from his teaching job at Boroughmuir and go and fight, but he was told that, if he did, his salary would no longer be paid, and he was supporting his family to a significant extent. And so, in the midst of this maelstrom of emotional and political affiliations, MacLean also shouldered responsibility for his siblings, and, as I say, his conduct was exemplary.

The whole story around the Scottish Eimhir is a rather murky affair. She would seem to have been what they call in French a *mythomane*, a mythomaniac, a woman who invented fascinating stories about what was happening to her. And one hopes that, when a biography is eventually written, shame can be overcome, the unneeded shame, and we can simply be told the truth, for the actual facts are the raw material from which the poetry was made and that transmuting is a crucial process. But the facts are important; they are of interest. In the introduction to the new collected poems, *Caoir Gheal Leumraich*, I quoted a Hungarian author speaking about Goethe and Thomas Mann who said that geniuses are not just important for their work. The way he or she acts from day to day has an effect on the people around and on the society – what I have in mind is the socially performative aspect of genius: the people they talk to, the things they say, the sexual and other relations they establish. And unfortunately, if you are a genius of this stature, all of that is part of the larger picture, so that I hope that when a biography of MacLean has to be written it will be an absolutely open one.

This is a very problematic area in Scotland. Alan Bold's biography of MacDiarmid constitutes a model because MacDiarmid's conduct was repeatedly shameful in a number of situations and this doesn't lessen the poetry, but Bold faces this head-on. And I hope that

MacLean's biographer will simply tell the truth about the lived material from which this wonderful poetry was made.

In the introduction to *Caoir Gheal Leumraich* there's quite a lot about a concert in December 1939 where Beethoven's 8th was played, which would appear to have given direct inspiration for *Dàin do Eimhir* XXIII, a very important poem. In the Aberdeen manuscript, it carries a subtitle: 'Eimhir and Beethoven's 8th'. One of the reasons that that concert is so significant is that so far it is the only documentary evidence for the name of the Scottish Eimhir. We know from the letters that MacLean considered dedicating the volume to AM, and – not in that concert programme but in a programme from the same series given by the same orchestra – someone whose name matches these initials appears among the second violins. The same name is still current in oral discourse in Edinburgh, and so quite a lot of people would associate it with the Scottish Eimhir. I don't know if that's enough to clinch the matter.

Another name current in oral discourse in Edinburgh is that of the other man, the '*gille-mirein*'. And I hope that whoever decides to do the biography will succeed in unearthing this rather lurid but very fascinating story about the kind of goings-on that were happening because, if the Scottish Eimhir was associating with a man who was a notorious homosexual in Edinburgh society, was she covering up for him? Exactly what was going on? Exactly what sort of hands did this poor, passionate, highly strung and rather naive Highlander from Raasay fall into? And in spite of all the suffering it caused him I can't find it in myself to regret this happening because of the poetry which emerged as a result.

IMD: You yourself have used the term *fabula,* as in 'a poet's *fabula*'. When I first came across MacLean's poetry when I was a schoolboy there seemed to be a fair consensus that the situation was, as might be thought from a reading of the poems, that he couldn't go to Spain because of his love for Eimhir. We then realised that there were more pressing reasons, in some ways more everyday reasons – economic reasons, because he was supporting his family. And you yourself have taken the debate a bit further – in that, clearly, these are love poems, love poems to an individual, in this case two individuals at least (maybe more!), but there is also something else involved, to do with the poet's realisation of himself as a poet, and to some extent this comes through in the poems as well.

CW: I absolutely agree with you that one of the dominant themes of the sequence is: 'I became a great poet by writing this piece of work.' That modelling oneself as a poet, as a figure, through the poems (Douglas Young refers to this too), is almost as important as the love story itself.

Patrick Crotty, in a very welcome and beautifully written review in the *TLS*, suggests that the sequence isn't so fundamental as a much larger group of Eimhir poems generally, and that it's not useful to reconstruct the sequence or pick it out. I think this is wrong. I believe MacLean had clear criteria for what could and could not go into the sequence. Any poem that reflected poorly on the Eimhir figure needed to be excluded. Poems expressing his subsequent disillusionment also couldn't find their way into the *Dàin do Eimhir* proper. It's also worth saying, still on this point, that it would appear that as MacLean was writing the poems he numbered them, so that when he composed a poem he knew this was Poem XXXVI or Poem LII. But he did make mistakes. There is no evidence that he actually destroyed anything. The missing VII, if you ask me, could be a simple oversight. Thanks to your own discovery of an unpublished poem among the Aberdeen papers, we now know he wrote *two* poems for No. XLVI. At quite an early stage he also started removing poems, but I think there are still huge arguments for reading the Eimhir sequence primarily as a unit, as a whole, and then having a larger, surrounding field, as it were, of connected and supporting poems still focusing on the love theme.

IMD: Yes, and there are several memorable poems on the same topic which are outwith the sequence. I think the one which starts 'An tè dhan tug mi uile ghaol' is an extraordinarily fine and beautiful poem. There are others too. But I'm not sure myself that what we now know as Poems XLVI and XLVII might not have sat more comfortably outside the sequence, as they bring in the personal to a very considerable degree. But that's just a thought.

CW: They are poems that express, in a very uncomfortable way, the erotic tension of the relationship, a suppressed erotic tension, and as you remember, there are three poems that appear to be closely related, Nos. XL, XLVI and XLVII – and in No. XL it is 'Mo Rùn Geal Dìleas' which he is rewriting.

IMD: Yes, these seem to have been regarded as particularly sensitive by MacLean and they weren't published until 1970 (in *Lines Review*). I don't have the same problem with XL as I do with XLVI and XLVII. In those it's as if a certain kind of autobiographical reality has broken in, broken through the sheen of the rest of the sequence. The sequence is influenced by what used to be called 'the Allegory of Love'; it has that behind it. You yourself have shown it has many other things behind it too.

CW: There's also the early poem, No. VI, which has been restored to the sequence, but was presumably removed because it makes explicit reference to the fact of there being at least two women behind the Eimhir figure. When he was preparing the sequence for publication, MacLean may have thought that was too dissonant, and so he pushed it into the *Dàin Eile*.

IMD: Another term you have used is *psychomachia*. How would you define that?

CW: I define that as personifying different elements of the poet's psyche and transcribing the dialogue between them – the way they speak to one another. The famous poem that begins 'Choisich mi cuide ri mo thuigse' is an example. There's a terrible sense of an eternal dividedness that cannot be overcome, and it's almost like staging the psychological conflict, making a play of it, making theatre of it. And, of course, it's a term that goes back to the study of medieval literature, doesn't it?

IMD: All that said, I think we can hardly be surprised that MacLean wondered about which poems to put in. He was corresponding with Douglas Young, who was a friend and advisor, and to some extent a mentor, I think – a sounding-board and, on the whole, a wonderful support for him – but MacLean kept changing his mind about the poetry: 'We'll put that one in …' 'No, keep these out …', and so on. I think that in view of the turbulence of his personal circumstances and the European situation and the depth of his feelings about all these matters, it's not surprising that he was pulled one way and then another. I wonder now if, looking down from wherever he is, he is probably on the whole happy that the whole sequence has been reconstituted and that all but one of the gaps that were there for a considerable time have been filled. And in addition, of course, a fair number of poems that had never seen the light of day have been published in *An Cuilithionn 1939 and Unpublished Poems* – forty-five of them, of which twenty-eight are reprinted in the new collected volume. And so we have a very full picture now.

CW: You've touched on a lot of different points. The MacLean–Young correspondence, of which Emma Dymock is preparing an edition, which is eagerly awaited – that's a milestone in twentieth-century Scottish literature. But by the time MacLean was writing to Young about the sequence he already knew how much he had been lied to by the Scottish Eimhir, and he would have been inhuman if this had not affected his attitude. The other thorny point is that we cannot honestly rely on MacLean's judgement of which are the best poems, because several that he wanted to exclude would now be regarded as high points of the sequence. I think No. XXII ('Choisich mi cuide ri mo thuigse') is one of them, and No. XIX ('Thug mise dhut bioth-bhuantachd') doesn't even appear in *O Choille gu Bearradh*.

IMD: I found that quite extraordinary too.

CW: This would imply that we cannot take MacLean as a reliable guide, that the choice, the exclusions, were not made on criteria of quality that we could subscribe to. And you're in a very difficult position when you're editing somebody's poems and you find yourself saying that the poet was wrong about what was good and what was not. I don't really see how we can get round this, as with the wonderful Cuillin praise poem in Section VII of 'An Cuilithionn' I've already mentioned. How could he possibly allow that to remain in manuscript! And so you do find yourself, if you like, correcting the poet willy-nilly.

Another problem is this whole issue of allowing your complete works to appear in parallel texts – Gaelic facing English. Now, it's possible that pragmatically, in 1989, this was the right thing to do, but retrospectively it can seem like a huge mistake. It's possible for poets on a world or European level to gain an audience in translation. The Greek poet Cavafy is a very good example – hugely read, hugely respected, and only a small proportion of the audience reads him in Modern Greek. But with MacLean it's different. If you read MacLean in English, you are reading him in the language which is suffocating and crushing the language of his poetry. That can never be innocent. And when MacLean allowed everything to appear, not just with a facing English translation but with his *own* English translation, he played into the hands of people who, for various reasons – laziness being one of them! – did not want to learn Gaelic, and also feel that the Gaelic text can be overlooked because he made his English translations for us; he made the job much easier – let's focus on the English poems.

Now in 1989–90, when it was important to gain a space for MacLean, this may have been a wise tactic. But I think we need to do some very, very strong back-pedalling now, both about the quality of MacLean's translations and about the whole issue of self-translation, when the language you are translating from is a threatened language, a language that is facing extinction. That is another reason why *O Choille gu Bearradh* is a very ambivalent book.

IMD: I suppose the poet is under pressure from the publishers. The template was set to some extent with *Reothairt is Contraigh*, the selected poems which came out in 1977, which did have parallel translations, many of the poems there having not been published with translation before. The 1943 *Dàin do Eimhir* has got a fairly small number of translations but they are tucked in at the back. And so one would make the point that, of course, he was probably under pressure from publishers.

CW: I do think that MacLean's practice then led to a number of other poets producing poems which are almost Gaelic and English done at the same time; and there's a huge temptation for a poet who is doing that then to move over to English, for all sorts of reasons. It's almost like a rolling ball that takes you in that direction. I consider that the vesture in which MacLean's poetry was presented is in part responsible for that tendency, which I would see as very detrimental to Gaelic poetry – Gaelic poetry in Gaelic, I want to say! – actually having a long-term future.

IMD: I think the poet himself was conscious of this because more than once a few years before he died I heard him saying – once on a Gaelic radio programme – that what mattered most to him was the reaction to his poems and the appreciation of them by native speakers of Gaelic, which was interesting. He seemed a little uneasy about the way things had gone.

CW: I hope you wouldn't exclude those of us who have learned Gaelic?

IMD: No, no, no! He referred to native speakers, but let's just leave it at 'speakers'!

What is the future of what you might call MacLean studies? How would you like to see these develop?

CW: I think the issue of the status of the English translation within the larger cultural picture and the picture of power relations is something that needs to be discussed.

Something else that would be wonderful to have would be a complete concordance of the *Dàin do Eimhir*, as MacLean writes his own special idiolect of Gaelic – in which a word like *leug* ('jewel'), for example, is fascinatingly important. A stage that needs to be gone through with *Dàin do Eimhir* is for someone to sit down and look at all the occurrences of, let's say, the twenty crucial terms in those sixty poems, and draw conclusions from that about the particular personal dialect that MacLean forged for himself from the Gaelic that was available to him.

IMD: Well, John MacInnes has made the point that the English translations give no indication of the sheer variety and range of registers of MacLean's Gaelic. It seems to me that sometimes MacLean's own translations follow the Gaelic so faithfully – so literally – that they give a slightly false idea of the Gaelic, and that the Gaelic may be thought to be more lumbering and more convoluted than in fact it is, whereas, as we know, it has a wonderful range and wonderful rhythm and just hits you between the eyes.

CW: It's a blindingly simple point, but this lovely word *àlainn* ('beautiful' in English) is a valid instance. Does it mean 'lovely', 'attractive', or 'appealing'? Gaelic has certain words that are not devalued, that have not lost their force, and they're crucially simple terms. That means that to some extent English is a very difficult language into which to translate Gaelic. I would feel much calmer if MacLean was gaining his reputation, like Cavafy's, through translation into seven or eight

different languages. But that's not the case, and the English translations are almost like a mould or a growth on the plant which in the
end will suffocate it and kill it. I'm sorry – this is my own feeling.

IMD: And, of course, you said at the beginning that you translated some
poems into Italian.

CW: Yes, yes. That was a very important stage in my own approach to
Gaelic because I lived in Italy for more than ten years. When I came
back to Scotland I couldn't write good English prose and I remember
teaching in Edinburgh and sometimes I knew exactly what I wanted
to say in Italian and I used to think: 'How can I put this in English?'
Even today, I occasionally suffer interference from Italian when using
English. Translating MacLean's Gaelic into what was then my everyday
language was a very important move.

I just have to say that my own involvement has been with the
original Gaelic text. I think MacLean's English translations deserve
prolonged consideration. It's not something I have been able to do
– I have never really sat down and looked at the English translation
and evaluated it as a rendering of the Gaelic. My task – and it's finished
now, I think – has been getting the body of Gaelic work into the
public domain. Having an English translation was a practical necessity
for publication reasons but I think that's another area that needs
opening up. I would be happy to see further translations of 'An
Cuilithionn' done by completely different hands. The more translations into English the merrier, and the more translations into
different languages the merrier. What is very problematic is giving
MacLean's English translations some kind of canonical status, simply
because they were done by the man who wrote the original. In the
preface to the 2002 *Dàin do Eimhir* I quoted Paul Valéry as saying
that the last person who should translate a poem is the one who
wrote it. But that would connect with my earlier point about what
happens to poets in this very, very complex relationship between the
Gaelic poem and its English equivalent, and the question of whether
they actually have equal status, whether one can stand without the
other. All of that needs talking about and clarifying. In MacLean's
case, I look forward to the time when it will be possible to publish
his poetry in a Gaelic-only edition. The fact that that's not possible

and doesn't happen at present says a huge amount about the conditions under which I have been working, and the conditions under which MacLean is being read.

As I've said, we need a concordance, a study of MacLean's vocabulary, and an honest and exhaustive biography, so that the raw material is available to us. We need those letters to Douglas Young, which are on the way, and more of MacLean's letters.

I would also like to see a development of George Campbell Hay studies because I think that the two met more than once at a crucial time, and MacLean felt a real affinity for Campbell Hay and felt he could talk to him. That would enlighten us as to the ambience in which MacLean was writing and would help to fill in the background. Developing MacLean studies is also about looking at the environment surrounding him – I mean, MacLean was in regular contact with George Davie, a hugely important intellectual. The intellectual environment he was moving in at that time – it's just a brief thing, a matter of a year or a year and a half – with people like James Caird – it's absolutely enthralling. We need a study of the intellectual stimuli which were there around the time the *Dàin do Eimhir* were written.

If I can move to a slightly different point, an important one is MacLean's bilingualism. The choice to write in Gaelic in 1939 has to be seen in terms of the languages that were available. Gaelic no longer subsisted in a monolingual context, so that MacLean's choice of Gaelic and use of Gaelic has to be conceptualised within a framework where writing in English was also possible. So what does it mean for a literary genius and an intellectual of huge importance to choose to write in Gaelic in 1939? Obviously there is the gut feeling of 'This is my true language', but it's also a strategy. I can't really say much more about it than that, but that's the context within which it has to be seen.

A while ago I read a lot about the Russian poet Joseph Brodsky, writing under the Soviet regime, and about the importance of ironic speech when you were writing in a context where language is so controlled and so loaded with implications of power. I think we need to develop some kind of an understanding of the multilingual possibilities in Scotland. And that's not just about English being stronger; it's about the meaning of the choice of a particular language. And, of course, the huge unacknowledged presence here is Scots, which would be the majority language – which *has been* the majority language in this country for the last two to three hundred years, a fact which is talked about so little. And so MacLean's choice of Gaelic has to be discussed. Studying Campbell Hay is useful because he wrote in all three languages and he modulates between them. This could shed a lot of light on the vexed question of the need to provide English translation. Self-translation is symptomatic of poets who are really pushed to the edge. Marina Tsvetaeva lived in Paris for fourteen years, and she was effectively a minority language writer, even though she was writing in Russian. French was all around her and she wrote in French and tried to translate herself into French – so there *are* parallels with what MacLean was doing.

All of these issues need to be brought into the open, and the kind of honesty that is essential when dealing with the antics of the Scottish Eimhir needs to be directed towards the linguistic behaviour (that's a good word, I think) around the emergence of these wonderful poems.

IMD: Would you like to say a little about the new collected poems published late in 2011, *Caoir Gheal Leumraich*?

CW: As you said, *An Cuilithionn 1939 and Unpublished Poems* had forty-five unpublished poems, but a selection only is provided in *Caoir*. And that was partly dictated by reasons of publishing *Realpolitik* because, if a book comes out in June, you don't render it obsolescent in November by putting everything in another book.

But it also includes the uncollected poems, poems that were published in MacLean's lifetime but didn't find their way into *O Choille gu Bearradh*. And some of these Emma and I had to translate ('Ach an Dà Theàrnaidh' is one example) because, I think I'm right in saying, there wasn't an extant translation by MacLean. These poems struck me as very fine indeed. It was a surprise to me that the 'written to order' poems, such as those for the Gaelic Society of Inverness, were so good. And it's a quite different MacLean from the MacLean of *Dàin do Eimhir*, the private writing. I would simply say that the difficulty of coming up with an English version took Emma and me into the complexities of these poems, and to me they are significant additions to the published corpus. This is another plus, and an advantage that *Caoir Gheal Leumraich* has over *O Choille gu Bearradh*.

There's also a poem you like very much, the last of the unpublished poems in *Caoir*, 'Tha na beanntan gun bhruidhinn'.

IMD: Yes, it's a classic statement, and I find it very moving. I'm really glad that's been published.

Now, it's common enough to gather up published but uncollected poems in a collected edition, but though it's not unknown, it's less usual to publish poems that have not appeared at all. How would you characterise your decisions about the poems that were in the notebooks and had not seen the light of day at all?

CW: Well, again, some misleading comments have been made. It's not as if the poet's family took us to Sorley's private desk and opened the drawers and let us leaf through these papers! In fact, for I don't know how many years – but it must be five or six – these unpublished poems have been in the National Library of Scotland. Anybody who gets a ticket can walk in off the street and look at them, so that in that sense they were already in the public domain. I touched on this earlier. I think that MacLean is such a fine writer that everything that we have is deserving of attention. And an editor's job is not evaluative. It's not his or her job to say, 'I looked through the unpublished poems and I think these are the ones which are worthy of attention.' An editor's job is to get a reliable text of everything into the public domain so that discussion can start. The unpublished poems had to appear. At the very lowest level they give us more information about what MacLean wrote, but there are several items there that can also give great pleasure. There's one poem which I had to edit in two versions because all we have are sketches, and it's almost like a combinatory problem. And that in its way is absolutely fascinating, as it does show us MacLean at work, not yet having reached a definitive version.

I also think that MacLean was quite chaotic with his papers. This is my impression. I believe the family was astonished at just how much material he had hung on to. A lot of things that we want to interpret as intentional were simply this brilliant man with so much going on in his head that he wasn't quite sure which poems were where. He wrote to Douglas Young in 1968 looking for some of the unpublished *Dàin do Eimhir* because he wanted to re-work them. I don't know why Douglas didn't say, 'Everything is in Aberdeen University Library.' Had they forgotten? Had Douglas forgotten? MacLean had clearly forgotten.

IMD: I suppose it's just possible, yes.

CW: Or did Douglas think: 'If I tell him they're there, God knows what he will do with them, so let's just leave them where they are'?!

IMD: We're always hearing how poets like Auden, say, have re-worked early poems. It's interesting that MacLean never, as far as I know, re-worked the *Dàin do Eimhir*. He left them strictly alone, I think.

CW: There are some papers in the NLS that show him – in the 1943 *Dàin do Eimhir* – actually rewriting. I can't remember which one offhand.

IMD: And, of course, he did revise some of them *before* publication. 'Ùrnaigh' (No. XVIII) is the obvious example, with the change in the first two lines.

What about any influence from MacLean on your own poetry? Would you say the work you have put in on editing him has affected the way you write yourself?

CW: I'm not sure that my own poetry as such is very connected with Sorley MacLean. It was a crucial step for me in 1984–85 when I put all of the *Dàin do Eimhir* that I knew at the time into Italian, which had been for about ten years my language of daily conversation and communication. And translation is a wonderful way of studying and analysing anyone's poetry, so to that extent I could say I learned Gaelic in order to read Sorley and Sorley brought me much closer to Gaelic. That being so, it's paradoxical that, of all the poets in my generation, I am probably the one least influenced by MacLean. I've certainly not made any conscious effort to imitate him or take up his heritage. I have a feeling that my own poetry comes from somewhere quite different and owes rather less to Sorley than, say, the work of Aonghas MacNeacail or Meg Bateman does – partly because my own poetry tends to be very personal in nature.

My poetry has very different roots. A Catholic upbringing amidst the rampant prejudice of Glasgow in the 1950s and 1960s, along with conscious assumption of the implications of my sexual orientation, meant I approached the language from a very different direction.

Moving abroad aged twenty-one offered me a safe place to find out about being gay. In a parallel way, I looked to figures like Rilke, Baudelaire or Pasolini for guidance about creating an expressive medium I did not believe was available back home in Scotland. Whereas MacLean was born at the heart of Gaelic society and could identify with it, while at the same time criticising, even rejecting it, I was someone trying to heal a wound, to repair the damage inflicted by a series of historical tragedies, as a result of which I grew up a monoglot in a language that meant nothing to my forebears.

IMD: Christopher, thank you very much.

The Contributors

Norman Bissell writes poetry and non-fiction and was awarded a Creative Scotland artist's bursary in 2014 to undertake research and professional development to write a novel. His poetry collection *Slate, Sea and Sky: A Journey from Glasgow to the Isle of Luing* (with photographs by Oscar Marzaroli) is published by Luath Press. A former principal teacher of history and EIS Area Officer, he is Vice-Chairman of the Isle of Luing Community Trust in Argyll and Director of the Scottish Centre for Geopoetics: **www.geopoetics.org.uk**

Tha am bàrd agus an sgrìobhadair **Maoilios Caimbeul** a' fuireach san Eilean Sgitheanach, is 's e an leabhar mu dheireadh a thàinig bhuaithe *Tro Chloich na Sùla* (CLÀR, 2014). Tha e air iomadach obair sgrìobhaidh eile fhoillseachadh – bàrdachd, ficsean agus eachdraidh-beatha.

Poet and writer **Myles Campbell** lives in the Isle of Skye. His latest book is the all-Gaelic poetry collection *Tro Chloich na Sùla* (CLÀR, 2014). He has produced numerous other works, including poetry, fiction and an autobiographical account.

Màiri Sìne Chaimbeul was born and raised in Plockton, Ross-shire, and attended school at a time when Sorley MacLean was Headmaster there. She obtained a degree in Celtic Studies at Aberdeen University, and while there undertook research on the Kintail poet Iain Mac Mhurchaidh which she has recently revisited with a view to publishing a volume of his poems. Her published work to date includes a Gaelic children's book, *Lee Ann,* and two for teenagers, *Àirigh Dhòmhnaill an Tàilleir* and *Ceann an Rathaid.* She has also written for television and radio and given talks, usually on Gaelic songs or traditional storytelling, one of these being a paper delivered at the twenty-second Celtic Symposium at Harvard in 2005. She has been a lecturer at Sabhal Mòr Ostaig for the past twenty-two years.

Professor Hugh Cheape has devised and teaches a postgraduate programme, MSc Cultar Dùthchasach agus Eachdraidh na Gàidhealtachd ('Material

Culture and Gàidhealtachd History') at Sabhal Mòr Ostaig. This followed a curatorial career in the National Museums of Scotland. His books include *Periods in Highland History* (1987) with I. F. Grant; *Tartan: The Highland Habit* (1991); *Witness to Rebellion* (1996) with Iain Gordon Brown; *The Book of the Bagpipe* (1999); and *Bagpipes: A national collection of a national instrument* (2008).

Emma Dymock completed her PhD on the subject of Sorley MacLean's 'An Cuilithionn' in 2008. She now lectures in the Department of Celtic and Scottish Studies at the University of Edinburgh, with her main research focusing on modern Gaelic literature. She is co-editor of MacLean's collected poems, *Caoir Gheal Leumraich / White Leaping Flame*, and is currently preparing the Sorley MacLean–Douglas Young correspondence for publication.

Douglas Gifford was Head of Department and is Emeritus Professor of Scottish Literature at the University of Glasgow. He has published widely in the field of Scottish literature, especially on Scott, Hogg, Gunn and Gibbon and on modern Scottish fiction. He is currently Honorary Librarian at Abbotsford.

Ian MacDonald is from North Uist and has had jobs there and in Birmingham, Glasgow, London and again Glasgow, where he worked for decades for the Gaelic Books Council. He has edited or translated many books in Gaelic and in English, among them the children's dictionary *Dealbh is Facal* and the first Gaelic version of the classic Welsh tales, *Am Mabinogi*. With Boyd Robertson, he compiled *Essential Gaelic Dictionary* (Hodder, 2004, 2010).

Murdo Macdonald is Professor of History of Scottish Art at the University of Dundee. He is a former editor of *Edinburgh Review*. He is author of *Scottish Art* in Thames and Hudson's World of Art series. His recent research has explored the art of the Scottish Gàidhealtachd, the cultural milieu of Patrick Geddes, Robert Burns and visual thinking, and Ossian and art.

Peter Mackay is a lecturer in Literature at the University of St Andrews. He is the author of *Sorley MacLean* (RHSS, 2010) and the co-editor of *Modern*

Irish and Scottish Poetry (Cambridge University Press, 2011) and *Sùil air an t-Saoghal* (Clò Ostaig, 2013). A collection of his poems, *Gu Leòr/Galore*, was published by Acair in 2015.

Timothy Neat (FASLS, HRSA) is a writer, film-maker, art historian and artist. His major contribution to Scottish culture has centred on a series of creative, 'symbiotic' relationships with revolutionary poets and artists – Burns, Mackintosh, MacDiarmid, Sorley MacLean, Hamish Henderson, Ian Hamilton Finlay, John Berger (his film with Berger, *Play Me Something*, winning Premio Europa, Barcelona, 1989). Neat's most recent book, *These Faces* (photographs and drawings), was published by Polygon in 2013.

Máire Ní Annracháin is Professor of Modern Irish in University College Dublin. Her main academic interests are literary theory and modern literature in Irish and Scottish Gaelic. Her PhD thesis was on the poetry of Sorley MacLean. She has written and edited many academic publications, most recently on the resilience of the Gaelic literary tradition. She has been chairperson of the community development organisation Glór na nGael and is a member of the board of directors of Sabhal Mòr Ostaig.

John Purser is a poet, playwright, composer and historian. He is best known for his book *Scotland's Music* and its eponymous radio series (both 1992 and 2007). He recently brought out three CDs of his music, and his new and collected poems, *There is No Night*, were published by Kennedy and Boyd in 2014. John is a researcher and part-time teacher at Sabhal Mòr Ostaig. He lives and crofts on the Isle of Skye.

Ronald Renton was Deputy Head Master of St Aloysius' College, Glasgow, until 2008. He is currently Convenor of the Education Committee of the Association for Scottish Literary Studies and Chair of the Neil Munro Society.

Alan Titley is Emeritus Professor of Modern Irish in University College Cork, former Head of Irish at St Patrick's College, Dublin City University, and a member of the Royal Irish Academy. He is the author of eight novels and three collections of stories, plays and poetry, and his selected essays were published in *Nailing Theses* (Lagan Press, 2012). One of his novels, *An Fear Dána*, recreates the life and times of Muireadhach Albanach Ó Dálaigh. His translation of the classic Irish novel *Cré na Cille* has recently been published by Yale University Press as *The Dirty Dust*.

Christopher Whyte's fifth collection of poems in Gaelic, *An Daolag Shìonach*, appeared in 2013. He is the author of the monograph *Modern Scottish Poetry* (2004) and has produced highly praised editions with commentary of *Dàin do Eimhir* (2002) and *An Cuilithionn 1939 and Unpublished Poems* (2011) by Somhairle MacGill-Eain/Sorley MacLean. His translations from the Russian of 180 poems by Marina Tsvetaeva appeared from Archipelago Press as *Moscow in the Plague Year* in 2014. A complete translation of her 1922 collection *Milestones* was published by Shearsman Press in spring 2015. Christopher lives and works full-time in Budapest.